£3.99

Water Music

Water Music

Music Making in the Spas of Europe and North America

Ian Bradley

OXFORD

UNIVERSITY PRESS

2010

OXFORD
UNIVERSITY PRESS

Oxford University Press, Inc., publishes works that further
Oxford University's objective of excellence
in research, scholarship, and education.

Oxford   New York
Auckland   Cape Town   Dar es Salaam   Hong Kong   Karachi
Kuala Lumpur   Madrid   Melbourne   Mexico City   Nairobi
New Delhi   Shanghai   Taipei   Toronto

With offices in
Argentina   Austria   Brazil   Chile   Czech Republic   France   Greece
Guatemala   Hungary   Italy   Japan   Poland   Portugal   Singapore
South Korea   Switzerland   Thailand   Turkey   Ukraine   Vietnam

Published by Oxford University Press, Inc.
198 Madison Avenue, New York, New York 10016

www.oup.com

Oxford is a registered trademark of Oxford University Press

Library of Congress Cataloging-in-Publication Data
Bradley, Ian C.
Water music : music making in the spas of Europe
and North America / Ian Bradley.
p.   cm.
Includes index.
ISBN 978-0-19-532734-2
1. Music and health resorts—Europe. 2. Music and health
resorts—New York—Saratoga Springs Region. I. Title.
ML160.B796 2009
781.5'3—dc22   2009013716

1 3 5 7 9 8 6 4 2

Printed in the United States of America
on acid-free paper

For my daughter Mary
With happy memories of the baths and music of Budapest

Wine needs conversation for its proper *dégustation*, water needs
music. Only then does it become true, as the quotation from
Pindar's Olympian Odes over the Bath Pump Room door states,
that 'Water is best'.
—Kenneth Young, *Music's Great Days*
in the Spas and Watering-Places

Preface and Acknowledgements

This book explores the influence of European and North American spas on musicians and music making between the early eighteenth century and the middle of the twentieth century. It is about the composers who came to spas, what they did and what they wrote when they were there, and the key role that music played in the social and cultural life and the therapeutic regimes of these pioneer resorts. It reflects a long-standing personal interest and passion of mine and the fact that several of my most memorable musical experiences have occurred in spa settings.

I am not the only writer who has found music to be at the heart of the spa experience. Music is a prominent theme in such classic spa novels as Ivan Turgenev's *Smoke*, based on Baden-Baden; Thomas Mann's *The Magic Mountain*, about life in a Swiss sanatorium; and Guy de Maupassant's *Mont Oriol*, set in an imaginary spa in the French Auvergne. In her book *Taking the Waters*, Alev Lytle Croutier writes of her time in Evian—during the day she was sprayed with water, wrapped in an algae bath, massaged under a douche, and received hydrotherapy in a giant bath tub, and in the evening she sat 'in a splendid *Belle Epoque* lounge surrounded by frescoes listening to two musicians play duets by Boccherini and Spohr as we supped Evian water—civilized, most civilized—in evening gowns'.[1]

Yet although music is widely recognized as an important element in the distinctive ambience and atmosphere of spas, the connection between music making and the cultural and social life of the fashionable watering places of Europe and North America has been largely unexplored. There has been surprisingly little study of the prominent role that taking the waters played in the lives of so many composers, nor of the music that was played in spas. This book will, I hope, begin to rectify this omission. It is not an exhaustive or comprehensive study of the subject. Rather it is designed to be representative, focusing on certain spas and composers. It is restricted to inland spas with natural mineral waters and does not attempt to chronicle the rich musical life that flourished in the English seaside resorts of Scarborough, Bournemouth, and Eastbourne (well covered in Kenneth Young's delightful book *Music's Great Days in the Spas and Watering-Places*), or in a city like Budapest with a long and well-established culture of bathing in mineral waters.

I have deliberately concentrated on a relatively small number of important and representative spas that have particularly rich musical connections. The geographical spread is deliberately wide to embrace North America as well as Europe and the approach is broadly chronological, beginning with Bath and Baden bei Wien, which both flourished in the eighteenth century, continuing through Baden-Baden, the spas of Bohemia and Bad Ischl at their height in the nineteenth century, and on to Buxton and Saratoga Springs, which had their glory days in the early twentieth century. A brief concluding chapter reviews the music in these spas today, including that which accompanies treatments in modern spas, now so ubiquitous and dominant a feature in the booming industry centred around health, well-being, and relaxation.

Many people have helped me in researching this book. Janice Furness and Chris Beedham have valiantly helped in translating German sources. John MacAuslan cast his eagle eye over the chapters on Baden-Baden and Bad Ischl and Peter Kemp checked the sections on Johann Strauss senior and junior. Emma Sutton suggested useful leads on Wagner, and Alexander Faris helped me with material about Offenbach in Bad Ems and Baden-Baden.

In Bath I had useful interviews with Stephen Clews, administrator of the Roman baths, and Robert Hyman, leader of the Pump Room

Trio. Anne Buchanan, local studies librarian at Bath Central Library, and Susan Fox and Rosemary Boyns at the Bath and North East Somerset Record Office generously made material available to me, and Kenneth James kindly allowed me to quote from his excellent thesis on music making in the city. While in Bath, I benefited from the excellent hospitality of James and Jane Bradby and Nicholas and Jane Ostler. Stephen and Alice Bates were hospitable and knowledgeable hosts in Tunbridge Wells.

My research in Baden bei Wien was greatly aided by Martina Spinka of the Tourist Office and Dr Christine Triebling-Löffler, who proved an expert guide. I also benefited from a conversation with Susanne Pfann and Margit Fussi, organists at St Stephen's Church. In Baden-Baden I received generous help from Simone Schmidt in the Tourist Office and Gunhilt Dame, who was another exemplary guide. Imo Quero-Lehman, custodian of the Brahms Haus, kindly let me spend a day in the library there. Peter Meanwell, producer of the BBC Radio 3 programme *Water Music* that I scripted and presented on the musical associations of these two spas, was a congenial companion whose suggestions and ideas I much appreciated. In Bad Ischl I benefited from the knowledge and enthusiasm of Carl and Helen Smith, founders and organisers of Operetta Heaven holidays.

My research in Buxton was greatly helped by Faye Jones, who produced much valuable material, and by the continuing and much-appreciated hospitality of Stephen and Rosie Shipley. I was able to try out two chapters of this book on the ever-appreciative and ever-patient audiences at the fringe events in the 2008 International Gilbert and Sullivan Festival and I thank them as well as Stephen Turnbull, the festival administrator and Ian and Neil Smith, the founders and organisers, for their support.

In Saratoga Springs I was aided by Ellen de Lalla from the local history room of the public library; Marianne Fitzgerald, the city historian; and Doris Lamont, archivist of the historical society.

My wife, Lucy, has cheerfully put up with my obsession with spas for nearly thirty years. She allowed me to drag her around the spas of what was then Czechoslovakia on our honeymoon, after an initial stay in Bad Ischl, where we enjoyed the lush romanticism of Lehár's *Der Graf von Luxembourg* just three nights after our wedding. Fifteen years later we were back there with our children to see Carl Zeller's

Die Vogelhandler, and we recently celebrated our twenty-fifth wedding anniversary by soaking in the mineral baths of Baden bei Wien and Bad Ischl and gorging ourselves on operettas, *kur concerts,* and one or two iced coffees and *Lehár schnitten—Schön ist Die Welt,* indeed!

Contents

Water Music

Introduction

For the French, they are *villes d'eaux* or *stations thermales,* for Germans *heilbäder, kurorte,* or *badeorte,* for Italians *terme,* and for Czechs *státní lázni* or *teplice.* North Americans tend to prefer the term *springs.* Perhaps most evocative and ubiquitous is the word *spa,* first adopted by a resort based around natural mineral springs and founded in 1326 in the wooded hills of the Ardennes, near Liège, in what is now Belgium. Its etymology is unclear. *Spa* may derive from the Walloon word *espa,* meaning a fountain, or from the Latin verb *spargere,* meaning to sprinkle or moisten, or it may be an acronym of the Latin phrase *sanitas per aquam* (health through water). The word was brought into wide currency by a visit to Spa in Belgium in the early seventeenth century by two English doctors, Sir William Paddy and Dr Richard Andrews. They applied the name to all those places possessing natural mineral springs to which people resorted to drink or bathe in the waters for therapeutic purposes.

Whatever their preferred local name, spas are mysterious, en-chanted, magical places, where springs and sources bubble up out of the ground and are channelled into baths and drinking fountains. Long venerated for their health-giving and curative properties, they are among the earliest identifiable sacred places and shrines. Since at least the time of the Romans, spas have been locations where people have congregated to bathe communally in natural warm waters and to which the rich and well connected have come not just to take a cure but to socialise, flirt, and be entertained and amused. Nowadays the word *spa* is used for leisure and treatment complexes, often annexed to hotels and based around swimming baths, whirlpools, Jacuzzis, steam rooms, saunas, and fitness suites, providing a hugely popular combination of sybaritic pampering and physical exertion.

The historic development and evolution of spas shows the successive influence of religious belief and superstition, the pursuit of health and well-being, and the rise of a leisured class and an entertainment culture. The idea that natural mineral springs that come gushing out of the ground are possessed of miraculous and magical properties was deeply embedded in primal religion and folklore. Among its expressions were Celtic water divinities, native American Indian incantations, and the votive offerings found around the Roman *thermae*. Several of the most fashionable and enduring European watering places owed their origins to the elaborate bathhouses built by the Romans where they found thermal springs. Vichy began as Vicus Calidus, established by Julius Caesar, Bath as Aquae Sulis with its temple to Minerva, and Baden-Baden as Aquae Aureliae. With the coming of Christianity, healing wells and springs were converted from their pagan associations, declared holy, and dedicated to local saints. During the Middle Ages many were taken over and administered by the churches and became important pilgrimage destinations. Spa in Belgium is a good example, being dedicated to St. Remaclus, bishop and apostle of the Ardennes, who reputedly possessed powers to purify fountains and generate springs.

With the ending of the veneration of shrines and holy places across much of Europe following the Reformation, spas became the focus for a new secular kind of pilgrimage, drawing visitors seeking health and well-being. The medical profession took over from the church, promoting them not for their supernatural and miraculous properties but their health-giving and therapeutic qualities. The first medical treatises on the benefits of both bathing in and drinking spa waters appeared in the sixteenth century. They analysed the mineral content of the waters, which were classified into three major types: sulphurous, saline, and chalybeate (with a high iron content). Following the lead of Bath, which had developed as the leading English resort in the late seventeenth century and early eighteenth century and was in many ways the pioneer spa, an array of fashionable watering places were established across Europe and North America. They included Vichy and Aix-les-Bains in France, Buxton and Malvern in England, Baden bei Wien and Bad Ischl in Austria, Baden-Baden and Bad Ems in Germany, Marienbad and Karlsbad in Bohemia (now the Czech Republic), and Saratoga Springs and Hot Springs in the United States. The nineteenth century saw the flourishing of these and other spas as kings, queens, and emperors, politicians and poets, businessmen and artists, soldiers and composers took up residence for several months every summer to take the waters, or, as they themselves often put it, to take a cure. Essentially, they were the first holiday resorts, providing the opportunity for their rich guests to unwind from stressful lives and escape polluted cities.

From the eighteenth century onwards spa towns were characterized by a distinct physical layout. At their centre were the thermal baths, drinking hall, and pump room built, often in classical style, over the natural springs and usually surrounded by elegantly laid-out parks and gardens and broad promenades. Other buildings to be found in the spa, or Kurpark, area often included a casino, theatre, assembly rooms, and concert hall. The architectural style differed from spa to spa, from the sweeping classical crescents of Bath and Buxton via the Biedermeir opulence of Baden bei Wien and Baden-Baden to the dazzling Romanesque and Oriental polychromy of the mountain spa of Le Mont Dore in the French Auvergne. But all shared a physical grandeur and magnificence that complemented and enhanced their fashionable ambience. Their appeal grew during the nineteenth century thanks to the popularity of the new medical science of hydrotherapy, pioneered in Grafenbürg in Silesia (now the Czech Republic) by Vincent Priessnitz, who cured himself of severe injuries occasioned when he was run over by a wagon by applying wet compresses to his chest for a year and drinking large quantities of water. Another advocate of hydrotherapy, Sebastian Kneipp, parish priest of Bad Wörishofen in Bavaria, claimed to have cured himself of tuberculosis by brief immersions in the freezing cold Danube, a vegetarian diet, and regular exercise, including treading barefoot in the dewy grass for five minutes every morning. Hydropathic establishments sprung up across Europe in which guests were made to drink copious draughts of water, wrapped in wet towels, and showered with high-pressure douches and sprays. Making the most of whatever particular resources nature had given them, spas developed specialist treatments based around bathing in highly sulphurous or iron-rich waters, covering the body with mud or peat, inhaling radioactive gases, sitting in rooms filled with steam and vapour, or being bombarded with electrical currents.

Although it was originally the healing waters that drew people to spas, increasingly what was on offer in the casinos, assembly halls, and ballrooms became their main attraction. From being places of pilgrimage for those seeking relief from debilitating and painful conditions, they became summer playgrounds for royalty, the aristocracy, and the haute bourgeoisie. While they still came ostensibly to take a cure and repair the ravages of a winter of overindulgence with a strict regime of sulphurous draughts, plunge baths, and enemas, most of those staying in spas by the mid-nineteenth century were in search of amusement, entertainment, diversion, and distraction. As the prototypes of the modern resort, spas played a significant role in the development of the institution of the holiday and the emergence of the leisure industry. They were devoted to the pursuit of pleasure at least as much as to the improvement of health.

Most of the crowned heads of Europe regularly decamped with their courts to spa resorts between the months of April and October, quitting the stuffy atmosphere and odours of their capital cities. Spa itself was the first to attract a royal clientele, successively luring Margaret of Navarre, Henry III of France, Christina of Sweden, Peter the Great of Russia, the fugitive English king, Charles II, and the Austrian emperor Joseph II, who described it as the café of Europe. Napoleon III established Vichy as the queen of the French *villes d'eaux* by bringing his entire court there for four successive years in the 1860s, building a magnificent row of Swiss-style chalets in which to house them and laying out the Parc des Sources with the imposing Thermal Establishment at one end and the Casino at the other. Baden-Baden established its reputation as the most fashionable of the German *kurorte* largely on the basis of its numerous royal visitors. They included Queen Victoria, who found the air there 'so becoming', Napoleon III, King Alfonso XIII of Spain, the emperors of Siam and Brazil, and several kings of Norway and Sweden. Kaiser Wilhelm I, who spent much of his life flitting between different spas and famously marched through the park in Bad Homburg snapping his fingers at trees he did not like, which were later felled, sojourned in Baden-Baden for forty summers. He also made twenty visits to Bad Ems, the favourite resort of Tsar Alexander II. The Austrian emperor Franz Josef spent eighty-three summers at Bad Ischl, where his mother had bathed in the brine baths to cure her infertility. Empress Josephine spent hours sitting on a vaporous hole at Plombières in the hope that she might produce an heir for Napoleon. Edward VII favoured Marienbad, where he romped in the bushes with young girls recruited by his trusty valet, and Bad Homburg, where he regularly lost as much as forty pounds in an evening at the gaming tables. Queen Emma and Queen Wilhelmine of the Netherlands, King Leopold II of Belgium, and King George I of Greece took their courts to Aix-les-Bains, while the Romanovs and the Hohenzollerns favoured Wiesbaden.

Largely because of the number of royal and other prominent visitors that they attracted, spas have played a key role in European politics and diplomacy. It was in the Bohemian spa of Teplitz that the rulers of Austria, Russia, and Prussia signed the Triple Alliance against Napoleon Buonaparte in 1813. Much of the detailed discussion in the Vienna Congress of 1814–15, which determined the settlement of Europe following the Napoleonic Wars, took place in Baden bei Wien. The Karlsbad Decrees, promulgated by Prince Clemens Metternich when he was staying at the Bohemian resort in 1819, inaugurated a thirty-year period of severe censorship and repressive rule throughout the Habsburg Empire and the German Confederation. A telegram sent from Bad Ems by Kaiser Wilhelm I of Prussia in 1870 following a meeting with the French ambassador Benedetti touched off the Franco-Prussian War. It was in the spa gardens at Bad Ems that Tsar Alexander II signed the Ems Edict of 1876 prohibiting the distribution of literary writings in the Ukrainian language. Kaiser Wilhelm II and Tsar Nicholas II had several meetings in Wiesbaden to discuss diplomatic alliances and stratagems, the most important of which in 1903 led to German backing for the Russo-Japanese War. It was at his summer villa in Bad Ischl that Emperor Franz Josef, having heard the news of the assassination of his nephew, Archduke Francis Ferdinand, in Sarajevo, signed the ultimatum to Serbia on 28 July 1914 that was to plunge Europe into the First World War. Spa in Belgium became the headquarters of the German Army in that war, and it was there that Kaiser Wilhelm abdicated in November 1918. Baden bei Wien served a similar function for the Austro-Hungarian forces, and it was from there that the last Habsburg emperor, Karl I, sent a telegram announcing their surrender to the allied forces. As commander of the allied forces in Germany during the Second World War General Dwight D. Eisenhower based himself in a house on the edge of the Kurpark in Bad Homburg.

Spas have also made a significant contribution to the literary life of Europe. Among those who regularly took the waters at Spa were Michel Montaigne, Victor Hugo, Alexander Dumas, Mark Twain, Sigmund Freud, Nicolai Gogol, and Fredreich Nietzsche. Baden-Baden attracted Dumas, Stendhal, Honoré de Balzac, George Sand, and Ivan Turgenev. The lure of the gaming tables took Dostoyevsky to Baden-Baden, Bad Ems, Bad Homburg, and Wiesbaden. From his first visit to Ems in 1774, apparently because of his scientific interest in the geological formations that produced the natural springs there, Goethe became a habitué of central European watering places, regularly taking the waters at Karlsbad, Marienbad, and Teplitz, where he spent extravagantly on 'balls, concerts and the like', provoking 'the savage indignation of his more radical critics'.[1] Marcel Proust made numerous visits to Evian. Herman Hesse went to Baden bei Zurich for twenty years and wrote many of his books there, including his spa novel *Kurgast*.

The influence that the watering places of Europe and North America have had on music making over the last three centuries is the particular subject of this book. An initial pointer to their significance can be gained by listing some of the works that were conceived or composed either in or for spas: Mozart's anthem *Ave Verum Corpus*; Beethoven's Ninth Symphony and A Minor String Quartet (Opus 132); Berlioz's opera *Béatrice et Bénédict*; Brahms's First and Second Symphonies, *Ein Deutsches Requiem*, Academic Festival Overture, Tragic Overture, Quintet in F Major, and *Gesang der Parzen*; Wagner's *Lohengrin* and *Die Meistersinger von Nürnberg*; most of Franz Lehár's operettas, including *Die Lustige Witwe*; and Offenbach's *Orphée aux Enfers* and *La Belle Hélène*.

Like other visitors, several composers and musicians frequented spas primarily in the hope of gaining relief from pain and therapeutic benefit for themselves or close family members. George Frederick Handel went to take the waters in Aix la Chapelle (Aachen), where the thermal springs were said to have been discovered by Charlemagne, after he had lost the use of his right arm through palsy in 1737. He was reported to have sat over a vapour bath 'near three times as long as hath ever been the practice'. Within a few hours of his quitting the bath, the nuns in a local convent heard him at the organ 'playing in a manner beyond any they had ever been used to' and concluded that he had undergone a miraculous cure.[2] He was on the point of going to take the waters in Bath in 1759 when he was stricken with what proved to be his final illness. Wolfgang Mozart's frequent visits to Baden bei Wien in the last three years of his life were occasioned by the fact that his wife, Constanze, spent much time there seeking a cure for an ulcerated leg and the complications associated with her almost perpetual state of pregnancy. Josef Haydn found himself in the same spa town for a similar reason, visiting his wife when she took the waters there in the hope of alleviating her rheumatism. Ludwig van Beethoven spent parts of at least fourteen summers at Baden on doctor's orders in an attempt to gain relief from the numerous ailments that afflicted him. Hector Berlioz's frequent sojourns in Baden-Baden were partially motivated by his desire to find a cure for the 'intestinal neuralgia' from which he suffered from 1856. Franz Liszt came as a patient to Karlsbad. Richard Wagner, who was an enthusiastic student of the new science of hydrotherapy and admitted that 'my fanatical agitation for a water diet and my polemics against the evils of wine' amounted to 'a new kind of religion', took the waters at Teplitz to ease his gastric troubles.[3]

Other musicians were drawn to spas not so much to take the waters for the relief of a specific ailment but rather to 'chill out' and de-stress in their calm and relaxing atmosphere. For composers and performers alike spas offered a chance to unwind from the pressures of frenetic lifestyles and pursue a quiet, disciplined, and healthy regime. Johannes Brahms hated the idea of a spa cure and never seems to have taken the waters during the many summers that he spent in both Baden-Baden and Bad Ischl. What drew him to these places was rather their tranquillity and healthy country air and, in the case, of Baden-Baden, the proximity of Clara Schumann. During the nine summers that he spent there he regularly rose at around four in the morning, walked in the woods for two or three hours, and then settled down to compose. Gaspare Spontini, the Italian opera composer and conductor, and Giacomo Meyerbeer both resorted to Spa for rest and recuperation. Meyerbeer became well known for riding a donkey along the Avenue of Trees, not the most eccentric form of transport favoured by guests in the 'Queen of the Watering Places'—the Duchess of Orleans rode around Spa on a camel. Franz Schubert regularly visited Bad

Gastein for its calming and relaxing atmosphere, and it was almost certainly a stay there that inspired his lost Gasteiner Symphony. Later this same resort attracted Arturo Toscanini and Bruno Walter for similar reasons.

Through the twentieth century, when less emphasis was placed on the direct benefits of taking the waters and more on the general restorative and 'detoxing' properties of spas, composers and performers continued to seek them out as places of renewal and retreat. Igor Stravinsky and Ida Rubenstein stayed at the Royal Hotel in Evian. Richard Strauss withdrew to Baden bei Zurich in 1945, writing his oboe concerto there and becoming well known in the locality for his long walks. George Szell recharged his batteries every summer at Bad Ragaz before conducting at the Salzburg Festival and then returning to the United States to take up his punishing winter schedule with the Cleveland Orchestra. Singers in particular seem to have found spas congenial places to relax and unwind and set up summer homes in or near them: Adelina Patti at Spa; Richard Tauber at Bad Ischl; Chauncey Allcott, the Irish-born American tenor famous for 'When Irish Eyes Are Smiling', at Saratoga Springs; and Marcella Sembrich, principal soprano at the Metropolitan Opera in the 1920s and 1930s, nearby on Lake George.

It was not just because of their therapeutic and relaxing atmosphere that spas attracted musicians. They also offered considerable possibilities for making money. This was partly because they were filled throughout the season by so many rich and influential visitors and offered composers opportunities for finding a wealthy patron and securing lucrative commissions. With their daily programmes of concerts, dances, and recitals to entertain the guests, spas also had an insatiable demand for music and provided much needed summer employment for professional musicians. Much incidental music was written or arranged specifically for pump room ensembles and kurhaus orchestras and bands. Spas provided conductors and instrumentalists with welcome employment in the summer months, when city opera houses and concert halls were often shut. Musicians who initially came to take a cure found themselves returning on an annual basis with a lucrative contract. This happened to Berlioz at Baden-Baden and Offenbach at Bad Ems. Both men were taken on for several seasons to conduct the kurhaus orchestra and supervise the musical entertainment provided for guests. Dvořák came five times to Karlsbad to supervise performances of his works. In 1821 the Congress Hall in Saratoga Springs became the first hotel in North America to employ a resident band when it hired Frank Johnson to provide a group of musicians throughout the summer season. By the end of the nineteenth century members of leading symphony orchestras were regularly decamping to spa resorts for the summer months. For ten years from 1902 Victor Herbert brought fifty-four players from the Pittsburgh Symphony Orchestra to Saratoga Springs to play every morning and evening on the piazza of the Grand Union Hotel.

Spa orchestras provided useful training for young instrumentalists seeking to improve their repertoire and ensemble playing. Franz Lehár had his first experience of playing in an orchestra at the age of twelve on the second violin desk of the twelve-piece spa orchestra at Bad Ullersdorf, which his uncle conducted. This youthful adventure confirmed him in his resolve to follow music as a career. His biographer Bernard Grun further suggests that the band's simple programme pieces 'sharpened his ear for the well-formed *cantilena*' and that 'from the limitations of the tiny orchestral combination grew his amazing skill in instrumental economy'.[4] Lehár's close friend Richard Tauber made his professional singing debut at Wiesbaden, where his father was producer and lead actor at the Court Theatre. The English bassoonist Archie Camden, who cut his performing teeth with the pavilion orchestra at Buxton, believed that playing in a spa ensemble superbly equipped recent graduates of music colleges for the sort of repertoire that they would have to cope with at the beginning of their professional careers: 'I have heard it said (and I endorse this) that a violinist, for example, will come out of college able to give an excellent performance of the Beethoven Concerto but completely unable to find his way round a Strauss waltz'. The spa-trained musician would have no such problems.[5]

Another factor that drew musicians to spa towns was the prospect of meeting interesting, important, and like-minded companions. Fashionable watering places attracted a Bohemian cliéntele of novelists, artists, poets, and musicians alongside royalty, aristocracy, and the haute bourgeoisie. They were places in which to be seen and make valuable contacts. Their popularity among creative people had a snowballing effect—when one came, others followed. Both Clara Schumann and Ivan Turgenev took up residence in Baden-Baden when their close mutual friend, the leading operatic mezzo-soprano Pauline Viardot-

Garcia, moved there in 1863. Brahms, in turn, made it his summer base to be near Clara Schumann. Malvern in the English Midlands, near where Edward Elgar was born and lived, became a magnet for British composers, including C. V. Stanford and Alexander Mackenzie. It was at spas that the giants of European music and literature met and conversed, as Beethoven and Goethe did at Teplitz and Karlsbad in 1812. It was also often where leading composers first heard the music of their contemporaries. Rossini's first encounter with the work of Wagner was when he heard a march being played by a kurhaus orchestra.

Live music played a central role in the daily regime of those taking the cure, from their early morning promenades in the pump rooms to the late night balls and dances. An important part of its function was to provide diversion and distraction during the long periods of enforced inactivity that made up a large part of the *curistes'* day and to counter the unpleasant effects of imbibing and bathing in evil-smelling and uninviting waters. Taking a cure was often a grim experience. Madame de Sévigné described bathing at Vichy in 1677 as 'a great rehearsal for purgatory. One is completely nude in this little underground place and there one finds a tube with hot water that a woman aims at different parts of her body. It is a very humiliating thing'. A visit to Buxton in the early 1720s led Daniel Defoe to make the same comparison: 'The smoke and the slime of the waters, the promiscuous multitude of the people in the bath, with nothing but their heads above water, with the height of walls that environ the bath, gave me a lively idea of the several pictures I had seen of Fra Angelico's in Italy of Purgatory'.[6]

It was in an effort to mitigate this hellish experience that spa owners and directors employed musicians to play in the early mornings and late afternoons while guests drank their prescribed dosage of mineral water or wallowed in the thermal baths. Dostoyevsky reported to his wife on his daily programme at Bad Ems in 1876: 'I get up at six and begin my drinking at seven. It takes an hour and a half. The band plays to an audience of six thousand. . . . At five o'clock I drink mineral water and listen to the band again'.[7] The early start to the music making was not always appreciated by guests. Lady Wolseley, wife of the swashbuckling Victorian general Sir Garnet Wolseley, complained during a visit to Marienbad in 1889: 'The band begins to play just outside the hotel at 6.30 and after that there is no peace. I drink three glasses, with intervals of 15 minutes, take an hour's walk in the woods, then come home to tea and dry bread.'[8] For others, however, the opportunity to hear live music from early morning to late at night was a major attraction. Touring German spas in 1920, S. L. Bensusan was particularly impressed with the daily programme offered in Bad Nauheim:

> The orchestra plays at between seven and eight o'clock in the morning, the hour varies with the month, for the benefit of the water drinkers round the Trinkhalle, and the programme always opens with a hymn. In the afternoons, the band plays on the terrace of the *Kurhaus,* and there again in the evening, unless the weather be wet, in which case the music is given in the large hall. Sometimes there are symphony concerts and then we learn that the players are capable of much finer effort than they display at normal times. Operas are frequently given in the season.[9]

As this observation indicates, music making at most spas expanded from its original purpose of accompanying the serious business of drinking and bathing in the waters to providing more general entertainment. Chamber music and vocal recitals were an important element in the elaborate round of social and cultural diversions established by Beau Nash in Bath in the early 1700s and later taken up by the major watering places of continental Europe. Spa managements vied with one another to provide ever-grander concert halls and more comfortable venues for orchestral and band concerts funded by subscriptions for the season. At Kissingen the spa orchestra played on a specially constructed turntable so that it could face the Kurgarten if the weather was fine and the inside of the promenade hall, with its flowers and palms, if it was wet. A vacuum dusting plant ensured purity of air in the hall, to which both warm and cold water was piped directly from the nearby Rakoczy Spring. Noting that the amount of carbonic acid in the waters used for some of the baths gave people the impression that they were bathing in champagne, Bensusan enthused that

> quite apart from its claims as a spa, [the town] has few equals as a resort for the amusement seeker. The concerts are given by a picked orchestra that plays in Munich during the winter; and

perhaps that fact says all that need be said as to its quality. There are fine operatic and theatrical performances, and the concert hall of the *Kurhaus* is not only finely designed and pleasing to the eye, but its acoustics are entirely satisfactory.[10]

The musicians who played every morning and afternoon in the kurpark or assembly rooms changed into more formal attire in the evening for concerts, dances, and balls. Dances were a prominent item in the daily spa routine and were often prescribed by doctors as an important part of the cure. Dr Kuhn, medical superintendent at the spa in Niederbronn, Alsace, advised in 1835 that 'the waltz, practised with a sweet abandon, is a precious adjuvant [help] for the cure' although he felt compelled to add that 'the gallop, the viennoise, the allemande and the sauteuse have little benefit'.[11] The therapeutic value of music more generally was also widely acknowledged, as in the opening lines of a song in *Les Eaux du Mont-Dor*, a vaudeville piece written by Eugene Scribe and first performed in 1822, in which a lover disguised as a doctor prescribes balls and concerts to his patients:

A concert treats migraine,
For the vapours, a ball is needed.

Increasingly music assumed an importance in the life of spas not just for its therapeutic benefits and accompaniment to the cure but as one of a number of seductive and entertaining diversions and amusements. As watering places became ever more fashionable, they attracted those who were not seeking a cure for a specific ailment but rather bent on pleasure and escaping from the cares and concerns of their everyday existence. Hedonism became as important a pursuit as health and spas became as well known for their decadent and romantic atmosphere as for their beneficial waters. As early as 1674 a character in Samuel Chappuzeau's satirical comedy *Les Eaux de Pirmont* had no doubt about what really motivated visitors to France's *villes d'eaux*: 'One plays, one dances, one laughs. For every four who drink, there are around twenty others who have come only in search of amusement'.[12]

High on the list of the amusements that drew visitors to spas was gambling. It was a particularly important element in the appeal and development of the leading German spas of Baden-Baden, Bad Ems, and Wiesbaden. For several decades in the mid-nineteenth century, when gambling in Britain, France, and other countries was banned or severely restricted, the roulette wheels and card tables in the German spa casinos were a magnet for gamblers from across Europe. Their lure is graphically illustrated in the life and writings of Feodor Dostoyevsky. After winning five thousand francs in the casino at Wiesbaden in 1863 he developed a reckless addiction to gambling in the German spas. In 1867 he spent seven weeks of 'sheer hell' in Baden-Baden losing night after night and ending hopelessly in debt. During the 1870s he made four disastrous gambling trips to Bad Ems and in Bad Homburg he squandered the advance which he had received for his novel *The Gambler*. Set in the imaginary German spa of Roulettenburg frequented by Russian, French, and English visitors, it gives a vivid picture of the life of a compulsive gambler.

The gambling culture in spas had its own impact on music making. Casinos often employed their own orchestras and bands and they were important venues for major musical performances. The opening of the new casino at Aix-les-Bains in 1849 was marked by a performance of Wagner's *Tristan und Isolde* in its great auditorium with Victor Emmanuel II and his wife as the guests of honour. The commission for Berlioz's *Béatrice et Bénédict* came from the manager of the casino at Baden-Baden. Several composers found the gaming tables almost as inviting as Dostoyevsky had. Arthur Sullivan, who was a regular habitué of the casinos of the French Riviera, serenaded their appeal in his wonderfully ebullient and infectious *café chanson* setting of the 'Roulette Song' in the *Grand Duke* in which the Prince of Monte Carlo recounts his recipe for escaping from debt by inventing the game of roulette. Celebrating the little ball as a 'true coquette' who flirts with both black and red, it ends with the sober reminder that whatever happens along the way, in the end 'the bank is bound to win'. While roulette and cards proved the major attraction for gamblers in the European watering places, North American spa goers were more likely to lose their shirts on horses. During his summer sojourns in Saratoga Springs Victor Herbert spent virtually every afternoon at the racecourse, losing much of the money that he had earned playing for concerts and dances the previous evening.

Gambling was not the only diversion of a more decadent kind that alleviated the tedium of the spa regime. Flirting was another. The prospect of amatory adventures and romantic liaisons came high on many guests' agendas. Close encounters with the opposite sex were encouraged by the mixed bathing facilities provided at several spas at least at an early stage of their development. Female visitors to the southern English spa of Tunbridge Wells, which developed a reputation for sexual licence, were promised in a ballad published in 1678 that it was not just the action of the waters that would cure their barrenness and stimulate fecundity:

Then you that hither childless come,
Leave your dull marriage behind you.
You'll never wish yourselves at home:
Our youth will be so kind to you.[13]

An account of the goings-on at the Cross Bath in Bath in the early 1700s suggests that music also played a contributory role in stimulating the pleasures of the flesh:

Here is performed all the wanton dalliance imaginable; celebrated beauties, panting breasts and curious shapes, almost exposed to public view; languishing eyes, darting killing glances, tempting amorous postures, attended by soft music, enough to provoke a vestal to forbidden pleasure.[14]

As they developed beyond their original narrowly therapeutic role, spas increasingly came to be seen as daring, naughty, enticing places where people did things they would never dream of doing at home. It was part of their liminal, enchanted aura. They were the perfect venues for affairs, elopements, and romantic entanglements. This element of their appeal is perhaps supremely epitomised by the amatory adventures of Goethe in the spas of Bohemia. A stay in Karlsbad in 1795, prompted by a bout of tonsillitis, saw him fall in love with a poetess, Friederike Brun, with whom he walked up and down the Pump Room drinking sulphurous waters. He rose at 5 a.m. every morning just so that he could be sure of accompanying her. On his first visit to Marienbad in 1821, at the age of seventy-two, he developed an infatuation with the seventeen-year-old Ulrike von Levetzow and became her regular companion on walks, at tea parties, and at balls over the next three summer seasons there. In 1823, also at Marienbad, he met and befriended a Polish pianist, Maria Szymanovska, whose musical talents he celebrated in the third section of his *Trilogy of Passion*. The Bohemian spas were especially famed for the romantic liaisons that they inspired, but they were by no means unique in encouraging amours. The affair between Marie-Louise, second wife of Napoleon Bonaparte, and Count Neipperg began in 1815 in Aix-les-Bains when her husband was on Elba. Emperor Franz Josef escaped every summer to Bad Ischl partly so that he could spend time there with the actress Katharina von Schratt. In 1848 Susan, Lady Lincoln, sparked off a major society scandal in Britain by leaving her husband and going to Bad Ems to embark on an affair with Lord Walpole. The physician whom she consulted there, Dr Celius, was well known for telling beautiful upper-class ladies that their illnesses would only be cured if they separated from their husbands. There were plenty of other spa doctors who could be relied on to offer similar advice.

Along with the wish to take a cure and make money, amatory adventure was one of the motives that took Jacques Offenbach back again and again to the German spa of Bad Ems. His experiences there illustrate the combination of factors that made spas so congenial for musicians in the nineteenth century. He first went to Bad Ems early in 1858 while touring with his Paris-based company, Les Bouffes. He returned in the summer at the suggestion of his doctor to take a cure to ease his rheumatism and was delighted to find the spa full of his French compatriots, many of whom had come for the gambling recently banned by Napoleon III in their native country. As well as taking the waters, he found the time to compose most of the score of *Orphée aux Enfers*. In 1862 Offenbach was given the contract to run the music in the concert hall in the Bad Ems Kurpark. He spent the next six summers in the resort where he found the atmosphere very congenial for composing. In his first season he completed *Bavard et Bavarde*, described by Saint-Saëns as 'a little masterpiece'. He also found romance on an excursion to the nearby spa of Bad Homburg, where he fell in love with a twenty-year-old singer, Zulma Bouffar, who was performing in the music hall. Infatuated by her gipsy looks and coquettish personality, he embarked on an affair which lasted for several years. She became his constant companion during summers at Bad Ems, while his wife, Herminie, stayed at home in Paris with the children. In 1863 he gave Zulma a leading role in *Lischen et Fritschen*, a short piece that he wrote within the space of a week as a result of a bet over dinner at the Bad Ems casino about how quickly he could compose a new work. Lindheim, the conductor at the Kursaal, conducted the first performance with the handle which had broken off the rake being used by the croupier to collect Offenbach's losses at the casino the previous evening. It became something of a talisman and was subsequently used by Lindheim to conduct the opening performance of *La Belle Hélène* in Paris.

Despite the excitement of his adulterous liaison, Offenbach seems to have followed a strict and regular regime at Bad Ems, at least according to a letter to his long-suffering wife in 1864 in which he reported getting up at 6:30 every day to drink the waters, rehearsing through the morning, devoting the afternoon to composing, bathing at 4 p.m., dining at 6 p.m., and spending the evening either conducting his works or in further rehearsals and composing. He used the small makeshift stage in the Kurpark concert hall and could only accommodate a few performers to preview small-scale pieces to be performed in the subsequent winter season by the Bouffes in Paris. Altogether, eight of his works were premiered at Bad Ems between 1862 and 1867, two in the presence of King Wilhelm I of Prussia. He also used his summer spa sojourns to work on his larger operettas, like *La Belle Hélène* which was substantially composed there in 1864. 'I find health and a certain inspiration at the same time', he told his friend Villemessant, adding that Ems compared favourably with the bigger and better known spas of Baden-Baden and Wiesbaden because 'neither luxury nor idle youth have yet invaded it'.[15] As time went on, he came to find the waters less effective in relieving the pain of what was, in fact, severe gout rather than rheumatism. 'The baths have done me harm, my palpitations and pains around the heart have come back strongly' he complained in 1867. Composing and conducting, however, remained wonderfully therapeutic: 'I am soaked in music. What a wonderful douche music is! The only one, besides, which my rheumatism permits me!'[16] In 1869 Offenbach took the Bouffes to Baden-Baden, where he premiered *La Princesse de Trébizonde*. He returned to Ems the following year, conducting *La Chanson de Fortunio* in the presence of Kaiser Wilhelm I just ten days before the issue of the famous Bad Ems telegram. The Franco-Prussian War forced Offenbach to switch from a German to a French spa and in 1873 he went to Aix-en-Provence. However, for his final visit to take the waters in 1879, just a year before his death, he was back in Germany at Wildbad.

If Jacques Offenbach serves as a good example of a composer who thrived in the atmosphere of a spa, Arthur Sullivan's diaries provide a more negative view. Although plagued by excruciatingly painful kidney stones for most of his life, Sullivan only resorted to spas in his latter years, and then only for two sustained attempts at a cure. For recreation he preferred the Riviera, to which he escaped regularly, lured principally by the gaming tables of Monte Carlo. When he did finally resort to taking the waters for medicinal purposes he found the whole experience very depressing. His first attempt at a spa cure involved spending thirty days at Contrexville in the summer of 1891. He arrived there on 21 July and the following day saw the doctor at 6:30 a.m., the usual time for medical appointments. He was prescribed baths at 7 a.m. and 3 p.m. and four glasses of water between 8 and 9 a.m. Otherwise, he walked, played a little tennis, took occasional carriage rides to nearby Aix les Bains, visited the theatre in the evenings and engaged in his passion for gambling. A diary entry for 23 July notes that the doctor had prescribed camphor pastilles to take before meals and chloroform to rub on his back in case of need and then triumphantly records 'won 100 francs at Bacc' (Baccharat—as prescribed by the Brigadier in Offenbach's *La Vie Parisienne*). At the end of his thirty-day cure, he complained that 'I still have the same pains as before'. He had also found it excruciatingly boring, as he told his friend the composer Ethel Smyth:

There is a constant delirious whirl of dullness here, the counterpart of which is only to be found in England at a Young Men's Christian Association Weekly Evening Recreation. I am up at 6 am, *masse'd* and douched, and drink 6 pints of the mineral water, walking all the time until breakfast at 10. Nothing more to eat and drink till 6 when we dine—then to bed at 10, to resume the same existence at 6 next morning. I need scarcely tell you that the two meals are the two great events of the day.[17]

It was to be another seven years before Sullivan tried another full hydrotherapy treatment, this time at Bad Gastein. On the day of his arrival, 17 July 1898, he noted that while he had been given a large and sunny room, 'the only drawback is that the band plays twice a day just under my window! It can't be helped. It's not a bad little band—

21 and the conductor'. In time, he grew to enjoy the band's performances and even persuaded them to rehearse his own *Henry VIII* suite and six 'short movements' from his operas. He was impressed by their sight-reading abilities. Despite having the company of Lord Rosebery and other British aristocrats who were fellow cure guests, the distraction of daily baths and massages and the application of a hot potato poultice on both thighs from 10 p.m. to 3 a.m., he again found the experience of taking a cure tedious. At the end of his stay he confided to his diary: 'My three weeks at Gastein has been very quiet and I think very beneficial. I feel much fresher and better. The place itself is beautifully situated but dull and expensive'.

Although he did not subject himself to any further Continental water treatments, Sullivan visited a noted British spa in what proved to be the last weeks of his life. His diary entry for 1 October 1900 reads: 'Felt very seedy all day—pain from kidney trouble. Left Victoria about 3 for Tunbridge Wells, awfully nervous and in terror about myself—very low'. He settled into the Wellington Hotel, which he had chosen because of its elevated and commanding position overlooking the common, had a good walk, and was having his postdinner coffee when he felt his old and familiar pain coming on.

> In half an hour I was writhing and bathed in sweat. I couldn't stand it any longer so sent for a doctor and in my note I told him what the trouble was. He came, got me into bed, and injected something—I don't know what but certainly not morphine, which relieved me directly and gave me a good night's rest.

During his stay at Tunbridge Wells, Sullivan managed a few walks and a drive to Penshurst, which he much enjoyed, but for most of the time he felt very low. On 14 October he wrote: 'I have been here just a fortnight and what have I done? Little more than nothing, first from illness and physical incapacity, secondly from brooding and nervous terror about myself'. The following day he noted: 'Lovely day . . . I am sorry to leave such a lovely day'. It is the last entry in his diary. His condition deteriorated rapidly; he returned to London and died a month later.[18]

The monotony of the spa regime and the role of music in alleviating it is a recurrent theme of Thomas Mann's great novel *The Magic Mountain*. The author himself compared his book to a work of music,

FIGURE I.1. The Wellington Hotel, Tunbridge Wells, where Sullivan stayed shortly before his death (author's photograph).

saying that it had been 'composed' rather than written. Its setting is the House Berghof, a sanatorium perched high on a mountain near the Swiss resort of Davos catering to sufferers from tuberculosis. Mann's wife had spent six months in a Davos sanatorium in 1912 and he also drew on his own experience of taking cures at Bad Gastein. The novel evokes powerfully the boredom induced in both sanatoria and spas by the long periods of enforced rest and inactivity and the effects of a predictable and prescribed regime in an insulated environment where time ceases to have much meaning. Music, in the form of the concert given every other Sunday morning after second breakfast on the terrace of the House Berghof, supplies one of the few elements of punctuation and this is what makes it so welcome to the guests.

> It is a pleasant change. It takes up a couple of hours very decently; it breaks them up and fills them in, so there is something to them, by comparison with the other days, hours, and weeks that whisk by like nothing at all. An unpretentious concert-number lasts perhaps seven minutes, and those seven minutes amount to something; they have a beginning and an end, they stand out, they don't so easily slip into the regular humdrum round and get lost.[19]

Later in the book, Mann describes a visit by sanatorium patients to the Kurhaus in the village:

> Here too there was music, a small, red-uniformed orchestra, conducted by a Bohemian or Hungarian first violin, who stood apart from the others, among the dancing couples, and be-laboured his instruments with frantic wreathings of his body. . . . [T]he dancing became much livelier as the evening advanced, and numerous patients from the sanatoria, as well as dissipated folk from the hotels and the *Kurhaus,* came later to join the fun. More than one serious case had here danced himself into eternity, tipping up the beaker of life to drain the last drop, and *in dulci jubilo* suffering his final haemorrhage.[20]

Perhaps the most powerful testimony to the importance of music in the life of those taking the cure is the huge significance of the arrival of a gramophone in the sanatorium. 'This was no childish peep-show, like those of which all the guests were sick and tired, at which no one ever looked after the first few weeks. It was an overflowing cornucopia of artistic enjoyment, ranging from grave to gay'.[21] The novel's hero, Hans Castrop, becomes the new gramophone's custodian and manager. On the first night of its installation, he stays behind after everyone else has gone to bed and plays over twenty records to himself. It becomes 'a new passion, a new enchantment and a new burden of love' releasing him from his ennui and out-of-sorts mood. He spends his evenings playing one record after another and his nights dreaming 'of the disk circling round the peg'.[22] He develops particular favouries—the closing scene of *Aida,* the second act of *Carmen,* the prayer from Gounod's *Faust* and above all Schubert's song *Linenbaum* (Linden Tree)—'ah, what power had this soul enchantment'.

An earlier novel set in a French *ville d'eau* similarly points to the key role played by music in the lives of those taking a cure. Guy de Maupassant's *Mont Oriol,* written in 1886 and set in the imaginary town of Enval in the Auvergne, begins with a description of the hydropathic establishment set up by Dr Bonnefille: 'medical waters, douches and baths were available on one storey; beer, liqueurs and music on the other'.[23] De Maupassant, who himself took numerous cures at Aix-les-Bains, Plombières, Luchon, and Châtel-Guyon, knew his spas well. Early on he describes the band of musicians encountered by the guests at Enval as they are wandering through the grounds of the casino:

> Round the corner of the building they came upon the orchestra in a Chinese kiosk. A fair-haired young man was frenziedly playing the violin and at the same time conducting a queer trio of musicians seated opposite him, with gestures of his head, his floating locks, and his whole body, which he managed to swing like a baton, bending it, straightening it and swaying it alternately to the left and to the right. This was Maestro Saint-Landri, with his assistants, a pianist, whose instrument was wheeled on castors every morning from the hall of the Casino to the kiosk, a flautist of enormous size, who seemed to be sucking a match and tickling it with his fat puffy fingers, and a double-bass of consumptive aspect. Together they laboured to produce a perfect impression of a worn-out barrel organ.[24]

De Maupassant is particularly good at identifying the mixture of magic and boredom found in spas, not least in their music making. Towards the end of *Mont Oriol* he has one of his central characters reflect:

> These watering places are the only true fairylands left on earth. In two months, more things happen there than during the remaining ten in the rest of the world. You would really think that the springs were not so much mineralised as bewitched. You meet specimens there of every race and class, magnificent adventurers, and such a medley of nationalities as you find nowhere else, and the most astonishing incidents occur every day.[25]

Yet this sparkling, enchanted quality coexists with a depressing drudgery and dreariness in the lives and the playing of the musicians who supply the guests with an important element of their magical spa experience. It is well brought out in another description of the band playing in the casino park:

> The orchestra was haltingly executing a dreary piece of classical music, punctuated with breaks and sudden pauses. The four musicians were worn out with playing in that solitude, day after day from morning till night, with no one to hear them save

trees and brooks; exhausted with trying to produce the effect of twenty instruments, and exasperated by never receiving their full pay at the end of the month. Petrus Martel always paid part of their salary in hampers of wine and bottles of liqueurs, which the patients never touched. Above the noise of the orchestra could be heard the click of billiard balls, and voices calling the score.[26]

Confirmation of the truth of this fictional observation is provided by numerous comments from spa musicians about their poor pay and conditions and the ignominy of having to perform background music to small audiences, most of whom had their mind on other things. Playing or singing to a largely empty park or room must have been particularly demoralising and it was by no means an infrequent occurrence. It was strikingly evident to a journalist who made a July evening visit to the spa gardens that the entrepreneur Thomas Keyse rather bravely established around a spring in the south London suburb of Bermondsey in 1765:

'Come', said Mr Keyse, putting his hand upon my shoulder, 'the bell rings not for prayers, nor for dinner, but for the song'. As soon as we had reached the orchestra, the singer curtsied to us, for we were the only persons in the gardens. 'This is sad work', said he, 'but the woman must sing according to our contract.' I recollect that the singer was handsome, most dashingly dressed, immensely plumed and villainously rouged; she smiled as she sang. . . . . As soon as the spa lady had ended her song, Keyse, after joining me in applause, apologised for doing so, by observing that, as he never suffered his servants to applaud, and as the people in the road (whose ears were close to the cracks in the paling to hear the song) would make a report if they had not heard more than the clapping of one pair of hands, he had in this instance expressed his reluctant feelings.[27]

Did spas inspire a particular kind of music among the composers and performers who frequented them? Was there, indeed, a distinctive 'water music' that came from contact with the mysterious springs and geysers bubbling up out of the earth and the rituals that surrounded the bathhouses and drinking halls? There are, of course, deep and primeval connections between water and music. The idea that springs and waterfalls have an inherent musicality is especially strong in Celtic mythology. In early Irish poetry water is often portrayed as having its own instrumentality or of being used as a musical instrument by a supernatural, unknown performer. Examples include the seven musical streams of the underwater well of Connla, the five melodious streams from a shining fountain in *tir tairngiri* (the land of promise) heard by King Cormac, and the waters of Assaroe in Munster, from which the music of *tir tairngiri* gushed out in a melody 'for the sake of which one would have abandoned the whole world's various strains'.[28]

There are, of course, several well-known pieces of music directly inspired by water. Among the most famous are Franz Liszt's *Au bord d'une source* and *Jeux d'eau à la Villa d'Este*, the latter piece composed in 1877 and inspired by the sound of the fountains at the Villa d'Este in Tivoli, near Rome, where Liszt stayed on several occasions. Perhaps the most evocative is Ravel's *Jeux d'Eau*, written in 1901 and inspired by Henri de Régnier's poem *Fête d'eau*, about the fountains at Versailles. At the top of the manuscript score, Ravel quoted a line from the poem 'Dieu fluvial riant de l'eau qui chatouille' (The river goddess laughing at the water which tickles her), a reference to the goddess, Latona, sitting naked on the back of a tortoise. The composer later wrote that this piano piece was 'inspired by the noise of water and by the musical sounds made by fountains, waterfalls and streams'.[29] Another water spirit, the nymph Undine, has inspired at least nine musical works: operas by E. T. A. Hoffmann, Albert Lortzing, Alexei Lvov, and Peter Tchaikovsky; ballets by Cesare Pugui and Hans Werner Henze; a flute sonata by Carl Reinecke; a piano prelude by Debussy; and the first movement of Ravel's *Gaspard de la nuit*. There is a rather fine statue of Undine in the middle of a fountain in the kurpark at Baden bei Wien, but none of these pieces were written there.

In fact, I cannot find a single piece of music either directly about or influenced by water that was composed in a spa. Neither Brahms's *Rain Sonata* nor Chopin's *Raindrop* Prelude were written when their composers were on one of their relatively frequent visits to a spa. The sound and presence of the natural mineral waters does not seem to have been a significant influence on any of the composers who wrote music while staying at spas. Johann Strauss found inspiration from the incessant rain in Bad Ischl and Franz Lehár from the River Traun

FIGURE I.2.
The fountain dedicated to Undine
in the Kurpark, Baden bei Wien
(author's photograph).

that flows through that spa town, but neither they nor any other composer seems to have found musical inspiration from drinking mineral waters or sitting in a thermal bath. Walks in the countryside were a much more fruitful source of inspiration during their sojourns in spas than the waters themselves. This is not, of course, to say that their spa setting was merely incidental to the many works composed there. The distinctive ambience, atmosphere, and companionship that spas provided were all vital to the creative process but the actual presence of the waters themselves was not a major influence.

Spas per se may not have inspired a distinctive musical style on the part of the composers who frequented them but did they cultivate one in terms of what was performed there? Can we extrapolate from the repertoire of kurhaus orchestras and pump room trios a distinctive and characteristic 'water' music? As the following pages demonstrate, there was a breadth and eclecticism in the music that was performed in the watering places of Europe and North America in their heyday. One of the more surprising features of spa concerts and recitals is the dominance of Wagner's music in the repertoire. I have already noted two indicators of his popularity among those taking the waters: the fact that Rossini first heard his music while staying at a spa and the choice of *Tristan und Isolde* for the opening of the casino at Aix-les-

Bains. Wagner was also extremely well represented in the repertoire of the Buxton Pavilion Orchestra (see page 157). On his last visit to Bad Ems in 1879 Dostoyevsky complained that the orchestra there would play no Mozart or Beethoven, 'only that utterly dreary scoundrel Wagner'.[30] Given Wagner's own considerable enthusiasm for water treatments and cures, it is perhaps not inappropriate that his music was so often played at spas.

Spa music could be quite demanding and 'heavy' in keeping with the mood of desperation and serious purpose that gripped many of those taking a cure in the hope of relieving constant debilitating pain and conscious of their mortality. This was also true of the music that was composed in spas. Some of Beethoven's deepest works, notably the *Missa Solemnis* and the Ninth Symphony, were written in Baden bei Wien. Brahms composed the most desolate of all his works, *Gesang der Parzen*, in Bad Ischl in 1882. The dominant mood of the music most often played in the spas of Europe and North America in their heyday, however, was light and perhaps best summed up in that phrase 'soft music' used by the rather scandalized visitor to Bath in the early 1700s. Waltzes, marches, gallops, polkas, and cotillions were the staples of the kurpark bands and pump room trios as they still are today. It was such 'soft music' that helped those taking the cure face the prospect of early morning promenades sipping evil-tasting waters, sent them gently to sleep as they sat in wicker chairs in kurparks and on hotel balconies after lunch, and encouraged their dancing, gambling, and amorous adventures in the evening. For many of their clients, often referred to in the German phrase as *kurgäste* (cure guests), spas were places to escape from mundane and unpleasant reality and pursue pleasure as much as health. Their purpose is encapsulated in a song from *Les Eaux du Mont-Dor*, a musical comedy set in the Auvergne spa:

Far from the town,
In this retreat,
What pleasure
To gather together!
In this retreat
Pure and tranquil,
Gaiety
Takes the place of health!

Those taking a spa cure because of agonising pain and desperation rather than for more decadent pleasures equally craved gaiety and escape in the form of music that was instantly appealing, easy on the ear and melodic. It was not surprising that the first record played on the new gramophone by the medical director of the Berghof sanatorium in *The Magic Mountain* should have been the overture to Offenbach's *Orphée aux Enfers:*

> A solo violin preluded whimsically; the bowing, the *pizzicato*, the sweet gliding from one position to another, were all clearly audible. It struck into the melody of the waltz, '*Ach, ich habe sie verloren*', the orchestral harmony lightly bore the flattering strain—enchanting it was to hear it taken up by the ensemble and repeated as a sounding *tutti*. The finish was abandon itself, a gallop with a drolly hesitating beginning, a shameless can-can that called up a vision of top hats waved in the air and flying skirts.[31]

If light music was what those engaged in the serious and tedious business of taking a cure needed and appreciated, it was even more appropriate as an accompaniment to the racier pleasures increasingly being pursued by other spa guests. A journalist describing the 1925 season in a French spa noted:

> Everywhere in the casinos light music is in full swing. Certain peevish spirits and some easily upset critics leave every year for the countryside against the fashion which gives the victory to easy music over heavily armed music, to the cavalry over the heavy artillery. And then? Why not admit that the public in these summer resorts has need of rest for the ear as well as rest for the intelligence and that it easily allows itself to profit from lullabies and restful melodies, from catchy and pretty rhythms?[32]

One particular genre does, I think, stand out as the quintessential 'water music'. Operetta, classically defined by Franz Lehár as 'something to be diverted by and then forgotten' and by Richard Traubner as 'basically designed to promote good feeling', perfectly fulfilled the prime purpose of the music played at spas.[33] It is not surprising that so many operetta composers found spas congenial and fruitful places to work: Offenbach in Bad Ems, where he wrote *Orphée aux Enfers*, described by Traubner as 'the first great operetta and the model for future operettas';[34] Karl Millöcker, Carl Zeller, Karl Komzak, and Carl Ziehrer in Baden bei Wien; Victor Herbert, the first American operetta composer of international importance, in Saratoga Springs; and above all, Franz Lehár, Emmerich Kálmán, Robert Stolz, Leo Fall, Oscar Straus, and the other leading figures of the 'silver age' of Viennese operetta in Bad Ischl. With their unreal, escapist, enchanted atmosphere, spas were quite often compared to operetta settings, as in Lady Wolseley's description of Marienbad in a letter to a friend: 'This place would bore you to death. It is extremely pretty, just like the scenery of an operetta, but the performers are those of a burlesque, grotesque from fat'.[35] The close links between spas and operetta continue. The four major operetta festivals in Europe all take place in spa towns: the Lehár Festival in Bad Ischl; the operetta festival in Baden bei Wien; the Offenbach festival in Bad Ems and the International Gilbert and Sullivan Festival in Buxton.

It is surely no coincidence that the two best-known and most popular operettas of all time, *Die Fledermaus* and *Die Lustige Witwe* should have been respectively set and composed in a spa. When Richard Genée reworked Henri Meilhac and Ludovic Halévy's three-act comedy *Le Revéillon* to produce the libretto of *Die Fledermaus*, he transferred the setting from Paris to 'a spa near a big city', almost certainly Baden bei Wien, where he himself had a villa. *Die Fledermaus* is not the only operetta to be set in a spa. In 1861 Halévy and Hector Crémieux wrote an operetta with music by Delibes set in Bad Ems and entitled *Les Eaux d'Ems*. *Pauline or the Belle of Saratoga*, written by Hart Pease Danks in 1874, recounts the lives and loves of a group of guests taking the waters over a summer season in Saratoga Springs.

Franz Lehár wrote substantial parts of the score of *Die Lustige Witwe* during his first visits to Bad Ischl, the Austrian spa he was to make his summer home for the second half of his life. He came closer perhaps than any other composer to producing a distinctive 'water music' influenced by and reflecting the unique culture and ambience of the European spa in its heyday. It is not to be found in the infectiously light and accessible melodies of *Die Lustige Witwe* but rather in the much darker, more haunting and bittersweet operettas he composed in his villa overlooking the River Traun in Bad Ischl in the 1920s. It is there, for me at least, above all in *Der Zarewitsch*, the tragic story of the heir to the Russian crown, which premiered in 1927. The hero is a figure all too familiar in the spas of Europe, imprisoned in a gilded cage, with all the outward trappings of wealth and power but tormented by loneliness, uncertain sexual feelings, and a sense of the transitory nature of pleasure and escape from the grim reality of life. The score of this particular operetta catches the ambiguity of the spa goer's experience and the mixture of desperation and decadence involved in taking the cure. At one level it is gloriously romantic, full of soaring Puccini-like cadences and escapism into a sunny, exotic world of tango dance rhythms. It is also full of wistful longing, melancholy, and a sense of impermanence and mortality. The oppressive atmosphere was superbly conveyed in the 2008 production at the Lehár Festival in Bad Ischl, where the stage was ringed by silver statues of soldiers carrying guns, amplifying the sense of the Crown Prince being confined and trapped, much as the *kurgast* is. The chorus wore masks and constituted a threatening presence, a reminder of the roles played out in spas and the frightening reality from which so many guests are seeking to hide. Like the hero's brief period of happiness with the girl he loves, which is cut short by his father's death, the spa experience can only be transitory and temporary. In the words of the most haunting song from this operetta: 'Warum hat jeder Frühling, ach, nur einem Mai?' (Why does every Spring have only one May?)

1

Bath

Bath was the first significant watering place in Britain and it established the model for spa life that was broadly followed across Europe from the mid-eighteenth to the early twentieth century. This model included a key role for music making. It was Bath that pioneered the tradition of music being played while people both drank and bathed in the thermal waters and of its becoming an essential adjunct to the cure. It was there, too, under the influence of Richard 'Beau' Nash, that the central features of social and recreational life for spa guests were developed. They included morning and afternoon promenades and social gatherings to exchange gossip in purpose-built assembly rooms and dances, balls, gambling sessions, concerts, and theatrical performances in the evening, all of which invariably had musical accompaniment.

The mineral waters at Bath flow at a rate of half a million gallons a day at a constant temperature of 48°C (120°F). Legend has it that they were discovered by Bladud, a British prince, who lived sometime between the ninth and fifth centuries BC and was banished from his father's court because he suffered from leprosy. He became a swineherd and wandered around the Avon Valley with his pigs, which also contracted a scrofulous skin disease. One day he came to a steaming swamp. The pigs plunged in and later emerged healed of their disease.

Bladud then ventured into the swamp and found that it cured his leprosy. He returned to his father's court and succeeded him as king, establishing his seat at the site of the mineral springs. Whatever the truth of this foundation legend, the springs at Bath were certainly an important site in ancient British times, being dedicated to the Celtic god Sul. Towards the end of the first century AD the Romans built cisterns to retain the healing waters, established baths, and named the town that grew up around them Aquae Sulis.

Bath seems to have been regularly resorted to by people seeking the cure-giving properties of its waters throughout the Middle Ages and continued to develop in the Tudor and Stuart periods. Among the diseases that its waters were thought to help were rheumatism, gout, leprosy, palsy, anaemia, digestive disorders, syphilis, and gonnorhea. The King's Bath, named after Henry I, was built soon after 1100 and was followed by other smaller open-air baths, including the Cross Bath and the Hot Bath. In 1597 a small rectangular bath was constructed for the exclusive use of women. It became known as the Queen's Bath after Anne of Denmark, wife of James I, bathed there for her dropsy.

From at least the mid-seventeenth century bands of musicians serenaded visitors as they bathed, drank the waters, and promenaded around the town. A sketch made in 1662 by Willem Schellinks shows a group of musicians playing at the foot of the steps leading up to the drinking fountain that had been set up the previous year at the corner of the King's Bath, so that people could drink the waters as well as bathe in them. Visiting Bath in 1668 the diarist Samuel Pepys recorded his unease at entering the Cross Bath at 4 a.m.: 'methinks it cannot be clean to have so many bodies together in the same water'. After two hours in the bath, he was 'carried away, wrapped in a sheet, home to bed, sweating for an hour, and by and by comes musick to play for me, extraordinary good as ever I heard in London'.[1] In the 1680s musicians occupying a specially constructed gallery were entertaining bathers in the open-air Cross Bath. Other musical entertainment was also being provided in the town, which, by the end of the seventeenth century, had become 'more famed for pleasure than for cures'. The earliest known reference to a public concert is one in 1700 to 'a consort of delicate musick, vocal and instrumental, performed by good masters'.[2] It seems to have taken place during the supper interval of a ball in the Town Hall.

It was following visits by Queen Anne in 1702 and 1703 that Bath became England's foremost resort, attracting those seeking health and pleasure and many of the social, political, religious, and artistic leaders of British society. Bath's preeminence lasted throughout the eighteenth century and brought thousands of rich and influential people to the small Somerset town. The man largely responsible for establishing that preeminence and instigating the complex rules and conventions that were taken up as a model by many Continental spas, Richard Nash, arrived in Bath in 1705 at the age of twenty-nine. Within a few months of his arrival, this fastidious Welsh opportunist found himself made master of ceremonies, after the incumbent was killed in a duel over a gambling dispute. Nash remained in his post until 1761 and his extravagantly dressed figure with fancy waistcoat and black wig topped by a jewelled cream beaver hat became a familiar sight around the town. He made Bath the premier spa not just of Britain but of Europe by imposing a rigorous code of dress and etiquette on all who came to take the waters and greatly improving the town's moral and physical atmosphere. Duelling and the carrying of swords by men were prohibited, begging was suppressed, and Nash personally supervised the cleaning, paving, and lighting of the streets as well as taking full personal control of all social activities.

Bath flourished under Nash's firm but benevolent rule, and by 1715 more than eight thousand people were arriving annually for the main autumn season, which lasted from late October until Christmas. A slightly less fashionable spring season ran from late January until early June. Later on in the eighteenth century, the two became merged and Bath was 'on heat' for much of the year with the season effectively lasting from autumn to early summer. Guests stayed for anything from two weeks to two months. Most came less for the therapeutic benefits of the waters than for the glittering social life and diversions. Daniel Defoe, visiting Bath in the early 1720s, noted that 'it is the resort of the sound, rather than the sick'.[3]

Bath was laid out according to classical principles in the early eighteenth century as an elegant Georgian resort town built around the central spa complex. A Pump Room was constructed next to the King's Bath in 1706, affording an elegant hall where people could drink the waters—three glasses each morning was the usual prescribed dose—in a sociable setting. The first set of Assembly Rooms was built nearby in 1709 near the Gravel Walks along which 'the company', as those spending the season at Bath came to be known, paraded. Another, larger building was established there in 1730, which came to be known as 'Old' or 'Lower' Assembly Rooms, especially after 1771 when what became known as the 'New' or 'Upper' Assembly Rooms were built to a design by John Wood near the Circus.

Life for 'the company' revolved around a series of regular and prescribed rituals. The day began early with guests being carried from their lodgings in sedan chairs at around six in the morning to one of the bathhouses so that they could bathe in the hot baths. They then gathered in the Pump Room to take their statutory three glasses of water and gossip. The Pump Room was substantially extended in 1751–52, with large windows put in to afford a good view of those wallowing in the adjoining open-air King's Bath, as described by Christopher Anstey in his *New Bath Guide* of 1766:

> Oh 'twas pretty to see them all put on their flannels,
> And then take the waters like so many spaniels:
> And though all the while it grew hotter and hotter
> They swam, just as if they were hunting an otter.[4]

Following breakfast at a coffee house or in the Assembly Rooms, a daily service at 11 a.m. (or sometimes noon) in the Abbey close to the Pump Room drew many of the 'company' as much for social as spiritual reasons. Most then either returned to the Pump House to mingle or promenaded along one of the parades in the early afternoon. Dinner, the main meal of the day, was taken at 3 p.m. or 4 p.m. followed by a further visit to the Pump Room, more walking, or tea in the Assembly Rooms. The evening was given over to card playing and entertainments. A typical week's programme during the season included dress balls on Mondays and Fridays, cotillion balls on Tuesdays and Thursdays, a subscription concert on Wednesday, and a visit to the theatre on Saturday. Sunday evenings offered a variety of church services and sacred oratorios. Oliver Goldsmith, writing in 1762 about Nash's achievements, noted: 'Bath yields a continuous rotation of diversions, and people of all ways of thinking, even from the libertine to the Methodist, have it in their power to complete the day with employments suited to their inclinations'.[5]

Music played a large part in virtually all these daily activities from the bands that serenaded the early morning bathers and drinkers to the orchestras that provided music for the balls, which ended, on Nash's orders, promptly at 11 p.m. The official musical life of the spa revolved around the Pump Room, where an orchestra played in the morning and afternoon, and the Upper and Lower Assembly Rooms, which were the venues for most of the concerts and balls, with more informal music making taking place in many other locations, including the churches, pleasure gardens, taverns, and coffeehouses. There were also numerous private concerts and entertainments in the grand houses that Bath's aristocratic and wealthy visitors rented for the season. Several of the guests brought their own musicians with them and not a few were themselves accomplished musicians. It was not uncommon for gentlemen amateurs to join professional musicians for concerts and recitals.

Nash himself was responsible for introducing what remains to this day the most conspicuous feature of the musical life of Bath spa, the band of musicians who play every morning and afternoon in the Pump Room. Nowadays their audience is more likely to be sitting drinking tea and eating Bath buns than parading up and down sipping the thermal waters, although these are still dispensed from a fountain at the side of the room. There has been an almost unbroken daily tradition of live music in the Pump Room for over three hundred years. The longest and fullest description of its origins comes from the pen of Francis Fleming, who was leader of the Pump Room orchestra from the early 1730s until 1778. In his account of the history of Bath from 1670, he noted that at the time of the construction of the Pump Room in 1706 'the band of music consisted of five only, most of whom Mr Nash disapproved, being very indifferent performers. They played in the Grove under some large trees'.[6] This seems to be a reference to itinerant musicians, probably little more than buskers, who entertained those walking through the town and seem to have largely relied on tips from passers-by that they divided among themselves every week. According to Fleming, Nash was prevailed on to have a proper band of musicians performing daily in the Pump Room by the doctors of Bath who argued that

The least stroke imaginable upon any musical instrument has such an effect on the human body as to move its component *machinulae* in all their parts, giving up the fibres of the whole body, more or less according to their degree of tension, correspondent concussions; and consequently the spirits are not only raised, or made finer, but the other animal fluids are also briskly agitated, and their preternatural cohesions and viscidities destroyed.[7]

Fleming expanded on this extraordinary piece of medical gobbledegook by adding his own endorsement: 'Music has this advantage above all exercises, that the concussions made upon the fibres by any instrument are short, quick and easy, whereby the nervous fluid is not only smoothly pushed on in its circulation, but also the natural contextures of all the animal threads are better preserved by their being never over strained.' After inviting his readers to consult the work of Dr Mead on the power of music in the poison of the tarantula, he went on to express his regret that music 'is not universally practised, as well for the amusement as benefit of the company where all other medicinal waters are frequented'.[8]

According to Fleming, Nash procured seven performers from London 'and in order to put them on a more respectable footing than the former band, permitted them to play in the Pump Room'.[9] Nash levied a subscription of two guineas to cover the cost of music both at the Pump Room and the evening balls. This sum was usually spent by Christmas, when another subscription was raised to allow the balls to go on until mid-January. Fleming notes that Nash granted a salary of two guineas a week to each performer, one guinea for attending the Pump Room and another for playing at balls. The musicians were required to play at the Pump Room from 8:30 to 10 a.m. in the winter season and from 8 a.m. until 10 a.m. in the spring season, every morning except Sunday. Other early accounts of the origins of music in the Pump Room substantially agree with Fleming's with minor variations. Oliver Goldsmith's *Life of Richard Nash*, published in 1762, notes that 'his first care when made master of the ceremonies, or King of Bath, was to promote a music subscription of one guinea each, for a band which was to consist of six performers, who were to receive a guinea a week for their troubles'.[10] A piece in the *Bath Chronicle* on 17 March 1803 dates the start of regular Pump Room concerts to 1710.

It is clear from these and other accounts that from very early in Nash's reign over Bath music of a high standard was being played every day as people gathered to drink water and converse in the Pump Room. The size of the group playing there fluctuated. A coloured

etching of the interior of the Pump Room reproduced on a fan usually dated to 1736 shows five musicians led by a trumpeter playing in
a small semicircular balcony, access to which was apparently gained
by climbing a ladder. In fact, this may possibly show a scene after the
1751 renovations, which provided a small gallery at the west end 'sufficient to hold a small Band of Musick for the Entertainment of the
Water Drinkers every Morning during the Seasons.'[11] By 1767, there
seem to have been nine musicians. The breakfast concerts had by then
been supplemented by recitals at noon. The musicians in the Pump
Room had to play against a background of chatter and the pouring
and clinking of glasses of water. Writing around this time, John Penrose
observed that it was hard to hear their 'tweedle-dum and tweedle-dee'
above the general hubbub. Lydia, a character in Tobias Smollett's
novel *Humphrey Clinker*, published in 1771, gives a similar impression in her description of the Pump Room in midmorning: 'the noise
of the music playing in the gallery, the heat and flavour of such a
crowd, and the hum and buzz of their conversation, gave one the
headache and vertigo the first day; but afterwards all these things became familiar and even agreeable.'[12]

Morning musical entertainment was not confined to the Pump
Room. There were also breakfast concerts in the Assembly Rooms,
where those not wishing to take the waters repaired after their early
baths to read and take coffee. One such concert on 11 October 1741
was marred by the death of Ralph Thicknesse, described by his brother,
Philip, as 'reckoned the best gentleman player on the fiddle in England'. He collapsed while playing first violin in one of his own concertos. The doctor who attended him gave the cause of death as a
stroke brought on by anxiety over the performance of his work, but
his brother reckoned that he died of 'the Bath waters' of which he had
drunk plentifully earlier in the morning before eating a hearty breakfast of spongy rolls.[13] Gentlemen amateurs like the unfortunate Thicknesse regularly performed alongside paid professionals from the Pump
Room and Assembly Room bands in the orchestras that played for
balls and concerts in the evenings. These evening ensembles often
numbered a dozen or more players, typically composed of four to
six violins, one or two violas and cellos, a double-bass, harpsichord or
organ, plus woodwind and brass, on which there was much doubling.

Formal dress balls constituted a major feature of the Bath social cal-
endar. Most took place in either the Lower or Upper Assembly Rooms

and fell into two distinct halves. The first part of the evening, which generally began around 6 p.m., consisted of French dances, including the bourée, courant, and especially the minuet. The long minuet, which opened proceedings and often went on for a considerable time, was a highly formalised ritual and more of an introduction than a dance. It was presided over by Nash, who, going in strict order of precedence, introduced each man present to a partner. The couple then danced a complete figure before the lady retired and Nash introduced the man to a new partner. The band played the same piece through-out, involving much repetition or the use of specially written tunes like 'The New Bath Minuet'. The second half, which followed after a lengthy supper interval, consisted of country dances. The dress code for the French dances was extremely formal, with gentleman required to wear dress wigs and ladies hoops and lappets. Around 1770 the cotillion, a formalised country dance danced in sets of four couples, arrived in Bath from Paris. It became extremely popular and there were regular cotillion balls for the rest of the century. In the 1790s Scottish reels and strathspeys and Irish jigs gained popularity.

Concerts were a regular feature of the Bath season from at least the 1740s. Their appeal was boosted in 1745 when legal restrictions on gambling made them the chief diversion on evenings when there were no balls. The Lower and Upper Assembly Rooms vied with each other to have the most enticing concert programme, and other venues were used, including the Town Hall and the Abbey, especially for sacred concerts. Evening concerts usually began at 6:30 p.m. and consisted of two distinct halves with a break in between for a substantial meal. From the middle of the eighteenth century, the programme for the first half increasingly focused on baroque music while the second half was made up of 'galant' or classical compositions or sometimes given over to a single oratorio or sacred work. Orchestral items were inter-spersed with instrumental solos and songs, primarily of English and Italian airs.

The concerts were financed by a separate subscription paid by those staying in Bath for the season. Nonsubscribers paid five shillings per concert, which was roughly double what subscribers were paying. The revenue raised in this way was basically inadequate to pay the pro-fessional musicians properly and most relied heavily on special benefit concerts, from which all profits went to a particular artiste. The bene-fit system was also used as the main means of rewarding visiting performers. Many local musicians supplemented their meagre earnings by keeping public houses and inns, taking in lodgers, giving music lessons, and pursuing a variety of other trades from brush making to sign painting. Although they often struggled financially, the spa offered considerable employment opportunities for professional musicians, and in the words of Kenneth James, who has written a doctoral thesis on the concert life of eighteenth-century Bath, 'it is doubtful if any other provincial centre in the country could boast of a more able nucleus of professional performers'.[14]

The concert repertoire was dominated by Handel, several of whose works were almost certainly heard in Bath before anywhere else in the United Kingdom. Virtually every eighteenth-century concert in the town for which there is a surviving programme or mention includes a piece by Handel. There were numerous performances of his oratorios, especially the *Messiah, Acis and Galatea, Judas Maccabeus, Israel in Egypt,* and *Solomon,* and of his solo songs and concertos. By the middle of the century the work of Italian composers such as Alberti, Corelli, Germiniani, and Giardini was becoming increasingly popular and from the 1760s J. C. Bach was often on the programme. The work of Haydn and Pleyel entered the repertoire of the Assembly Room orchestras in the 1780s—on 1 January 1784 a benefit concert featured Haydn's *Stabat Mater*—but there was relatively little Mozart until the 1790s, when his overtures began to appear on the progammes. The earliest appearance of Mozart in a Bath concert seems to have been with a piano concerto in 1785. Among British composers, only Arne, Boyce, Purcell, and Webbe appeared with any frequency and were mostly represented by songs.

The orchestras for evening concerts, made up of the Pump Room band augmented with other professional and amateur players, were supplemented by visiting artistes and soloists. Italians were especially popular. Among the first was Elizabetta de Gambarini, who came in 1746 to play the harpsichord and to sing. There was considerable rivalry between visiting Italian musicians and local players. This reached a peak in the 1750s when Giuseppe and Christina Passerini sought to dominate Bath's musical life and put on rival performances of Handel oratorios shunning local players. In the autumn season of 1757 they attempted to usurp a benefit concert in aid of Daniel Sullivan, a local singer, and turn it instead into one entirely for their own advantage. A local harpist, Mr Roberts, retaliated by putting on his own benefit

concert at which he promised 'no foreign fiddlers, nor foreign squeek-
ers; I have reason to despise them, as all English musicians ought to
do'.[15] Frustration with the Passerinis came to a head in December 1758
when Giuseppe demanded a fee of ten guineas for his wife and three
guineas for himself for a performance of Handel's *Solomon* in which
he expected local players to perform without payment. The wrath of
the entire Bath musical establishment turned against them and they
were forced to depart. Less controversial were the infant prodigies
from home and abroad who were regularly brought in to play in concerts. William Crotch performed on the harpsichord and violin in
1784 when he was just nine, and J. B. Cramer made his debut in a subscription concert in 1786 at the age of fifteen playing a Mozart concerto. In 1789 a ten-year-old black violinist, Master Bridgtower, billed
as the grandson of an African prince, caused a particular sensation.

A succession of prominent and accomplished musicians, several
of whom achieved national fame, directed the musical life of Bath
throughout its eighteenth-century heyday. The first was Francis Fleming (1715–78), who was appointed leader of the Pump Room orchestra soon after he came to Bath in 1732. He held this position until his
death, became the first director of the subscription concerts, led the
theatre orchestra, and was also much involved with balls and dances.
Himself a dancing master, he visited Paris every summer to keep up
with the latest dances in the fashionable ballrooms there. Fleming
effectively superintended music making at the Old (later Lower) Assembly Rooms from 1744 until shortly before his death, although
others challenged his supremacy at various times, notably Passerini
through the 1750s.

Thomas Chilcot (1707–66) was the leading keyboard player in
Bath until the 1750s. He was organist of the abbey from 1728 and a
member of the Pump Room orchestra. It was Chilcot who principally
introduced the music of Handel to Bath. He himself wrote harpsichord concertos and songs. One of his pupils, Thomas Linley senior
(1733–95), became a leading figure on the Bath musical scene, writing
numerous songs that were regularly sung at concerts and by glee
clubs and directing many concerts in Bath from the mid-1750s until
1774, when he went to London to become director of music at Drury
Lane Theatre. His daughter, Elizabeth, a noted soprano, appeared at
Covent Garden and eloped to France with Richard Sheridan in 1772.
His son, Thomas Linley junior (1756–78), was an infant prodigy who

became known as the English Mozart. At the age of eight he played the solo part in a violin concerto at a public concert in Bath. After studying with Boyce and then in Italy under Nardini, where he met Mozart, he returned to Bath, where he led the orchestra for the subscription concerts held in the New Assembly Rooms from 1771 to 1776. After his death in a drowning accident in Lincolnshire, Mozart described him as 'a true genius' who, had he lived, 'would have been one of the greatest ornaments of the musical world'.[16]

The two other leading figures in the musical life of Bath in the later eighteenth century both hailed originally from the Continent. William Herschel (1738–1822) was born in Hanover and first came to Britain when the band of the Hanoverian Guards, in which he was an oboist, was stationed in Kent in 1756. He moved to Bath in 1766 to be organist of the Octagon Chapel, one of several privately owned proprietary chapels built to cater to the spiritual needs of the Bath 'company'. A polymath, he taught the harpsichord, guitar, and violin and later devoted himself to astronomy, discovering the planet Uranus. Like Chilcott he was a devotee of Handel and the first performance that he conducted in Bath was of the *Messiah* in October 1767 to mark the opening of the organ at the Octagon Chapel. He was organist there until 1782 and conducted numerous sacred works. A particularly notable concert in 1772 included Allergi's *Miserere*, Pergolesi's *Stabat Mater*, and the first performance in England of Palestrina's *Reproaches*. Herschel promoted a series of outdoor concerts in baths and pleasure gardens, sang as principal vocalist in many oratorios, and wrote symphonies, concertos, chamber sonatas, glees, and catches. He had an uneasy relationship with Thomas Linley junior, whom he accused of failing to provide him with a music stand whenever he was playing in the New Assembly Rooms. As a result of what Herschel took to be this deliberate slight, he claimed that he had to drag his own stand the considerable distance from the Pump Room or the Old Assembly Rooms every time he had a concert there. In 1776, he succeeded Linley as musical director at the New Assembly Rooms and presumably at last got his own music stand.

Perhaps the most significant contributor to music making in Bath during its golden age, and certainly one of the spa's most colourful characters, was the Italian-born castrato Venanzio Rauzzini (1746–1810), for whom Mozart wrote his motet *Exultate, Jubilate* in 1773. He settled in Bath in at 1780 as a well-established composer, having already been engaged for concerts in the town in the late 1770s. From 1780 until his death thirty years later Rauzzini directed several of Bath's major musical activities. He organised and conducted the subscription concerts at the New (Upper) Assembly Rooms, directed, accompanied, and composed for the gentlemen's singing clubs, and conducted and performed at many private concerts and soirées. He wrote much music for the theatre and several cantatas, including *The Genius of Britain,* written to celebrate the recovery from illness of George III in 1789, and *Old Oliver: or the Dying Shepherd* in 1796. Rauzzini also penned numerous instrumental works, overtures, and marches that were played at subscription concerts, including several written to encourage patriotism during the Napoleonic Wars and boost the spirits of local volunteers, like his 'March Dedicated to the Volunteer Corps of Bath', performed in the first concert of the 1798–99 season.

During the three decades that he dominated the musical life of Bath, Rauzzini did much to improve its standards and make it more fashionable. He brought several leading Continental musicians to the town, including the Italian violinst Giovanni Viotti, who had a clause inserted in his contract with the London Italian Opera Company allowing him to perform in Bath during the 1794–95 season. Rauzzini also promoted local artistes, including the soprano Anne Cantelo, a pupil of J. C. Bach, and the flautist Andrew Ashe. Idolised by the ladies, one of whom, Lady Gooch, who was married with two children, was said to have offered him £10,000 'to go off with her', Rauzzini was one of the few Bath musicians to be seriously wealthy. He had both a town house and a substantial villa on the outskirts where he entertained visitors, including Haydn. He always maintained, however, that his subscription concerts left him on the verge of bankruptcy and was constantly trying to get the subscriptions put up to what he regarded as a more realistic sum that would properly cover costs. In February 1794 a special benefit concert was arranged to compensate him for losses sustained at the season's subscription concerts, where his own pupils were the principal performers. By then the price of admission to each evening concert had risen from 5s to 7s 6d, with subscribers effectively paying half that price per concert.

As well as the regular subscription and benefit concerts, there were also charity concerts put on 'in aid of the industrious poor'. An interesting insight into the economics of these events comes from a detailed account of a charity concert performed in June 1781 in the Town Hall.

For carrying music and instruments to and from different parts of the town, chairmen received 16s. For bringing, putting up, taking down, and carrying back staging and stands for the orchestra, porters and carpenters were paid 12s. Tuning the harpsichord cost 5s and a guinea was shared between six people who checked tickets, cleaned the concert room, put out the benches, and distributed the concert bills. With the musicians giving their services free, total costs came to only £2.14.0 and the charity received the proceeds of over £46.

On the whole, there was much more interest among Bath concert-goers in who was playing and singing than in the works being performed. Notices advertising concerts in the local newspapers quite often failed to make mention of what would actually be played, while giving prominence to the names of the performers and sometimes also to the composers represented. A typical notice advertising Miss Cantelo's benefit concert on 1 January 1789 simply promised music by Handel and Cimarosa. There were a good number of recitals by soloists, sometimes of an unusual nature, such as that advertised for 1 January 1784: 'Mr Cartwright performs on musical glasses at New Assembly Rooms'. On 6 January 1785 the New Assembly Rooms hosted 'Mademoiselle Denis on Pedal harp' and on 4 January 1787 a triple harp concert.

Despite Nash's best efforts, the behaviour of the audiences at Bath concerts often left much to be desired. Fighting among servants trying to secure the best seats for their employers led eventually to a ban on the reserving of seats and unruly behaviour among the footmen and chairmen waiting for passengers at the end of concerts led to all servants being banned from the entrance to the Assembly Rooms.

It was not uncommon for people to walk into concerts halfway through a piece being played and walk out long before the end. Kenneth James comments that 'for the majority of Bath's company music was of no greater importance than a means of spending an idle hour, or providing further social contact'.[17] A cartoon by Thomas Rowlandson of a concert in the 1780s shows several members of the audience chatting and at least one sleeping through a recital by a female singer accompanied by a fifteen-piece orchestra. At a concert in the New Rooms on 15 April 1778 the radical politician John Wilkes was 'seen to be paying more attention to the fire in Mrs Stafford's eyes than to the silvery voice of Miss Cantelo or to the graceful rendering of selections from the *Messiah*'.[18] The composer Charles Dibden complained

FIGURE 1.1. Cartoon by Thomas Rowlandson of a concert in Bath in the 1780s (Bath Central Library).

after a midday concert in March 1787 that the Bath audience greeted all performances 'with a vacant gravity, an unfeeling stare, a milk and water indifference' and added 'Heaven defend me from such a set of insipid, vague, unmeaning countenances'.[19]

Dibden was generally unimpressed by the atmosphere in England's leading spa, writing after his visit that 'at Bath everything is superficial . . . everything gay'.[20] Other leading musical luminaries who visited it were more complementary. Josef Haydn, who stayed with Rauzzini in 1794, accompanied by the Venetian composer Giambattista Cimador, thought it 'one of the most beautiful cities in Europe' and showed his appreciation by writing a round to serenade his host's dog 'Turk'. Carl Abel, the German bass viol player and friend of J. C. Bach, was a regular visitor. While many of the visiting musicians were drawn principally by the spa's social and cultural pleasures, some came specifically for the waters. The French composer and violinist François-Hippolyte Barthélemon came in 1767 to accompany his sick wife, who was taking the waters. He found himself drafted to lead and conduct the Gentlemen's Public Subscription Concerts, for which he was paid with a benefit concert. Handel visited Bath to take the waters in 1749 and returned again in 1751, possibly to receive treatment from the local physician, Dr Pierce. On 12 April 1759 he was preparing to go to Bath for a cure but became too ill to travel and two days later he died.

Alongside the formal serious music provided by the subscription concerts in the Assembly Rooms and Town Hall, there was much informal music making. Several catch clubs and glee clubs met in taverns and coffeehouses. They were usually all-male affairs but held regular ladies' nights. Singing took place from 7 to 9 after which a substantial cold supper would be served, with port and sherry to drink, followed by more singing until 11 p.m. Several bands played in the town's pleasure gardens. A wind band of horns and clarinets played at breakfast time in Spring Gardens. The City Waits, whom Nash had snubbed in favour of London players for his Pump Room band, also continued to make their presence felt throughout the town. As well as playing along the gravel walks where visitors paraded they also serenaded newly arrived guests outside their lodgings and demanded a tip, traditionally half a guinea from a nobleman and five shillings from a commoner. Orders issued by the town corporation in 1774 instructed the Waits 'to desist from playing at lodging houses to the great disturbance of the sick and others who resort to this place'.[21] Even the churches sought to cash in on the distinctive musical welcome that they could offer guests. The arrival of visitors for the season was often greeted by the bells being rung in several of the town's churches, with the campanologists expecting a handsome tip for their labours.

Bath's musical life reached its apogee in the closing years of the eighteenth century. The *Bath Chronicle* of 15 December 1796 proudly described the standard and range of musical performances in the town as being 'without competition in the kingdom'. The opening subscription concert of the 1799–1800 season drew an audience of over seven hundred, one of the best houses ever and by all accounts more attentive than they had been for much of the preceding century. The Pump Room was further extended in 1795. Its continuing role at the hub of the spa's musical life was well captured in the *Bath Herald* of 2 November 1799:

> The Pump Room Band is one of the oldest and best establishments of this place; it draws the visitor and inhabitant from the most distant parts of the city to one general place of morning rendezvous; there long-parted friends indulge in unexpected

meetings, whilst the inspiring melody of the orchestra spreads a general glow of happiness around.

Before leaving the eighteenth century, it is worth making a brief detour about 150 miles east from Bath to another English spa put on the map by Beau Nash. Tunbridge Wells, on the Kent and Sussex border, never attracted more than four thousand visitors each season compared to the twelve thousand who flocked to Bath at the height of its popularity. Yet during the seventeenth century, when its chalybeate (iron-rich) springs were visited by Queen Henrietta Maria, King Charles II, and the future Queen Anne, Tunbridge Wells was, if anything, more fashionable than its later better-known rival. Nash was appointed master of ceremonies there in 1735 and for the next twenty-six years he divided his time between the two spas, helped by the fact that the Tunbridge Wells season was largely concentrated in the summer months when Bath was at its quietest. He established a similar programme of entertainments with two balls a week in the Assembly Rooms and a weekly subscription concert.

There was no pump room in Tunbridge Wells, where the cure was based on drinking the waters dispensed by a lady known as 'the dipper' from the spring at the far end of a paved walk laid out at the end of the seventeenth century and known as the Pantiles. The spa band, paid for by subscription and ensconced in a charming little first-floor gallery that still survives just a hundred yards or so along the Pantiles from the spring, provided musical accompaniment as guests paraded up and down sipping their cups of water. They played three times every day: in the early morning when most people took the waters and then 'practised the necessary exercise of walking'; after a break for morning prayers when 'the company' took to the Pantiles again to promenade and converse; and finally after dinner when many returned to stroll in the evening air and show off their 'full and splendid attire'. Like Bath, Tunbridge Wells prospered throughout the eighteenth century and went into a slow decline in the nineteenth. When the novelist William Thackeray walked through the Pantiles in the early 1850s, he had a distinct sense that the glory had departed:

There are fiddlers, harpers, and trumpeters performing at the moment in a weak little old balcony but where is the fine company? Where are the earls, duchesses, bishops and magnificent embroidered gamesters? A half-dozen children and their nurses are listening to the musicians; an old lady or two in a poke bonnet passes; and for the rest, I see but an uninteresting population of native tradesmen.[22]

Bath and Tunbridge Wells both suffered in the nineteenth century from the rise of a new kind of cure, sea bathing, and the consequent growth in popularity of coastal resorts. Royalty were among the first to forsake inland spas for seaside towns, the prince regent going to Brighton in 1783 and George III choosing to recuperate after a long illness at Weymouth. Along with the other English spas, Bath went into a slow decline, with inevitable consequences for its musical life. The subscription concerts, direction of which was taken over on Rauzzini's death in 1810 by Andrew Ashe and later in 1838 by John Loder, came to an end in the early 1840s. In addition to the declining audience and the long-standing difficulty of raising sufficient funds through subscriptions, they seem to have been killed off by the proliferation of amateur musical performances for which there was no charge. Perhaps they also finally fell victim to the long-standing indifference and bad manners of the Bath audiences and their preference for flirting or gossiping rather than listening to good music.

Jane Austen's last novel, *Persuasion*, begun in 1815, includes a scene set at a fashionable Bath concert. For the heroine, Anne Elliott, amatory considerations come before musical ones: 'Anne's mind was

FIGURE 1.2.
Music Pavilion in the Pantiles, Tunbridge Wells (author's photograph).

in a most favourable state for the entertainment of the evening: it was just occupation enough: she had feelings for the tender, spirits for the gay, attention for the scientific and patience for the wearisome; and had never liked a concert better, at least during the first act.'[23] While she was able to explain the words of an Italian love song to her cousin, Mr Elliot, affording him a frisson of excitement, it is on Captain Wentworth that her eye and her thoughts are fixed during the performance. Unfortunately he did not seem to enjoy the concert and also, she felt, seemed jealous when later Mr Elliot asks her to translate another Italian song. Before the end of the concert, Captain Wentworth bids Anne goodnight. 'Is not this song worth staying for?', she asks, hoping that she might persuade him to remain with her. 'No!' he replies, 'there is nothing worth my staying for' and he walks out before the end of the evening's entertainment in the best traditions of the Bath concert audiences.[24]

Despite the disappearance of the weekly subscription concerts, Bath continued to attract leading musical luminaries throughout the nineteenth century. Niccolò Paganini played three times in the 1831–32 season. Joseph Joachim performed frequently. Johnann Strauss the elder came to the Upper Assembly Rooms with his orchestra for two concerts in the summer of 1838. Franz Liszt gave three recitals in September 1840. Louis Jullien conducted twelve Promenade concerts in November 1840. Jenny Lind gave four recitals between 1847 and 1862 and Clara Schumann appeared six times between 1867 and 1873. In 1867 Arthur Sullivan conducted his oratorio *The Golden Legend* at the Theatre Royal with a 250-voice choir and 70-strong orchestra. In the same year there were also two concerts given by the American Slave Troupe and Brass Band, made up of freed slaves.

Much music making still went on in people's homes and at dances and glee clubs. An indication of its vitality can be gained by browsing through the catalogues of John Charles White, who published and sold sheet music at his music warehouses at No.1 Milsom Street and No.3 George Street. His 1815 catalogue shows what was particularly popular in Bath at the time.[25] It is divided into six categories:

1. Piano pieces—predominantly rondos, waltzes, and marches
2. Quadrilles 'by the best modern composers with their proper figures in French and English, as danced at the Bath Rooms and Nobilities Assemblies'

3. Dances 'as performed at all fashionable assemblies and arranged for pianoforte'
4. Harp pieces—predominantly rondos and waltzes, some arranged for harp, piano, and flute or violin
5. Vocal items—predominently Handel's songs
6. Sacred pieces—'a selection of the most admired hymns and psalms as sung in all places of worship'

White also composed the music to love songs, such as 'Ah Edward, why didst thou consent?'—a particular favourite sung by Mr Ashe at the Bath concerts—and turned out numerous dance tunes for the Bath assemblies with titles like 'The Dandy Beaux' and 'The Fairy Queen'. They were published as single sheets of music with brief instructions for the dance printed at the bottom.

Music continued to be provided in the Pump Room throughout the nineteenth century. The 1815 edition of *The Original Bath Guide* described the Pump Room orchestra as 'a nursery for good musicians which encourages professors of superior merit to settle here'. However, standards had slipped by the time Augustus Granville, the Italian-born doctor who wrote extensively about the spas of England, made his first visit to Bath:

> Formerly, the Bath Orchestra and its Pump Room musical performances were the theme of general commendation in England. With the decline, however, of the renown of the Spa, its musical attractions declined likewise; until at length the mere semblance of an orchestra remained, such as I myself heard as late as 1839, to scrape upon a few sorry cremonas the same eternal bars of Corelli and Handel every day at two o'clock.[26]

Granville attributed the poor quality of the music to the fact that the Pump Room was open free of charge and attracted 'a score or two of idlers, many of them of the lowest order'. However, when he returned to Bath in 1840, he was pleased to note that 'the establishment of a moderate rate of subscription has enabled the managers to introduce, for a six-month season, Promenade concerts'. As a result, 'the influx of visitors has greatly increased in number, as well as respectability, and the promenade in the great Pump Room, at the noon tide hours of fashion, is become *une affaire de rigueur* for the elite and the elegant of this beautiful city'. He noted grandly that 'the last thrill of the corneto' having sounded from the gallery band, 'the fashionable throng is sallying out of the saloon to spend an hour or two in visiting or walking, in observing and being observed'. He also expressed delight with 'the recently introduced first-rate military band, which performs daily during the season, from two till four o'clock, the choicest productions of Rossini, Auber, Strauss, and the other favourite composers'.[27] The Promenade concerts proved popular: in 1855 they were taking place, apparently free of charge, on Tuesday, Thursday, and Saturday afternoons.

Detailed surviving records of the Pump Room band give a fascinating insight into its fortunes in the later nineteenth century. Here, for example, is the balance sheet of income and expenditure for the 1859–60 season:

Subscriptions and donations	£117.14.0
Single tickets	£57.4.2
Benefit concert proceeds	£16.12.6
Total income:	£185.10.8
Salary to band	£160.0.0
Printing & advertising	£13.4.10
Bill posting	£19.0
Cleaning pump room	£5.5.0
Two doorkeepers	£4.0.0
Gratuity	£2.0.0
Sundries	£1.10.0
Total expenditure	£185.10.8[28]

For the 1865–66 season the orchestra had fifteen players and performed sixty concerts through the winter, with a subscription for the whole series costing just 5s. Individual admission was 6d per concert. The money coming in from subscriptions and admission fees was not sufficient to cover costs and Bath Corporation (i.e., the Town Council) was obliged to provide an annual subsidy of around £100 to meet the shortfall in receipts. In 1869 the Corporation debated, not for the first or last time, the wisdom of continuing with the Pump Room orchestra. One councillor asked, 'Do we have to pay them? They only have to saw and blow'. His view did not prevail and the councillors agreed to maintain a thirteen-piece orchestra made up of wind and string players. Bath Corporation continued to subsidise the Pump Room orchestra at the rate of £80 a year through the 1870s. In 1876 a voluntary committee of Bath citizens appointed to manage music in the Pump Room agreed that 'appealing as it does to a refined audience, it should be of an attractive and superior character and worthy of enlightened support'.[29] A thirteen-piece orchestra was engaged to play for two hours on three afternoons a week for a twenty-week season beginning in mid-November. Subscription rates were fixed at 5s for a single and 7s 6d for a double ticket and nonsubscribers could attend a concert for 6d. In 1877 the Corporation agreed to daily concerts but in 1880 reverted to holding them on alternate days.

William Salmon, who conducted the Pump Room orchestra from 1869 to 1884, was very popular. He was succeeded by Herr Van Pragg, who continued until 1892, being replaced by Max Heymann, who shot himself in the garden of his home in 1911 after finding out that he was incurably ill. Frank Tapp then took over and played through the First World War with a repertoire that included at least sixty symphonies. He noted that Beethoven's (of which he played all nine) were the pivot around which all else revolved and Tchaikovsky's the biggest draw, followed by Brahms's four symphonies, Dvořák's *New World*, and César Franck's Symphony in D. Tapp brought Stanford, Elgar, and German to Bath to conduct their own works and established a weekly routine in the Pump Room with Thursday afternoon being the time for symphonies, Thursday evening for light classics, and Saturday evening for operatic selections. He was relieved of his position in 1917, according to some sources because he had introduced the work of Schönberg to Bath, and succeeded by the clarinettist George Robinson, who was paid £278 for his first season.

Overcrowding in the Pump Room in the early 1890s, by which time there were daily concerts again, led to calls for it to be improved and enlarged. Comparisons were made between the cramped facilities at Bath and the spacious provision for music making in Continental spas: 'In almost all foreign watering places the Pump Room is a main feature, but at Baden Baden and other spas it is made entirely subservient to the means provided for health, recreation, promenade, reading and more especially music'.[30] A report from the Corporation noted that while the Bath Pump Room 'is a fine room most successfully built for music', trying to use it both for water drinkers and daily concerts meant that 'one branch or other must necessarily suffer'. A committee set up to look into the question concluded that 'the present Pump Room should be devoted exclusively to the drinkers with provision for readers of the daily papers and other literature' and in 1897 an extension to the Pump Room was built as a concert hall. It is now the entrance lobby for the Roman Baths.[31] The programme for an afternoon concert between 3 p.m. and 5 p.m. on 9 November 1899 under Max Heymann shows that in its new home the Pump Room orchestra was offering a substantial classical diet:

Part 1
Prelude: *Colomba* Mackenzie
Overture: *Leonore* No. 3 Beethoven
Traume (violin solo) Wagner
Piano Concerto, No. 2 in D Minor Mendelssohn (first performance in Bath)
Part 2
Septet for Strings, Trumpet and Piano Saint-Saëns (first performance)
Song: Love Sleeps Only Rebelly
Cradle Song Mozart
Fantasie: The Marriage of Figaro Mozart

The repertoire in 1899 included some major works—Beethoven's *Eroica* Symphony was played on the afternoon of 16 November—but also embraced lighter fare. The evening concert that day included a Suppé overture, selections from Sullivan's *The Yeomen of the Guard*, and Offenbach's *Orphée aux Enfers*, the intermezzo from *Cavalleria Rusticana*, and a xylophone solo by Dietrich. In its new concert hall, the Pump Room orchestra gave afternoon concerts daily and evening concerts on Tuesdays, Thursdays, and Saturdays. There were also public rehearsals between 12 and 1 p.m. on Mondays, Wednesdays, and Fridays. Throughout the summer a military band, usually the band of the First Volunteer Battalion of the Somerset Light Infantry, played in the pleasure gardens at Hedgemead Park. A contract made with this band in 1897 stipulated that 'the band shall play not less than eight tunes between the hours of 7 & 9pm'. The 1901 contract required the bandmaster to provide 'lamps and oil during the performance'.[32] Visiting bands also came to Bath, notably Sousa's in 1911.

For the 1908–9 season the Pump Room orchestra numbered twenty-one players plus a conductor. They were paid at varying rates between £1.1.0 and £4.15.0 a week. The composition was three first violins, two second violins, viola, cello, double bass, flute, oboe, two clarinets, bassoon, two horns, two cornets, trombone, timpani and drums, and a keyboard accompanist. The orchestra was contracted to play for thirty-three weeks from 26 September. In the summer months from 18 May to 12 September a military band played every afternoon and evening from Monday to Saturday and on Tuesday, Thursday, and Saturday mornings in various locations around the town. A good number of its members were drawn from the ranks of the Pump Room orchestra. In 1909 the Corporation again reviewed Bath's musical provision. A special committee was set up to consider the desirability of employing the orchestra throughout the year rather than just on a seasonal basis. Max Heymann told the committee when he appeared before them that this would provide a much better standard of music and pointed out that 'whilst 10 years ago a second-rate military band used to suffice for places such as Margate, Folkestone, Brighton, Bridlington etc at the present all these places vie with one another to have the best string orchestras'. The orchestras at Buxton and Harrogate were bigger and better paid than the one at Bath. He suggested that instead of charging 5s for two hundred concerts, the Corporation should think of charging 5s per concert: 'If a tradesman gave away his wares in that fashion he would be considered a lunatic'.[33]

The committee approached other resorts and found that they had substantially bigger orchestras: Bournemouth had forty-five players, Buxton thirty-three, and Bridlington twenty-six. It recommended that Bath should have a larger orchestra playing throughout the year. The Corporation, however, was unwilling to take on a larger deficit than it already incurred in running the existing smaller seasonal orchestra. The accounts for the 1907–8 season showed that the orchestra cost £2,397, with only £1,796 being raised through subscriptions and ticket sales, leaving a £701 deficit. So the Pump Room orchestra continued to be hired on a seasonal basis. The contract with Frank Tapp in 1911, for example, stipulated that for a total salary of £250 and the proceeds of two benefit concerts he would engage musicians and prepare concerts for thirty-three weeks from the end of September. In 1917 a different arrangement was tried with a smaller group of musicians performing for fifty weeks of the year. An eighteen-piece orchestra was contracted to perform for six afternoon and two evening concerts of two hours each in the Pump Room through the winter and

FIGURE 1.3. The Bath Pump Room orchestra in 1917 (Bath and North East Somerset Record Office).

for a total of twenty-four hours each week during the summer, with a quintet of piano, two violins, cello, and bass playing additionally every morning in the winter. The contract stipulated that each player 'shall appear five minutes before the commencement of each concert in black coat and vest and dark trousers, dark tie and black boots at morning, afternoon and outdoor evening concerts and in evening dress with black-tie, dress shirt with stiff front and black boots at the evening concerts'. The Corporation agreed to provide tubular bells and a piano but all other instruments were the responsibility of the musical director. Members of the orchestra were paid £2.16.0 for first instruments and £2.12.6 for second instruments.[34]

The Pump Room orchestra fluctuated considerably in size during the 1920s, at one stage being reduced to a septet but later expanded to fifteen players under the direction of Jan Hurst, who remained until 1929. The first time Hurst conducted César Franck's symphony, an elderly lady dropped dead in the Pump Room. Just before the next performance of the work, a few months later, the cellist tripped on his way to the platform and broke his leg. During Hurst's third performance of this symphony, someone drowned in the baths. He never attempted to conduct the work again. In 1929 Thomas Beecham was invited to conduct the Pump Room orchestra while taking tea with the dowager Duchess of Somerset. He obliged with the dances from Stravinsky's *Prince Igor*. In 1930 a Festival of Contemporary Arts in the Pump Room opened with an afternoon concert by an augmented Pump Room orchestra conducted by Edward Dunn, who took over from Hurst. It included Elgar's overture 'In the South', Delius's Concerto for Violin and Orchestra, Holst's 'St Paul's Suite for Strings', and Quilter's 'Three English Dances'. Subsequent concerts in the festival included Walton's *Façade* with Constant Lambert, Eric Coates conducting some of his own work, a piano recital by John Ireland, three concerts devoted to the work of Albert Ketelbey conducted by the composer, much music by Delius, Howells, and German, and a tribute to British composers of the past, which included Sullivan's *In Memoriam* overture, excerpts from the *Beggar's Opera*, Purcell's Suite for Strings, and works by MacKenzie, Brewer, Coleridge-Taylor, and Bishop. Audiences at Bath were notably more avant-garde and progressive than those in other spas and seaside resorts and were accordingly treated to several contemporary British compositions little heard elsewhere. As Kenneth Young reflects, 'What other resort would have put on *Bethlehem* by Rutland Boughton—the eccentric composer who lived at Glastonbury—or even his much better known *The Immortal Hour* (in costume)?'[35]

Under Edward Dunn and his successor, Maurice Miles, the Pump Room orchestra was expanded to eighteen players and provided a remarkably varied repertoire through the 1930s. Monday evenings were given over to popular music and included modern dance tunes such as *Tiger Rag*. The Tuesday programme was light classical and on Wednesday a full symphony concert was performed at both 3 p.m. and 8 p.m. Miles instituted Thursday evening Promenade concerts and on Saturday the orchestra was joined by solo vocalists, including Anne Zeigler and Elisabeth Schumann. Concerts from the Pump Room were regularly broadcast live by the BBC.

The orchestra was disbanded in 1939 and music making was suspended during the Second World War, when the Pump Room was used as a shelter for those bombed out of their homes. It took some time after the war for regular music making to resume and when it did so it was on a much smaller scale than before. In the early 1950s a Pump Room Trio was formed, led by Sidney Jones, who was one of the first musicians to play for silent films in Britain. The trio is now a well-established feature of the Pump Room, playing seven days a week, both morning (10–12) and afternoon (2:30 to 4:30) in summer and on mornings only in the winter at a total cost to the local council, which continues to employ the musicians, of around £70,000 a year. The postwar period also saw a more general revival in Bath's musical life with the founding in 1948 of the 'Bath Assembly' as a festival devoted to eighteenth-century music. In 1959 Yehudi Menuhin was appointed its artistic director. He was succeeded by Michael Tippett from 1970 to 1974 and William Glock from 1975 to 1984. It has recently incorporated jazz and contemporary music and as the Bath International Music Festival fills the spa town with music during the last two months of May every year.

2

Baden bei Wien

Thanks to its proximity to Vienna, patronage by successive Habsburg emperors, and close links with both Mozart and Beethoven, Baden bei Wien had an important role in the cultural and musical life of Austria in its imperial heyday. Almost certainly the intended setting for *Die Fledermaus*, it became the favourite resort of a number of operetta composers in the late nineteenth century and is now one of the main European venues for operetta performance. Just twenty-six kilometres south of the Austrian capital on the edge of the Vienna Woods, the small spa town lies on a geological fault through which more than one and a half million gallons of highly sulphurous water erupt every day at temperatures ranging from 24° to 36°C (80° to 97°F).

As in Bath, the naturally hot mineral waters at Baden were enjoyed and exploited by the Romans. In 70 AD the grateful soldiers of the Thirteenth Legion, finding that the waters gave some relief from the rheumatism they suffered in the cold damp air far from their Mediterranean homeland, dedicated a tablet to the nymphs of the spring. By the reign of Emperor Diocletian at the end of the third century AD, the small township that grew up around the thermal baths fed by the hot springs appeared on maps under the name *Aquae*. During the Middle Ages Baden acquired a racy reputation, with men and women bathing together naked in communal baths. In 1480 Emperor Friedrich III, who often frequented the waters, gave Baden a coat of arms depicting a man and woman sitting naked in a small circular bathtub. A treatise on taking the waters in Baden, written by Dr Wolfgang Wintperger in 1512, was the first book in German devoted to a spa. In 1531 Emperor Ferdinand I gave the springs now known as 'Frauenbad' and 'Karolinenbad' as a present to the town and granted the inhabitants the right to levy a charge of two pfennings for each visitor to the baths. An imperial edict in 1626 sought to prevent mixed bathing and establish separate bathhouses for men and women but it was overruled by the town councillors, who clearly knew what was good for business.

The sulphurous waters at Baden have always been used predominantly for bathing rather than for drinking, although they were sometimes mixed with milk or whey and prescribed to be drunk for catarrhal affections of the gastrointestinal and respiratory organs. Bathing in the waters has long been recommended for those with gout, rheumatic conditions, and skin diseases. Although the atmosphere in the bathhouses became less licentious following the Reformation and Counter Reformation, with long ankle-length white linen bathing robes being made compulsory for men and women, communal bathing continued and there was much conviviality with meals and drinks being served to bathers who often spent several hours together in the water. Baden's proximity to Vienna made it an ideal retreat from the city during hot and dusty summers and attracted an increasingly fashionable clientele in the eighteenth century, led by Emperor Francis I and Empress Maria Theresia. The first spa gardens were laid out in 1792 and named the Theresia Gardens in her honour.

It was imperial patronage that put Baden firmly on the map as a leading spa in the early nineteenth century. In 1796 Francis II, the last Holy Roman emperor (and first emperor of Austria), came to take the waters. He enjoyed the experience so much that he continued coming for stays of two to three months virtually every summer until his death in 1835. Baden became the summer residence of the imperial court and as a result attracted leading figures from the worlds of politics and the arts. Elegant colonnaded bathhouses, hotels, and villas were built in the Biedermeier style. In 1812 a new theatre replaced the hall erected by the town council in 1767 for plays and concerts. The spa's popularity did not wane following Francis II's death. Although his successor, Ferdinand I, did not patronise Baden, having been put off the place by an assassination attempt in 1832, an increasing number of Viennese made the relatively short journey from the ever-more crowded and polluted capital to take the waters and relax in the Kurpark. In 1897 a direct tram route from Vienna opened, reducing the journey from three and a half hours to less than an hour. The Badener Bahn still runs from the Vienna Opera to the Josefplatz in the centre of Baden. The town continues to be a major spa resort today, with around 420,000 overnight guests staying every year, of whom over 200,000 are taking a cure, the majority being financed by insurance schemes. A range of treatments are carried out in the Kurmittelhaus, to which thermal water from fifteen springs is channelled through a central pipe.

Music assumed an early importance in the life of the spa, which was described by an early visitor as 'a miniature Vienna in watercolours'. There are accounts of lusty and bawdy singing among bathers in the sixteenth and seventeenth centuries. Imperial patronage brought more refined music making to Baden in the late eighteenth century. Francis II was himself an enthusiastic amateur musician and played second violin in a string quartet that met regularly in the home of Ernst Trost, the mayor. The emperor's brother, Archduke Karl, remembered as a formidable military commander who triumphed over Napoleon at Aspern, employed Ludwig von Köchel, the assiduous researcher and collector of Mozart's works, as tutor for his children. As a result, Köchel spent fourteen summers at Weilburg Castle at the entrance to the Helenental Valley on the outskirts of the town. The first prominent composer who came to Baden primarily to take the waters was Christoph Gluck, who took a cure in 1781 following two strokes. He reported that as a result he had 'once more escaped from the jaws of death'.[1]

Baden's most famous musical guest in the eighteenth century did not himself take the waters. Wolfgang Amadeus Mozart first visited in August 1773 when he and his father, Leopold, were staying in Vienna for two months in the hope, vain as it proved, that he might obtain an appointment at the imperial court. They hired two carriages and drove out to Baden after lunch one Saturday with two other families, returning on the Sunday evening. This visit seems to have been purely for social and sightseeing purposes. Mozart came to Baden again in June 1784 to visit Count Johann Thun, who was taking a short cure there. He became a much more regular visitor later in the 1780s on account of the illness of his wife, Constanze, whom he married in 1782 when she was just twenty. Between 1783 and 1791 she gave birth to six children, only two of whom survived infancy. The strain of almost constant pregnancy and complications surrounding most of the births put her into a state of poor health. Early in the summer of 1789 she developed a serious infection in her foot, which became ulcerated and led to her being confined to bed. A series of lengthy cures involving bathing at Baden was prescribed, and between 1789 and 1791 she spent several weeks at a time there, often staying with her son, Karl, who had been born in 1784, and sometimes accompanied by her husband's pupil, Franz Süssmayr. Although Mozart remained at home in Vienna working, he regularly visited her.

The expense of these cures exacerbated Mozart's considerable financial difficulties and he was forced to ask for help from his friends and patrons. A letter to Michael Puchberg, a Viennese textiles manager and fellow Freemason on 17 July 1789, begged for financial support because of 'the very heavy expenses in connection with the cure my wife may have to take, particularly if she has to go to Baden'. It ended with the coda: 'My wife was wretchedly ill again yesterday. Today leeches were applied and she is, thank God, somewhat better'.[2] Puchberg immediately sent 150 gulden in response. A week or so later he received another letter with the news that Constanze's condition had eased 'and if she had not contracted bed-sores, which make her condition most wretched, she would be able to sleep. The only fear is that the bone may be affected. She is extraordinarily resigned and awaits recovery or death with true philosophic calm'.[3]

Soon after she was installed for her first cure in the middle of August 1789, Mozart visited Constanze in Baden and stayed for three nights. She remained there for two and a half months. Mozart was not inattentive, visiting when he could, sending her an infusion, electuaries, and ants' eggs to hasten her recovery and insisting that she should never go out walking alone, but pressure of work and rehearsals for a revival of The Marriage of Figaro demanded his presence in Vienna for much of the time. The absence of his wife allowed him to press on with work. While she was in Baden he finished his Piano Sonata (K.576), wrote his String Quartet in D (K.575), and probably also began work on his Clarinet Quintet (K.581) and his opera Così fan Tutte. Constanze returned home to Vienna in November and gave birth to a baby girl who survived for just an hour. After another winter and spring of illness, she was back again in Baden in late May 1790. Returning to Vienna to conduct Così Fan Tutte after visiting her in early June, Mozart wrote to Puchberg, 'my wife is slightly better. She already feels some relief, but she will have to take the baths sixty times—and later on in the year she will have to go out there again. God grant that it may do her good'.[4] Puchberg responded by sending 25 gulden.

Although there is no evidence that Mozart himself ever tried bathing in the Baden waters to ease the rheumatic fever from which he suffered in his latter years, he seems to have been an enthusiast for spa treatments despite their heavy cost. Writing to Constanze from Munich in November 1790 he suggested that the two of them should make a journey further afield to some German spas 'so that you may try some other waters'.[5] It was, however, to Baden that she returned the following year, now pregnant with their sixth child. Her cure was partly financed by the 50 ducat advance that Mozart had received for the Requiem commissioned by Count Franz Walsegg-Stuppach for his wife, who had died aged twenty.

During his earlier visits to Baden Mozart had struck up a close friendship with Anton Stoll, the town's school teacher, choir master, and organist at the parish church. The two men regularly drank together and Stoll performed Mozart's masses in the church with the composer himself sometimes conducting the choir in the organ loft. It seems quite likely that Constanze lodged in the organist's house during her first two stays in Baden. By the time of her third cure, however, her deteriorating condition dictated a change of lodgings. At the beginning of June 1791 Mozart wrote to Stoll: 'Will you please find a small apartment for my wife? She only needs two rooms, or one room and a dressing room. But the main thing is that they should be on the ground floor'. His first choice was for rooms next to the butcher's shop but failing that the ground floor of the town notary's house would also do very well. Given the state of her leg, the other key requirement was 'for something fairly near the baths'.[6] Stoll acted quickly and on 4 June Constanze and Karl were installed in ground-floor rooms at *Zum Blumenstock*, the notary's house in Renngasse, close to the Antonsbad where she would be taking her baths. Three days later Mozart, who was in the middle of composing *Die Zauberflöte*, wrote to her expressing delight at her report that she was in good health 'and that, very sensibly, you were not taking baths every day'.[7] In another letter he counselled:

When you are bathing, do take care not to slip and never stay in alone. If I were you I should occasionally omit a day in order not to do the cure too violently. I trust that someone slept with you last night. I cannot tell you what I would not give to be with you at Baden instead of being stuck here. From sheer boredom I composed today an aria for my opera. I got up as early as half past four.[8]

Constanze remained in Baden through June and the first half of July. Mozart made frequent brief visits to Baden to see her, often leaving Vienna at 5 a.m. There is a well-established local story that one night he arrived very late and, finding it impossible to rouse anyone by knocking on the door and ringing the bell pull, attempted to gain entry to her ground floor apartment through an open window. One version has it that he was accosted by an army officer who lived in the house opposite and had taken a fancy to Constanze, another that he was apprehended by a drunken guard who hauled him off to the local police cells, provoking Mozart's reflection: 'It was the cheapest night I ever spent in Baden'. In fact, he found Constanze's rooms, which abutted straight onto the street, too noisy and when he himself stayed overnight in Baden, he took a small room in a cottage in the courtyard of the notary's house. It was while staying there on 17 June 1791 that he composed his exquisite setting of the ancient communion hymn *Ave Verum Corpus* (K.618). Just forty-six bars long and scored for SATB chorus accompanied by strings and organ, this jewel-like piece, as it has been described, received its first performance in Baden parish church under Stoll's direction six days later on the feast of Corpus Christi. There is some debate as to whether the work was commissioned by Stoll or written by Mozart either in lieu of rent owed for Constanze's lodgings the previous year or simply as a thank-you present for the choirmaster's help in arranging her accommodation. It is perhaps significant that aside from the unfinished Mass in C Minor and the Requiem, it is the only piece of church music written by Mozart during the last ten years of his life.

The expense of this third and longest cure led Mozart yet again to write begging money from Puchberg, who stumped up another 25 gulden. On 30 June Mozart wrote entreating his wife 'to take the baths only every other day, and only for an hour. But if you want me to feel quite easy in my mind, do not take them at all, until I am with you again'. She does not seem to have heeded his advice, for two days later he was writing in response to a report that she had a stomach upset: 'Perhaps the baths are having a too laxative effect? My advice is that you should stop them now! Today is the day when you are not supposed to take one and yet I wager that that little wife of mine has been to the baths. Seriously I had much rather you would prolong your cure well into the autumn'.[9]

Mozart continued to make regular visits to Baden to see his wife. During a stay from 9 to 11 July, he attended the parish church on Sunday morning where his *Missa Brevis* in Bb Major (K.275) was sung with Stoll's eleven-year-old sister-in-law as the soprano soloist. His letters to Constanze were full of medical advice as well as tender sentiment. In one he promised to enquire at the court chemists 'where the electuary may perhaps be obtained. . . . Meanwhile, if it is necessary, I should advise you to take tartar rather than brandy'.[10] Constanze took his advice about prolonging her cure and, following the birth of their sixth child, Franz, on 26 July and after taking a break when she and Mozart made a visit to Prague together for the first performance of *La Clemenza di Tito*, she returned to Baden at the beginning of October shortly after the opening of *Die Zauberflöte* in Vienna.

As before, her husband made frequent brief visits but he told her that he found it impossible to work in Baden. Continuing financial problems made it imperative for him to go on composing and this meant he had to remain in Vienna. In her absence, he regularly rose at 4:30 a.m. and worked on until midnight, completing his Clarinet Concerto in A (K.622) and his Requiem. He continued to express a keen interest in the progress of her cure, writing on 8 October: 'I hope that these baths will help to keep you well during the winter. For only the desire to see you in good health made me urge you to go to Baden. I already feel lonely without you'.[11] He also sent her almost daily bulletins on the progress of *Die Zauberflöte*. On 14 October he sent her a long letter detailing the enthusiastic comments of Antonio Salieri and his mistress, Caterina Cavalieri, on his new opera: 'they both said that it was an *operone*, worthy to be performed for the grandest festival and before the greatest monarch'.[12] It is the last known letter of Mozart's to survive. The following day he and Karl went to Baden to bring Constanze home and on 17 October they returned to Vienna. He was exhausted from overwork and over the next few weeks became progressively more ill, apparently with rheumatic fever. He died on 5 December, just seven and a half weeks before what would have been his thirty-sixth birthday.

Did Baden have any influence on Mozart's music? Apart from his miniature masterpiece *Ave Verum Corpus,* he does not seem to have composed anything while visiting his wife there. The indirect influence of Baden on his music making, however, was arguably considerable. It is not wholly fanciful to suggest that the need to make money to pay for Constanze's cures, the enforced solitude and leisure that her protracted absences in Baden produced, and the heightened emotion reflected in his letters to her combined to make the summers of 1789–91 among the most productive of his career. Some of his most lyrical work, including much of *Die Zauberflöte* and the clarinet quintet and concerto, were composed while she was away undergoing the cure. In his biographical study Wolfgang Hildesheimer raises the question of whether in fact Mozart packed Constanze off to Baden to be rid of her. He also speculates as to whether she had an affair with Süssmayr while there and wonders why her husband sent his young assistant off to be with her rather than keep him in Vienna to work on copying out opera parts. It is difficult to make a judgement on these questions. Although Mozart seems to have been manoeuvred into marriage with Constanze by her mother, he had a genuine affection for her and the letters he wrote almost daily while she was staying in Baden display much tenderness and affection. They also show his interest in the minutiae and mechanics of spas. Perhaps the more intriguing question is whether he would have survived longer if he had himself taken a cure.

As it was, Constanze outlived her husband by fifty-one years, marrying the Danish diplomat Georg Nissen and dying at the age of eighty in 1842. She went on visiting spas but switched in later life from Baden to Bad Gastein near Salzburg where, coincidentally, Mozart's mother had taken a four-day cure in 1750. There, in the words of Hildesheimer, 'she spent many weeks each year, mindlessly vegetating'. Certainly a diary entry from 1829 that he quotes suggests a dull regime, consisting of bathing, taking short walks, lying down, and knitting. The only remotely exciting event that she reports is delaying arrival for her 8:00 bath until 9 a.m. 'because the stranger, who will take my letters with him to London and whose name I still do not know, bathes in the nude and I cannot as a respectable woman bathe with him'.[13]

Mozart was not the only major composer whose wife resorted to Baden for her health at the end of the eighteenth century. Josef

Haydn's unloved and unloving wife Anna Maria spent considerable periods there in her latter years seeking to alleviate her rheumatism. In 1793 Haydn complained that she was 'ailing most of the time and always in the same bad temper'.[14] Writing to a friend in November 1799 he noted that she had gone to Baden ,'where she intends to spend the winter because of the baths', taking with her a portrait of himself, not because of any wifely affection but because it was the work of her lover, Ludwig Guttenbrunn.[15] This visit was, in fact, destined to be her last. On 20 March 1800 she died in the home of Anton Stoll, with whom she had often lodged while taking the waters. Stoll admired Haydn almost as much as he admired Mozart and often performed his masses with his choir in the parish church. Unlike Mozart, Haydn did not visit his wife, except when she was dying. An admirer hailed him over his wife's deathbed as 'creator of the divine *Creation* in which every sound is harmony and consonance, every phrase the expression of the creator's noble, sensitive, soul'.[16] It must have been some consolation for what was otherwise a grim time—the end of forty years of unhappy marriage. A sad little postscript is provided in a letter written by Haydn to Stoll on 7 July 1800 enclosing nine gulden due to the Baden Town Mortuary.

Ludwig Van Beethoven was undoubtedly Baden's most regular and distinguished musical visitor in its belle époque. It was probably curiosity that first drew him there shortly after his move to Vienna in 1792. He seems to have come on a number of occasions in the 1790s, lured by the fame of the spa, with its recently opened kurpark and Roman ruins exposed as a result of recent excavations, not to mention its Mozartian associations. He struck up a friendship with a distinguished Baden resident, Count Johann Browne, to whom he dedicated twelve variations in 1797. In his exhaustive article on the subject of Beethoven's connection with Baden, Dr Theodor Frimmel writes that 'there is no doubt that Beethoven mixed with the Brownes in Baden in 1801' but admits that there is no evidence that he stayed with them there or composed in their house.[17]

For the remainder of his life, Beethoven established a pattern of leaving Vienna for several months almost every summer. Baden was his favourite summer retreat, although he also went to other outlying villages like Döbling, Mödling, and Heiligenstadt and to more distant spas, notably Teplitz in Bohemia. Frimmel suggests that he made substantial stays in Baden during seventeen of the twenty-three years between 1803 and 1825. In fact, this is probably a slight exaggeration. We cannot be completely certain that he was there in 1803, 1808, or 1817, all of which are included in Frimmel's list. He did certainly so-journ in Baden in fourteen of these years and it is possible that he made short visits in others. His practice was to take lodgings in the fashionable centre of the town for several weeks or months, return-ing to Vienna for a day once a week. Although much is now made of the Beethoven connection in Baden, at the time he came he was not a welcome guest, particularly with his landlords. His moodiness and de-termination to play music at all hours made him an unpopular lodger and few wanted him back—over fifteen stays he went through seven different lodgings.

Undoubtedly one of the main reasons why Beethoven chose to stay in Baden so often was in order to take the waters. He was in poor health for most of his life and also suffered from severe hypochondria and constant fear of mortal illness and an early death. He never really recovered from a serious illness, variously thought to be rheumatic fever or typhoid, contracted in 1794 just two years after he came to Vienna. Early symptoms of the deafness that was to afflict him with increasing intensity for the rest of his life manifested themselves in 1798 when he first complained of a buzzing and humming in his ears. This tinnitus-like condition was accompanied from 1801 onwards by almost permanent colitis with abdominal pain, constipation, diarrhoea, and wind. The symptoms are suggestive to me of the condition that we now call irritable bowel syndrome, which would also be conso-nant with Beethoven's generally nervous and agitated state. They were compounded by persistent and severe catarrh and recurrent hepatitis and jaundice. Among the various diagnoses that have been made by modern medical practitioners, perhaps the most common is of a pro-gressive connective-tissue disease and immunopathy. The doctors whom Beethoven himself consulted, while less ready to make a ge-neric diagnosis, were mostly in agreement in recommending a cure that involved taking baths. His first experience of such a cure was not encouraging. The cold baths prescribed by a doctor, whom he con-sulted in 1801 and described simply as 'a medical ass', made his con-dition worse. He fared better later in the same year at the hands of Dr Gerhard von Vering, an army surgeon, who 'prescribed the luke-warm Danube bath, into which each time I had to pour a little bottle of strengthening stuff'.[18] This treatment brought about a marked improvement in his health but did not stop him changing doctors again in 1802, this time to Dr Johann Schmidt, the author of a number of scholarly works. It was almost certainly Schmidt who first prescribed a cure at Baden.

It is difficult to form a judgement from the many letters that he wrote about his treatments in Baden and elsewhere just how enthusiastic Beethoven himself was about the therapeutic benefits of spas. Martin Cooper, in his book about the last decade of the composer's life, is in no doubt: 'Beethoven was a great believer in mineral baths both for his general health and for his deafness which he was probably right in believing was intimately connected with the state of his bowels'.[19] Many of his letters suggest, however, that he often found the process of taking mineral water baths irksome and not always efficacious. There is, indeed, a strong suggestion in his writings that the main attraction for him in Baden was not so much the healing waters as the country air and scenery and the many opportunities for long walks through wooded valleys and hills. He went there, in his words, 'to be a peasant for half the year'. In a letter sent from Vienna to his friend Therese Malfatti on the eve of his departure for Baden in 1810, he wrote: 'How delighted I shall be to ramble for a while through bushes, woods, under trees, through grass and around rocks. No one can love the country as much as I do. For surely woods, trees and rocks produce the echo which man desires to hear'.[20] While staying in Baden he regularly rose early in the morning to go out on long solitary walks, taking with him bundles of folded music paper on which he would scribble phrases and melodies when they came to him. An observer noted 'when he became excited by some musical idea, he waved his hands and screamed melodies, occasionally frightening horses and unsuspecting strangers.'[21] His favourite walk was through the Helenental Valley to the west of Baden and up its thickly wooded steep slopes to the romantic ruins of the thirteenth-century Rauhenstein Castle. The path through the valley following the course of the Schwechet River is now known as the Beethovenweg.

Although his main summer retreat in 1803 was the Viennese suburb of Oberdöbling, his biographer A. W. Thayer writes that 'at the beginning of the warm season Beethoven, as was his annual custom, appears to have spent some weeks in Baden to refresh himself and revive his energies after the irregular, exciting and fatiguing city life of the winter'.[22] The thematic catalogue of Beethoven's works compiled by Kinsky-Halm records that he composed the major part of his *Eroica* Symphony in Oberdöbling and Baden. There is, however, no other record of this stay, and his first well-documented visit was in July 1804. He does not seem to have found it a wholly satisfying experience, writing to his pupil and friend Ferdinand Ries on 14 July: 'We are having bad weather here, and at Baden I cannot protect myself against people. I must run away if I want to be alone'.[23] Ries himself gives an intriguing account of what happened when he turned up one evening at Beethoven's lodgings for a piano lesson:

> I found a handsome young woman sitting on the sofa with him. Thinking I might be intruding, I wanted to go at once but Beethoven detained me and said: 'Play for the time being.' He and the lady remained seated behind me. I had already played for a long time when Beethoven suddenly called out 'Ries, play some love music'; a little later, 'Something melancholy!' then, 'Something passionate!'
>
> From what I heard I could only come to the conclusion that in some manner he must have offended the lady and was trying to make amends by an exhibition of good humour. At last he jumped up and shouted: 'Why, all these things are by me!' I had played nothing but movements from his works, connecting them with short transition phrases, which seemed to please him. The lady soon went away and to my great amazement Beethoven did not know who she was. I learned that she had come in shortly before me in order to make Beethoven's acquaintance. We followed her in order to discover her lodgings. We saw her from a distance but suddenly she disappeared. Chatting on all manner of topics we walked for an hour-and-a-half in the beautiful valley adjoining. On going, however, Beethoven said: 'I must find out who she is and you must help me'. A long time afterwards I met her in Vienna and discovered that she was the mistress of a foreign prince. I reported the intelligence to Beethoven but never heard anything more about her either from him or anybody else.[24]

Beethoven did not return to Baden in 1805 or 1806 but was back there in June 1807, when he stayed near the Johannesbad, one of the main bathhouses in the centre of town. His visit does not seem to have been an unmitigated success in terms of improving his health. In a letter to Baron von Gleichenstein on 13 June he complained: 'Yesterday and today I have been very ill, and I still have a terrible headache' and ten days later he told the same correspondent that 'after Schmidt's diagnosis I must not stay here any longer' and asked the baron to arrange for him to drive back to Vienna.[25] It is not clear what Schmidt diagnosed but Beethoven seems to have ignored his advice and stayed on in Baden until the end of July, working on the Mass in C (Opus 86) which had been commissioned by Prince Nikolaus Esterházy. The fact that amongst the sketches for the Mass are notes for his Sixth Symphony has led scholars to assume that he was also working on that while at Baden. The Helenental Valley, through which he took walks, has often been linked to the natural occurences recorded in this symphony, especially the storm in the third movement. However, Dr Alfred Willander, in his study *Beethoven und Baden* (Baden, 1989), counsels caution over the story that this movement was inspired by a storm experienced by Beethoven while walking in the valley in the vicinity of the Cholera Chapel, and near the spot now marked with the 'Beethoven stone'.

Beethoven may possibly have remained in Baden to keep in contact with another patron, Archduke Rudolph, brother of Francis II, who stayed there every summer and became his pupil on the piano and his only pupil in composition. The two men sometimes appeared together at social gatherings. One such appearance at the casino in Baden that probably took place in 1807 was later recalled by Therese von Hauer:

> Once as a young girl, I was taken along as Beethoven was expected to perform on the fortepiano. He appeared, refused requests for a time but finally stepped up to the piano, pulled a miserable face but then played, improvising fantasies of intense feeling and considerable skill on themes suggested by a few of the ladies, so that afterwards everyone left the room delighted and most satisfied.[26]

There is no definite evidence that Beethoven stayed in Baden during the summers of 1808 and 1809, although Thayer asserts that he was there in September 1809. An undated letter that may possibly originate from this visit complained that 'the post from Baden is the most wretched of all; it resembles the whole Austrian state'.[27] In his study of Beethoven in Baden Willander suggests that he may have worked on the Piano Concerto No. 5 in E major, Opus 73, and his Piano Sonata 'Les Adieux', Opus 81a, while there. Beethoven undoubtedly came to Baden in August 1810 and stayed until early October, working on his String Quartet in E-flat, Opus 74, tidying up his Fifth Symphony in C Minor, Opus 67 (a letter refers to the removal of two bars from the scherzo), and composing two works for military band: the Polonaise in D Major and March in F Major (WoO 21 and 19). There is no mention of bathing in the letters that he wrote during this stay. By now, he had a new physician, Dr Giovanni Malfatti, who had taken over after the sudden death of Dr Schmidt in 1809. Malfatti seems to have been particularly keen on the therapeutic properties of the Bohemian spas and it was at his instigation that Beethoven forsook Baden in 1811 and 1812 for Teplitz, Karlsbad, and Franzensbad (see pages 115–18). He retained a soft spot for the Austrian spa, however. While staying at Karlsbad at the end of July 1812, he received news of a disastrous fire that destroyed Baden's archducal palace, theatre, casino, parish church, and 117 houses. On 7 August he put on a special concert, which raised just under a thousand florins for relief and restoration efforts.

While staying at Teplitz in the summer of 1812 Beethoven met and acquired a new physician, Dr Jacob Staudenheim, who attended him until 1824. After initially prescribing cures in various Bohemian spas, he seems to have been happy to countenance the composer returning to his favourite Austrian summer retreat in 1813. Beethoven arrived in Baden at the end of May in what he described as 'a state bordering on mental confusion'. Archduke Rudolph arranged lodgings for him in the Sauerhof in Weilburgstrasse, a Biedermeier masterpiece built by the Austrian architect Josef Kornhausel on the foundations of a fifteenth-century palace. Beethoven wrote to Rudolph on his arrival that the town is 'still very empty so far as people are concerned; but all the more fully and lavishly is Nature decked out in her profusion and ravishing beauty. . . . I am convinced that the glorious beauties of Nature and the lovely surroundings of Baden will restore my balance'.[28] Apart from a few weeks in July and occasional day visits back to Vienna, he remained at the Sauerhof until mid-September.

It is clear from descriptions of those who visited him during this stay that he was in a bad way both physically and mentally. His old friends Nanette and Andreas Streicher found him 'in the most de-plorable condition with reference to his personal and domestic com-forts. He had neither a decent coat nor a whole shirt' and described his state of mind as at 'the lowest ebb' it had been for many years. The artist Blasius Höfel recalled that he often saw Beethoven at an inn near the Sauerhof, 'sitting in a distant corner, at a table which, though large, was avoided by the other guests owing to the very uninviting habits into which he had fallen. . . . [N]ot infrequently he departed without paying his bill, with the remark that his brother would settle it. . . . He had grown up so negligent of his person as to appear there sometimes positively *schmutzig* (dirty)'.[29] Gradually, the Streichers induced him again to mingle in society, from which he had almost completely withdrawn into a state of melancholy isolation following the emotional crisis that appears to have triggered the letter to 'the Immortal Beloved' penned in Teplitz (see page 116). This crisis also brought his musical productivity to a halt and he wrote no work of any significance during 1813 until late in the summer, when the in-ventor and entrepreneur Johann Nepomuk Mälzel brought him the idea and a partial draft of a new composition celebrating Wellington's victory over Napoleon in the Peninsular War at the Battle of Vittoria. He responded by composing 'Wellington's Victory' (Opus 91). The piece was almost certainly started while he was still in Baden but probably completed in Vienna.

Beethoven returned to Baden in 1814 for a relatively brief stay, whether at the Sauerhof or near the Johannesbad is not entirely clear, during which he worked on the Piano Sonata in E minor, Opus 90, dedicated to Prince Moritz Kichnowsky. In 1815 he was back for sev-eral weeks over the summer, working on his two sonatas for piano and cello (Opus 102) and spending much time with the English pianist Charles Neate, who took a room near him. Neate later recalled that Beethoven's habit when in Baden was to work in the morning, dine at 12 or 1 p.m., and towards evening go for a walk, sometimes up the Helenental Valley but more often through the fields. The two men often walked together and Neate told Thayer that he had never met a man who so enjoyed nature: 'Nature was like food to him, he seemed really to live in it'.[30] Beethoven was also in Baden for part of October. The following month his brother Carl died of consumption at the age of forty-one, leaving Ludwig as joint guardian with his widow of their nine-year-old son, Karl. Over the next four years Beethoven was locked in a bitter dispute with his sister-in-law to obtain legal guardianship of his nephew, which he eventually won. His health was considerably affected by both his brother's sudden death and his worsening relations with his sister-in-law, and from the end of 1815 he was almost permanently ill with a series of infections that continued until his death. Recurrent colitis and diarrhoea was accompanied by intermittent hepatitis and jaundice and increasing deafness, which necessitated those conversing with him writing everything down from 1818 onwards. He also suffered from depression and irritability and underwent what amounted to a progressive nervous breakdown between 1816 and 1818.

Beethoven was anxious to flee Vienna for Baden in the summer of 1816 and join his friend and patron Archduke Rudolph there but he had to wait for the all clear from his doctor about the state of his chest. By the middle of July he was able to report: 'I am at present in Baden and in excellent health—thanks not to the company here, but most certainly to the really lovely natural surroundings'.[31] This time he lodged at Breitnerstrasse 26, later known as Schloss Braiten, where he remained, with the usual occasional brief trips back to Vienna, until mid-September. While staying in Baden he composed his Piano Sonata in A Major, Opus 101. In the words of Martin Cooper, 'it was a particularly bad time for Beethoven, who was deeply disturbed emotionally by the new responsibility for his nephew and by his fears and guilty feelings about the boy's mother. The sonata in A major seems like an oasis in this wilderness, the escape into an ideal world from cares that only find, perhaps, an occasional echo in the finale's fugato'.[32]

Although Frimmel lists 1817 as one of the years when Beethoven stayed in Baden, I can find no clear evidence of this. Rather, he seems to have been in Nussdorf for most of that summer. In 1818, 1819, and 1820 he forsook Baden for the nearby spa of Mödling, where he stayed in each of these three years from early May to the end of October. Within two days of his arrival in 1818, he had begun taking thermal baths and was also hard at work on his Piano Sonata in B-flat (Opus 106). Physical exercise was also a priority: in June he reported that 'I am rambling about in the mountains, ravines and valleys here with a piece of music paper and scrawling several things for the sake of bread and money'.[33] During his lengthy stays in Mödling in 1819 and 1820 he laboured on his *Missa Solemnis,* inspired by Archduke Rudolph's election as archbishop of Olmütz and intended to be sung at his enthronement. Progress on this great work was slow, however, largely because of his illness. 'I am not at all well', he explained to Rudolph in a letter from Mödling in August 1819, 'and for some time now I have again had to take medicine. Hence I can scarcely devote myself for a few hours a day to Heaven's most precious gift to me, that is, my art and the Muses'.[34]

Following this four-year absence, Beethoven was back in Baden every summer between 1821 and 1825. Arriving in September 1821 after an attack of jaundice to take a cure prescribed by Dr Staudenheim, he had the usual problems finding lodgings. He was having dinner at the inn Zum Schwarzen Adler when he heard of available rooms just across the road in Rathausgasse. He immediately rushed off to secure them. The innkeeper called the police to have him arrested for leaving without paying his bill, but Beethoven was let off when he proved his identity and paid up. He remained in the upstairs rooms, which belonged to a coppersmith, Johann Bayer, until the end of October, working on what he described as 'potboilers' and continuing to labour on the *Missa Solemnis.* The stay was not a success in terms of its main objective. 'The weather soon became chilly', he wrote to a friend, 'and I started such violent diarrhoea that I could not stand the cure and had to rush back to Vienna'.[35] Despite this, he was back in September 1822, staying first at the inn Zum Goldenen Schwan and then back in the rooms in Rathausgasse. Describing himself to one friend as 'living here in the waters of the Styx', he told his brother Johann: 'about my state of health I cannot declare with certainty that there has been a definite improvement. All the same I fancy that thanks to the good effect of the baths the trouble will be arrested, though not completely cured'.[36] The music critic Friedrich Rochlitz recorded his impressions of a visit from Beethoven during this stay:

He arrived looking quite neat and clean, even elegant. Yet this did not deter him from going for a walk—and it was a hot day—in the Helental. This meant taking the main road, used by the Emperor and his family among many others, who crowd along what is usually a narrow footpath. Undismayed by this, Beethoven took off his fine black frock-coat, slung it on a stick over his shoulder and wandered along in his shirt-sleeves. . . . His talk and his actions were one long chain of eccentricities, some of them most peculiar.[37]

During this stay Beethoven worked on music for the opening of the Josephstadt Theatre, Vienna, commissioned by its director, Carl Friedrich Hensler, who also ran the theatre in Baden. This involved revising and extending his music for *Die Ruinen von Athen*, which had been written for the opening of a theatre in Pesth in 1812, in order to fit it for the revised version of the play, entitled *Die Weihe des Hauses*, which was to open the Josephstadt Theatre. His friend Anton Schindler has left this vivid account of how he composed the overture for the new piece:

> One day while I was walking with him and his nephew in the lovely Helental near Baden, Beethoven told us to go on in advance and join him at an appointed place. It was not long before he overtook us, remarking that he had written down two motifs for an overture. At the same time he expressed himself also as to the manner in which he purposed treating them—one in free style and one in the strict, and, indeed, in Handel's. As well as his voice permitted, he sang the two motives and then asked us which we liked better. This shows the roseate mood into which for the moment he was thrown by the discovery of two gems for which, perhaps, he had been hunting a long time. The nephew decided in favour of both, while I expressed a desire to see the fugal theme worked out for the purpose mentioned.[38]

Beethoven returned to Vienna in early October 1822 to conduct the opening performance of *Die Weihe des Hauses* and then came back to Baden for another two weeks, staying at a house in the Magdalenahof in Frauengasse and working on his Ninth Symphony.

In 1823 the perennial problem of finding suitable lodgings in Baden was compounded by the fact that he made a very sudden decision to exit Vienna in order to finish his Ninth Symphony in Baden. Johann Bayer was unwilling to have him in his house in Rathausgasse but eventually Anton Schindler persuaded the reluctant coppersmith to take in his distinguished but difficult former lodger once again. Bayer made just one stipulation—if the composer wanted the first-floor rooms overlooking the street that he had occupied before, he must provide his own window shutters. Schindler later discovered the reason for this seemingly strange condition:

> Beethoven was in the habit of scrawling all kinds of memoranda on his shutters in lead pencil—accounts, musical themes, etc. A family from North Germany had noticed this the previous year and had bought one of the shutters as a curiosity. The thrifty smith had an eye for business and disposed of the remaining shutters to other summer visitors.[39]

Beethoven's 1823 sojourn began in the middle of August when he described himself as 'in a very poor state of health'. A few days after his arrival, he wrote to his nephew Karl:

> I came here with catarrh and a cold in my head, both serious complaints for me. I fear that this trouble will soon cut the thread of my life or, worse still, will *gradually* gnaw it through. Moreover my abdomen, which is thoroughly upset, must still be restored to health by medicines and dieting. . . . Only today did I begin again *properly* to serve my muses. After all the baths are more inviting, at any rate to me and tempt me to enjoy the beauties of nature.[40]

Financial strictures dictated that, despite the lure of the baths and country walks, he must go on composing. He expressed his plight to his friend Ferdinand Reis on 5 September: 'My health, when all is said and done, is very shaky and, good heavens, instead of enjoying as others do the pleasures of bathing, my financial straits demand that I should compose every day. And as well as taking the baths I have to drink mineral waters'.[41] His stay at Baden, which continued until early October, in fact proved very productive. He supervised the copying of scores of his *Missa Solemnis*, corrected for publication the Diabelli Variations (Opus 120) and the Pianoforte Sonata in C Minor (Opus 111), and composed the slow third movement and possibly also other portions of his Ninth Symphony (Opus 125). This last achievement is commemorated by a plaque on the wall of the house in Rathausgasse, now known as the Beethoven Haus. The small entrance hall, bedroom, and study used by the composer, together with two larger first-floor

FIGURE 2.1. Waxwork figure of Beethoven working on the Ninth Symphony, Beethoven Haus, Baden bei Wien (author's photograph).

rooms, have been turned into a museum that contains facsimiles of all the pieces that he worked on while in Baden. In his former study a re- markably lifelike waxwork figure sits at a desk poring over the Ninth Symphony.

Beethoven often received visitors while staying at Baden. One of the most distinguished was fellow composer Carl Maria von Weber, who drove out from Vienna with his son Max and the English com- poser Sir Julius Benedict in early October 1823. They dined with Bee- thoven and his nephew Karl in the elegant surroundings of the Sauer- hof, which were in marked contrast to the state of the apartment in Rathausgasse as described by Weber: "Everything in the most ap- palling disorder—music, money, clothing on the floor, the bed unmade, broken coffee cups upon the table, the open pianoforte with scarcely any strings left and thickly covered with dust, while he himself was wrapped in a shabby old dressing-gown".[42]

The following day Beethoven wanted to take his guests on a walk through the Helenental but the weather was inclement. Weber spent the afternoon with the composer in his apartment: 'This rough, re- pellant man actually paid court to me', he later reported to his wife, 'served me at table as if I had been his lady. It was uplifting for me to be overwhelmed with such loving attention by this great genius. How saddening in his deafness! Everything must be written down for him. We inspected the baths, drank the waters, and at five o'clock drove back to Vienna'.[43]

In 1824 Beethoven was back in Baden for a long stay lasting from late May to mid-October with the customary brief forays to Vienna. This time he stayed in the Hermitage, near the main baths and close to what is now the Hotel Gutenbrunn, where a plaque inside records his stay. As usual, many of the letters that he sent while taking the cure were full of grouses. He wrote to Archduke Rudolph on 23 August, 'It is impossible when one is taking these baths to command one's physical strength as usual' and subsequently complained that 'the bad weather has prevented me from taking my baths' and that 'at Baden I can scarcely find anything to eat unless I eat at home'.[44] His mood gradually improved, however, and by the end of September he was commending the mountainous countryside 'where one would like to strengthen one's constitution by walks and learn to meet the coming worries of town life by enjoying the open air and the lovely countryside' and telling the Viennese harp manufacturer Johann Stumpff, 'I think that you ought to take more exercise in the form of walking'.[45] Stumpff allowed himself to be led on a morning walk through the Helenental Valley.

In April 1825 Beethoven suffered a serious abdominal illness with acute intestinal inflammation. His new physician, Dr Anton Braunhofer, prescribed an early departure to the country for fresh air and 'natural milk' and a severe diet: 'no wine, no coffee; no spices of any kind. . . . I'll wager that if you take a drink of spirits, you'll be lying weak and exhausted on your back in a few hours'.[46] While Beethoven had no trouble following the first part of his doctor's orders, beginning his summer sojourn in Baden much earlier than usual on 7 May, he found the restriction on wine irksome, as he indicated in a letter to Braunhofer on 13 May:

> Still very weak and belching and so forth. I am inclined to think that I now require a stronger medicine, but it must not be constipating—Surely I might be allowed to take white wine diluted with water, for that poisonous beer is bound to make me feel sick—my catarrhal condition is showing the following symptoms, that is to say, I spit a good deal of blood, but probably

only from my windpipe. But I have frequent nose bleedings, which I often had last winter as well. And there is no doubt that my stomach has become dreadfully weak, and so has, generally speaking, my whole constitution. Judging by what I know of my own constitution, my strength will hardly be restored unaided.[47]

He closed this grim and graphic account of his symptoms with a plea set to music: 'Doktor sperrt das Tor dem Tod! Note hilft auch aus der Noth' (Doctor close the door to death! Music will also help in need). Despite his poor physical state, and the cold weather which meant, he told his nephew, Karl, that 'I can scarcely move my fingers to write', he managed during the second half of May to compose the slow third movement of his A Minor String Quartet, Opus 132, the second of three quartets which had been commissioned by Prince Galitzin. He wrote on the score: 'Heiliger Dankgesang eines Genesenden an die Gottheit' (An invalid's hymn of thanksgiving to God on his convalescence). Over the remainder of his stay in Baden, he completed the A Minor Quartet and also composed the third of the Galitzin quartets, Opus 130 in B-flat major.

As so often in his life, Beethoven achieved this great surge of creativity while at a very low ebb both physically and emotionally. He became increasingly paranoid about his nephew, Karl, who was himself in a state of emotional turmoil, and ever more certain that his own death was looming. Rapidly changing diets seem to have been a more important component of this particular cure than either bathing in or drinking the Baden waters. In mid-May Braunhofer prescribed a drinking chocolate that was apparently unavailable in Baden. An urgent request to Karl to send some over from Vienna was accompanied by the rueful comment: 'Tomorrow no doubt I shall have to drink coffee. Who knows, perhaps it will be better for me than chocolate' and a tirade against Braunhofer for telling him to eat asparagus—'after the meal at the inn I am suffering a good deal today from diarrhoea'.[48] Another letter to Karl on 24 August complained 'since yesterday I have eaten nothing but soup and a couple of eggs and have drunk only water; my tongue is quite yellow; and without bowel motions and tonics my stomach will never be cured'. Yet two days later he was reporting: 'I must not drink red wine *only* but *white wine with water as well*'.[49]

Despite these successive assaults on his digestive system, Beethoven's health improved through the summer and several of his many visitors found him in excellent spirits. He remained in Baden until 15 October 1825, making this his longest stay ever. It was also his last. Baden was to be the scene of one further and very unhappy episode in his life. On 29 July 1826 his nephew Karl pawned his watch in Vienna and bought two pistols with the intention of committing suicide. He drove out to Baden that evening and the following morning he walked through the Helenental Valley and climbed to the ruins of Rauhenstein, where he had so often gone with his uncle. He loaded the guns and put both to his temple. The first bullet flew harmlessly past, while the second ripped up his flesh but did not penetrate his skull. When he was found lying in the ruins, he asked to be taken to his mother's house. The combination of Karl's attempted suicide and return to his mother devastated Beethoven. At the end of 1826 he developed liver disease and intestinal bleeding and died on 26 March 1827 at the age of fifty-six.

What did Beethoven gain from his numerous and increasingly lengthy stays in Baden? Although his comments suggest a certain ambivalence about the value of bathing in the waters, he does seem to have found his summers at the spa therapeutic and beneficial in soothing his numerous physical ailments and troubled spirit. The country air and the walks in the nearby fields and through the Helenental Valley were, perhaps, the main attractions. Certainly he was not seduced by the more decadent pleasures to which other composers succumbed when they frequented spas. He did not dance, he did not socialise very much, he drank only moderately, and he certainly did not gamble—in the words of Thayer: 'he does not appear to have known one playing-card from another'.[50] It is difficult to assess the influence that Baden had on Beethoven's music. The piece most clearly and directly related to his experience of taking the cure there is the third slow movement of the String Quartet in A minor (Opus 132) with its very specific dedication. As musicologists have pointed out, it portrays the experience of healing and recovery in a way that is not found in any other works by Beethoven or his predecessors, namely through the use of the Lydian mode and the creation of a chorale melody that serves as a basic prayer and is then elaborated in variations.[51] It is the most obvious and direct 'product' of his time and experiences in Baden but it is surely not the only part of his output to have been influenced by them. Several important ideas and themes clearly came to him while he was walking in the surrounding countryside with his sheets of manuscript paper at the ready. The list of major works either partially or substantially composed while he was at Baden is impressive and suggests that the atmosphere there was conducive to serious as well as to lighter work.

Beethoven was Baden's most distinguished and most regular musical visitor in the early nineteenth century but he was not the only composer to frequent the spa in this period. Antonio Salieri, master of music to the imperial court, came for several summers in an effort to cure his rheumatism. His first documented visit was in 1805, when he stayed in Renngasse just a few doors away from the house where Constanze Mozart had lodged during her last cure. In 1818 he stayed at the Augustinian convent in Frauengasse where Francis II was based and during a visit in 1820 he composed a fugue for soprano and bass in E major. In 1823 he stayed at the Sauerhof to recover from a bad bout of gout. Unfortunately he fell down the stairs, injuring his head, and never fully recovered. He died two years later. Franz Schubert spent a night at the tavern Zum Schwarzen Adler in June 1828 along with his friend Franz Lachner, organist at the main Protestant church in Vienna, and the publisher, Herr Schick. Over supper Schick suggested that the two musicians should compose something to play on the famous organ at the Cistercian Abbey at Heiligenkreuz, where they were travelling on to the following day. Fortified by beer, the two men sat down and each wrote a four-hand organ fugue. They had finished by midnight and were up at 6 a.m. the next day for the coach ride to the Abbey. The two-manual organ on which they played, with its 3,700 pipes and 50 registers, is still in the Abbey Church at Heiligenkreuz.

Johann Strauss the elder regularly played at Baden, notably at the Schwarzen Adler, a centre of music making and dancing, and also in the Hausweise meadow at the entrance to the Helenental Valley. Two of his waltzes were inspired by and decicated to Baden: *Souvenir de Baden*, Opus 38 (1830), and *Mein Schönster Tag in Baden*, Opus 58 (1832). Josef Lanner, the other founding father of the Austrian waltz, also regularly gave concerts in the town and wrote both the *Badener Ringeln* Waltz, Opus 64 (1832), and the *Schwechat Landler*, Opus 32 (1832). A bronze statue of the two waltz kings stands in the middle of the Kurpark. Among other musicians who took the cure at Baden

FIGURE 2.2. Statue of Johann Strauss and Josef Lanner in the Kurpark, Baden bei Wien (author's photograph).

in the mid-nineteenth century were Felix Mendelsohn-Bartholdy; Conradin Kreutzer, master of music to the imperial court; and Otto Nicolai, the founder of the Vienna Philharmonic Orchestra. Richard Genée, librettist of *Die Fledermaus*, stayed for a while at Schloss Braiten, where Beethoven had lodged in 1816.

A number of leading light music and operetta composers settled in Baden in the latter part of the nineteenth century. Karl Millöcker (1842–99), for ten years principal conductor at the Teater an der Wien, composed his operetta *Der Bettelstudent* while staying in Baden and lived in a villa in the town for the last five years of his life. Carl Zeller (1842–98), composer of *Der Vogelhändler*, came to Baden after a bad fall that led to paralysis in his arms and spent the last two years of his life living in a house in Engengasse. Karl Komzak (1850–1905), a Hungarian-born military bandsman who founded the band of the Eighty-fourth Infantry Regiment in Vienna and was the first conductor to introduce stringed instruments to a military band, moved to Baden in 1892 for health reasons. He took over as conductor of the Kurorchester, spending spring and summer in Baden and winter in Mostar. His many compositions include the popular waltzes *Badener Madl'n* and *Mein Baden*. He died on Easter Sunday 1905 at the age of fifty-four when he fell under the wheels of a departing train at Baden station. Other pieces dedicated to Baden by composers who visited the spa include the *Badener Park Polka* by Carl Ziehrer (1843–1922) and *Souvenir de Baden* by Edouard Strauss (1835–1918).

Partly in an effort to distinguish itself from Vienna and find a specialist niche, Baden increasingly established itself through the twentieth century as a centre for operetta performance. The outdoor summer theatre built in 1841 over the site of the original spring discovered and exploited by the Romans was replaced in 1906 by a large arena with a moveable glass roof. The 657-seat Sommerarena still houses the annual summer operetta festival. In 1909 the Kaiserjubiläums-Stadttheater, designed by the theatre architects Helmer and Fellner, was built to replace the 1812 Biedermeier theatre. It remains the principal venue for operettas and musicals from October to April. Baden's musical life continued to sparkle through the early decades of the twentieth century with recitals by Richard Tauber and Maria Jeritza. In 1925 Pietro Mascagni conducted his own *Cavalleria Rusticana* at the theatre. A new casino, the largest in Austria, was built in 1934 to cater to the more sophisticated leisure market which developed as spa cures became focused less on health and more on hedonism. Baden continued to inspire musical tributes. One of the best known, a light romantic duet 'Ich kenn ein kleines Wegerl in Helenental' from the 1940 operetta *Brillianten aus Wien* (Diamonds from Vienna) by Alexander Steinbrecher, was taken up for the footpath along the Helenental Valley, which is waymarked with signs featuring the opening bars of the song.

Although most of the music now heard in the Kurpark and in the indoor and outdoor theatres at Baden is of a light variety, the spa's more serious musical legacy is not forgotten. As well as the statue of Strauss and Lanner, the Kurpark contains a small neoclassical temple

FIGURE 2.3. Bust of Beethoven in front of the
Sauerhof, Baden bei Wien (author's photograph).

dedicated to Mozart and a much larger concrete domed temple erected
by the Kurkomission in 1927 to mark the centenary of Beethoven's
death. Echoes of Beethoven are to be found throughout the town.
Almost every other street in the centre boasts a plaque indicating that
he stayed there. The town's cinema is called the Beethoven Kino.
When I was there it was somewhat incongruously showing *Sex and
the City* and *Indiana Jones*. Perhaps even more incongruously, posters
outside the Beethoven Haus advertized a production of *Les Mise-
rables* in the KaiserjubiläumsStadttheater. A bust of Beethoven by the
sculptor Sockel stands in the gardens in front of the Sauerhof, now
a luxury hotel. The hotel's bedrooms have been given names that

commemorate Baden's rich musical legacy. I was fortunate enough to stay in the Joseph Lanner room. Next door was Johann Strauss Vater, and along the corridor Karl Komzak, Karl Millöcker, Carl Zeller, Franz Schubert, and Antonio Salieri. Mozart and Beethoven's names each appear on two rooms, a testament to the important role that Baden played in their lives and compositions.

3

Baden-Baden

Set on the edge of the Black Forest in southwest Germany at an elevation of 650 feet, blessed with abundant hot thermal waters, and surrounded by wooded hills affording shady walks, Baden-Baden established itself as the leading spa of Europe for much of the nineteenth century. Eugène Guinot, society editor of the influential French newspaper *Le Siècle,* observed in 1845: 'In Europe there are two capitals, Paris for the winter and Baden-Baden for the summer'. His countryman Gérard de Nerval described the setting of the elegant spa in his 1852 novel *Lorely, Souvenirs d'Allemagne* as 'arranged as for a pastoral opera'. In the mid-nineteenth century Baden-Baden attracted a large number of musicians and artists, chief among whom was Johannes Brahms, who made it his summer retreat for nine successive years.

The mildly radioactive springs, of which there are more than twenty, rise from a depth of 6,500 feet and vary in temperature between 112° and 154°F. They were well known to the Romans, who called them Aquae Aureliae. Emperor Caracalla (r. 211–17) personally laid out the baths with a bottom layer for ordinary soldiers, a middle layer for officers, and a top layer of baths for the exclusive use of the emperor. The ruins of the Roman baths are still visible next to the ultramodern Caracalla Spa complex. The thermal waters at Baden-Baden, which have to be cooled before they can be drunk or bathed in, have a comparatively weak mineral content. The spring chiefly used for drinking, the Hauptstallenquelle, has per litre 2.0 grammes of sodium chloride, 0.16 each of calcium chloride and carbonate, 0.053 of lithium chloride, and 0.0007 of arsenate of lime. These minute traces of lithium and arsenic are supposedly important in the treatment of gout. Other conditions for which the Baden-Baden waters are recommended are rheumatism and other affections of the joints, disorders of the nervous system, loss of muscular power, consequences of injuries to bones and joints, chronic skin infections, and chronic catarrh and they are recommended as well for convalescence from malaria and other infective disorders.

As at Baden bei Wien, bathing has always been a more important part of the cure than drinking in Baden-Baden. When the waters were prescribed for drinking and gargling, as they were in the spa's mid-nineteenth century heyday, they were often fortified with other salts imported from Marienbad and Carlsbad. A magnificent Trinkhalle was built in 1842, fronted with sixteen massive Corinthian columns and a long gallery with murals showing local legends and stories. It now houses the Tourist Information Centre and there is a fountain inside where visitors can drink the piping hot water. The main bathing establishment, the Friedrichsbad, opened in 1877 and is still operating today (another, the Kaiserin-Augustabad, was later opened for ladies only); it offered thermal water baths at varying temperatures, vapour baths, hot-air baths, mud baths, douches, electric baths, grape and milk cures, and compressed-air chambers. Several of the grand hotels around the town had their own bathhouses and there were also private sanatoria. Walks were laid out around the town for those taking the *'Terrain-kur'*. A visiting English medical practitioner described Baden-Baden as 'a sort of invalid's compendium, where various kinds of physical and other treatments can be applied in addition to the treatment by the thermal waters'.[1]

Even more than for its therapeutic and curative properties, Baden-Baden became known for its elegance and ambience. A 1904 guide to mineral springs and climatic resorts across the world noted that 'the hotel and other accommodation probably exceeds that of any other town in Europe and amusements and distractions of all kinds are provided'.[2] Chief among these amusements and distractions was gambling. The earliest official mention of licensed gambling in Baden-Baden is in 1748. In 1809 a gaming room was opened in the Konversationshaus on the Market Square (now the Town Hall). In 1824 a Kurhaus was built with designated gambling rooms. King Louis Philippe's decision in 1838 to close all gaming houses in France gave a huge boost to Baden-Baden as Frenchmen flocked across the border to play the tables there, with roulette taking over from card games as the main attraction. From 1838 the casino was managed by Jacques Bénazet, who had previously run the Palais Royal in Paris. He and his son Edouard, who took over after his father's death in 1848, had the strong support of Grand Duchess Stéphanie, an adopted daughter of Napoleon Buonaparte, and invested huge sums in the casino. Between 1854 and 1858 four new gaming rooms were built onto the side of the Kurhaus. Decorated with gilded stucco, extravagant red plush, and massive chandeliers by the theatrical designers of the Paris Opera, they consisted of a white hall in Louis XVI style, the Salon Pompadour or yellow hall (Louis XV), a red hall in Louis XIV style, which served as a stage for theatrical productions, and the green hall (Louis XIII), which was also used as a ballroom. The casino played a major role in the musical life of mid-nineteenth-century Baden-Baden, hosting concerts and sponsoring the kurorchester.

Edouard Bénazet did much else for the town. He built a large theatre in 1862 designed by the Paris architect Charles Séchan in the style of the Paris Opera. He substantially endowed the first Protestant Church in Baden-Baden, surely one of the few places of worship to have been built out of the profits of a casino. Above all, he laid out the grounds around the Lichtentaler Allee, a path running along the banks of the River Oos and connecting Baden-Baden with the thirteenth-century Cistercian Abbey at Lichtental 2.3 kilometres away. In the seventeenth century the ground around the path had been planted with oak trees. Bénazet developed it as an elegant promenade. The first stretch, starting from behind his theatre, he turned into an English parkland with fountains shaded by oaks and beeches. Further along the Oos he created a much more formal French garden and then a broad avenue lined by lime trees with meadows alongside. Elegant hotels and villas were built all along the Allee, their gardens running down to the clear shallow waters of the Oos. The Lichtentaler Allee became the centre of Baden-Baden social life, the place in which to engage in the favourite sport of visitors, to see and to be seen. More conventional and muscular sports were also on offer there, thanks to the initiative of Archibald White, vicar of the Anglican Church of All

FIGURE 3.1. Theatre at Baden-Baden (author's photograph).

FIGURE 3.2. Casino and Kurhaus at Baden-Baden (author's photograph).

Saints, established in 1867 to cater for the growing number of English-speaking guests. He introduced tennis, golf, and football to Baden-Baden. The tennis club he founded in 1881, the first in Germany, still exists in the Lichtentaler Allee, its courts defiantly sited just opposite the French gardens. For other more hearty guests who did not just want to bathe, promenade, or gamble, there was abundant shooting and hunting in the adjoining Black Forest.

Fashionable Europe flocked to Baden-Baden, led by several crowned heads and the aristocracy of Germany and Russia. So many Russians came that a Russian Orthodox church was erected in the town. Among them was the novelist Feodor Dostoyevsky, who lost all his earnings at the casino and described his experiences there in his 1866 novel *The Gambler.* King Wilhelm I of Prussia (from 1871 Kaiser Wilhelm, the first German emperor) made forty summer visits, always arriving with twelve black horses and twelve coachmen and staying in the Hotel Messmer, which changed its name to Maison Messmer during his residence, as protocol forbade the emperor from staying in a hotel. Tsar Alexander II lived in similar splendour during his stays and Napoleon III lodged at the spacious Villa Stephanie. Queen Victoria, by contrast, occupied three austere rooms in a modest wooden house belonging to a relative, Prince von Hohenlohe. Her son and grandson, the future King Edward VII and King George V, came while Princes of Wales. The Aga Khan was attracted to Baden-Baden largely by the ninety-eight varieties of patisserie made by the local baker. As well as enhancing the atmosphere of exclusivity and grandeur, the royal visitors also attracted danger and conspiracy. A visiting Russian prince was killed by his mistress and Prince Stourdza of Rumania was assassinated by a group of anarchists disguised as priests.

Like all spas, Baden-Baden in its heyday was a mixture of glittering decadence and sordid desperation. The cure was not taken just by Europe's rich and famous, who did not really need it and for whom it was a kind of holiday, but also by those seeking escape from terrible illness and addiction. One of the most pathetic figures to come there was Helen Gladstone, sister of the British Liberal politician William Ewart Gladstone. Addicted to opium and suffering from severe religious mania, she arrived in the early 1840s having already tried a cure at Bad Ems. Her condition did not improve and Gladstone went out in the autumn of 1845 with the purpose of bringing her back home. He stayed there for five gloomy weeks, witnessing many distressing scenes, such as when she had to be held down by force while leeches were applied after she had taken three hundred drops of laudanum and become partially paralysed. On another occasion, she locked herself in her room after drinking a bottle of Eau de Cologne mixed with water. This was the other side of Baden-Baden. Gladstone found the

whole atmosphere so torrid that while staying there he drew up an extraordinary memorandum listing the channels through which sexual
depravity came to him (thought, conversation, hearing, seeing, touch,
and company), the times when he was especially receptive to sexual
temptation (idleness, exhaustion, absence from usual place, interrup-
tion from usual habits of life) and effective remedies (prayer, realis-
ing the presence of the Lord Crucified and enthroned, and immediate
pain—which in his case meant severe self-flagellation). Many other
visitors indulged in sexual peccadilos without Gladstone's agonising
introspection and guilt.[3]

Music played an important role in the spa's social and cultural life.
From early on in the nineteenth century there were regular concerts
to entertain guests taking the cure. In 1824 a concert kiosk was built
opposite the Kurhaus and an orchestra of Bohemian musicians was
engaged to play annually through the season. Leading musicians were
attracted to Baden-Baden from the same mixture of motives that
brought them to other spas. Some came seeking patronage, like Carl
Maria von Weber, who made a visit in 1810 when Crown Prince Ludwig of Bavaria was staying, in the hope of securing some concerts in
Munich. In the event, no concert dates resulted from their encounter
but Weber conducted a performance of *Don Giovanni* in Baden-
Baden and had a very agreeable time with the crown prince, especially
on night wanderings with a guitar singing serenades to ladies. Touring virtuosi and composers found it a lucrative venue for performances and composers a good place to showcase new works. Paganini
played there in 1830 and Liszt made the first of several appearances in
1840. Rossini's *Stabat Mater* was performed in the Kurhaus Theatre
in 1842, shortly after its Paris première. In 1854 the French composer
Louis Clapisson's *opera comique Le Sylphe* was premièred there and
the following year the newly renovated Konversationshaus opened
with the première of his *Les Amoureux de Perrette*.

In 1854 Baden-Baden acquired a permanent resident orchestra, as
distinct from musicians engaged annually for the season. A winter orchestra of sixteen players gave a weekly Sunday concert in the Konversationshaus. The programme for one of the first of these concerts,
on 20 November 1854, survives and features overtures and extracts
from operas by Donizetti, Haydn, Auber, Rossini, and Wagner. In summer the orchestra was doubled to thirty-two players and there were

daily evening concerts. The orchestra also played for balls throughout the year and wind players were stationed at the Trinkhalle at 7:00 every morning to serenade guests taking the waters. In 1859 a large and elaborately decorated wrought-iron pavilion, designed, like the new theatre, by the French architect Séchan, was built in front of the Kurhaus to accommodate the enlarged orchestra.

The first major composer to have a close association with Baden-Baden was Hector Berlioz. He first came in 1852 to give a concert during the summer season. He returned for nine of the next eleven years to conduct at the invitation of Edouard Bénazet. One of the attractions of regular visits to Baden-Baden for Berlioz was almost certainly the opportunity they gave him to seek treatment for the severe nervous disorder, diagnosed as 'intestinal neuralgia', from which he suffered and which caused him acute pain. He also enjoyed climbing to the ruins of the old castle above the town and gazing down over the valley of the Rhine. In 1856 he was appointed conductor of the annual music festival that had recently been established in Baden-Baden for the month of August with the new orchestra. He held this post until 1863, conducting a full performance of his opera *Harold en Italie* and extracts from *Les Trojans* and *La Damnation de Faust*. As his memoirs indicate, he was more than happy with the arrangements provided by the casino manager:

> M. Bénazet has let me have everything I could possibly want for the performance of my own works. His munificence in this respect has far surpassed anything ever done for me even by those European sovereigns whom I have most reason to be grateful to. 'I give you carte blanche', he said again this year. 'Get the artists you need from wherever you please, and offer them whatever terms you think will satisfy them. I agree to everything in advance'.[4]

In August 1860, during a stay in Baden-Baden, Sir Charles Hallé, the English-based pianist and conductor, wrote to his wife: 'I have met here Berlioz, Richard Wagner, Danton, Sivori, Wolff, Cosmann, Piatti and several other old acquaintances. I spent nearly the whole day yesterday with Berlioz; we went through the score of *Armida* and, from memory, the whole of *Iphigenia*'.[5] Some days later, he wrote expressing his concern at Berlioz's condition following a rehearsal that he had conducted:

> Poor Berlioz gave me the greatest pain. I never saw a man so changed and, but for a miracle, he would surely be in his grave before this time next year. He knows it himself, and speaks of it with a sadness that pierces one's heart. He was so pleased to see me and to be able to open his heart in talking of music; he told me he had not felt so well for a long time as during those two days.[6]

From remarks made by his good friend Ernest Legouvé, it seems that Berlioz's affliction was one of the heart and that, like so many other musicians caught up in the heady, romantic spa atmosphere, he had fallen for a much younger woman. He reported on a meeting with Berlioz in the woods below the castle at Baden. 'He seemed different, aged and sad. We sat on a bench, for the climb tired him. He was holding a letter, which he clutched convulsively. It was from a young and pretty girl in love with him but he said regretfully: "I am nearly 60. She cannot love me—she does not love me"'.[7]

If Baden-Baden gave Berlioz a broken heart, it also provided him with an important commission that brought about his last great composition. In 1860 Bénazet asked him to write an opera for his new theatre and suggested that he might base it on an episode from the Thirty Years War with Edouard Plouvier as the librettist. Berlioz, however, decided to go back to an idea that he had first hatched in 1833 for a comic opera based on Shakespeare's *Much Ado About Nothing*. He provided his own libretto based on a translation of the play by Benjamin Laroche and focusing on the characters of Beatrice and Benedict. *Béatrice et Bénédict* was premièred in Baden-Baden on 9 August 1862. During the performance, Berlioz suffered violently from neuralgia, which, he said, blotted out emotion and interest. 'The result of this eccentric coolness', he wrote later to a friend, 'was that I conducted better than usual'.[8] This original production had a very short second act. It was expanded for a revival in Baden-Baden in 1863. That year Berlioz initiated the rediscovery of Pergolesi's works with a revival of *La Sera Padrona* at Bénazet's theatre. It was his last season at Baden-Baden. Too ill to come in 1864, he recommended Ernest Ryer to succeed him for the 1865 season. He died in 1869.

FIGURE 3.3.
Plaque commemorating the first performance of Berlioz's *Béatrice et Bénédict* in Baden-Baden, 1862 (author's photograph).

Hector Berlioz was not the only distinguished musician whom Edouard Bénazet lured to Baden-Baden. In 1860 he persuaded Charles Gounod to première his opera *La Colombe* there, six years before it received its first performance in Paris. The Czech bandmaster and composer Miloslaw Koennemann, who took up residence in Baden-Baden in 1852, also had several works premiered there, including *Der Fremersberg*. This musical tribute to a mountain just outside the spa opens with a hunting scene and ends with the monks intoning a *Te Deum* in the nearby monastery. In 1859 Bénazet appointed Koennemann leader of music in the Konversationhaus, a position he held until his death in 1890.

Richard Wagner came to Baden-Baden in 1860 not because of a commission from Bénazet but in an attempt to ingratiate himself with the leading royal family in Germany and ease his rehabilitation in the country from which he had effectively been banned because of his revolutionary views since his involvement in the Dresden uprising of 1849. Hearing that Princess Augusta of Prussia, wife of the future king and emperor Wilhelm I, was in the spa, he hastened there from Frankfurt. Abandoning his wife, Minna, and her companion 'to the seductions of the roulette table', he availed himself of a letter of introduction to one of the princess's ladies-in-waiting 'through whom

I hoped to be presented to her exalted patroness'. His account of the visit continues:

> After a little delay I duly received an invitation to meet her in the Trinkhalle at five o'clock in the afternoon. It was a wet, cold day, and at that hour the whole surroundings of the place seemed absolutely devoid of life as I approached my momentous rendezvous. I found Augusta pacing to and fro with Countess Hacke, and as I approached she graciously stopped. Her conversation consisted almost entirely of assurances that she was completely powerless in every respect.

Having been 'dismissed with an air of indifference' by his potential royal patron, Wagner left 'the much praised paradise of Baden without carrying away any very friendly impression'.[9]

It was perhaps partly the unhappy memories of this visit that led Wagner to turn down the town council's offer of a free plot of land in Baden-Baden on which to erect his theatre to launch the Ring cycle in 1871. Several friends suggested it would be an ideal location for the new theatre and festival to showcase his works with its plentiful supply of summer visitors and the capacity to accommodate them. To all of them, however, he turned a deaf ear. In the words of his biographer Ernest Newman, 'the merely pleasure-loving crowds in popular resorts were not the material out of which he hoped to form his ideal audience'.[10] His choice of Bayreuth as the location for his new purpose-built theatre was made partly on the grounds that it was not a fashionable spa or summer resort.

A snapshot of the musical life in Baden-Baden at the height of its popularity can be gained from perusing the pages of *Badeblatt* for the summer of 1869. This newspaper, which came out daily during the season and carried prominently on its front page the official list of guests staying in the main resort hotels, was dominated by advertisements for and reviews of musical performances. The highlight of the 1869 season was the debut appearance of the Bouffes Parisiens under the personal direction of Offenbach, who had made his first visit to Baden-Baden in 1856 as a cellist. Their performances in the theatre from 7 July to 2 August included the première of Offenbach's *La Princesse de Trébizonde*, which was rapturously received. As well as accompanying the Bouffes in the evening, the Kurorchester played every morning and afternoon on the Promenade or in the kiosk in front of the Konversationhaus. They also tackled more substantial works in free Friday classical matinée concerts. The band of the Fourth Regiment of Infantry played every Sunday afternoon and Thursday evening in the kiosk. Their programme for Sunday 18 July began with Strauss's "Radetzky" March and included the overtures to Weber's *Oberon* and Rossini's *Guillaume Tell* before concluding with a 'Brilliant Fantasy for Three Cornets à pistons' by Koennemann. There were numerous extra evening musical events, like the Grand Vocal and Instrumental Concert in aid of the Protestant Church, which featured a female vocalist from Richmond, Virginia, and included movements from Max Bruch's First Violin Concerto and Weber's Piano Concerto, arias from Gluck's *Orphée*, Meyerbeer's *Le Prophète*, and Mozart's *Titus*, Schubert lieder, and piano pieces by Pauline Viardot.

Badeblatt promised a feast of music in September 1869 to celebrate the anniversary of the birth of the grand duke of Baden, including performances of French and Italian operas, balls, and concerts with well-known soloists and choirs. In order to take the strain off the resident Kurochester, which as the paper pointed out, would be playing regularly from 7 a.m. until midnight, the spa administration had engaged a second orchestra, consisting of more than forty instrumentalists from the bands of the First, Third, and Fourth Infantry Regiments of Baden, to play throughout the month of September. With strings as well as brass and woodwind, it would provide music for balls, in the kiosk, and at other special occasions. There were also to be some grand military band concerts featuring over a hundred players from the three regimental bands.

Aside and quite separately from the music making centred around the Kurhaus and the theatre and designed for spa guests, Baden-Baden became a mecca for more serious musicians who came regularly in the 1860s and early 1870s to recharge their batteries and enjoy one another's company. They included the pianist Anton Rubinstein, who regularly rented a summer villa and spent much time in the casino, the violinists Hugo Heerman and Joseph Joachim, the baritone Julius Stockhausen, and the composer Theodor Kirchner, a disciple of Robert Schumann. The pianist-composer Jakob Rosenhain, who was highly regarded by both Schumann and Mendelssohn, took up permanent residence in the town. They formed a distinct social circle, which included other artists such as the engravers Gustav Doré and Julius

Allgeyer, and the painter Anselm Feuerbach, who came annually for several weeks with his mother. They came for the social and cultural ambience rather than to take the waters or to make money. Indeed, when Joachim's wife, Amalie, developed bad rheumatism, or what he called 'flying gout', in 1866 it was not the local waters that were prescribed by the doctor but rather the salt-water baths of Harzburg. The couple duly went off there and she quickly recovered. For them, as for many others, the appeal of Baden-Baden lay in its relaxing and elegant atmosphere rather than the efficacious properties of its thermal springs.

At the centre of this select musical and artistic circle was Pauline Viardot-García, the Spanish born mezzo-soprano and star of Italian opera companies. A pupil of Liszt and friend of Chopin, she had formidable musical talent and connections. In 1863, aged forty one and fresh from a triumphant performance in Gluck's *Orphée et Alceste* at Paris Opera House, Viardot-García and her liberal-minded French husband, Louis, an impresario and director of the Théâtre Italien in Paris, moved to Baden-Baden in semi-retirement to escape the imperial regime of Napoleon III. She was known there simply by her married name, Viardot. She had earlier sung in Baden-Baden as a soloist in Berlioz's *La Damnation de Faust* conducted by the composer in 1860. The couple built a spacious villa in the Thiergartenstrasse (now Fremersbergstrasse) just off the Lichtentaler Allee. Inside, a picture gallery contained paintings by Spanish and Dutch masters and her most treasured possession, Mozart's autograph score of *Don Giovanni* enshrined in a special casket. In the spacious gardens Viardot built what she called her 'Palace of Arts', a theatre and music room complete with pipe organ, which was used for regular performances. An engraving of a musical soirée there shows Anton Rubinstein playing the piano to an audience that included King Wilhelm I and Queen Augusta of Prussia, Otto von Bismarck, and Gustav Doré. Viardot regularly entertained her guests by singing or playing her own compositions. On 10 March 1866 she performed her 'Petite Suite pour piano, violon, tambourin et triangle' with herself on the piano, her son on the violin and her two daughters, aged twelve and fourteen, on the percussion instruments.

It was because of the Viardots that the Russian novelist Ivan Turgenev came to Baden-Baden. He was almost certainly her lover and later lived in a ménage-à-trois with her and her husband. Turgenev

FIGURE 3.4. Engraving of a musical evening at the Viardot villa with Anton Rubinstein at the piano (author's collection).

arrived very shortly after the Viardots in May 1863, taking lodgings close to their villa on the first floor of a large house in Schillerstrasse. He later moved in 1868 to his own large villa in Thiergartenstrasse to be even closer to them. He was captivated by the atmosphere of the spa, writing to Flaubert in 1865: 'Do come to Baden-Baden. Here are the most magnificent trees I have ever seen. They do wonders for the eyes and the soul'. Baden-Baden was the setting for his novel *Smoke*, written between 1865 and 1866 and published in 1867. It perfectly captures the atmosphere of the spa with its motley collection of 'Italians, Moldavians, American spiritualists, smart secretaries of foreign embassies, and Germans of effeminate, but prematurely circumspect physiognomy'.[11] The central character, Gregory Mikalovitch Litvinov, a retired Russian official, finds himself in Baden-Baden because his fiancée's aunt, Kapitolana Markovna Shestov, despite being a fierce democrat and opponent of aristocracy 'could not resist the temptation of gazing for once on this fashionable society'. The musical life of the spa is captured well in the novel. Sandwiched between descriptions of the Konversationhaus and the gambling saloons in its opening pages is an account of 'the orchestra in the Pavilion playing first a medley from the Traviata, then one of Strauss' waltzes, then "Tell her", a Russian song, adapted for instruments by an obliging conductor'.[12] There are also some delightful vignettes of the aristocratic guests and their attempts at music making:

> Here was Count X, our incomparable dilettante, a profoundly musical nature, who so divinely recites songs on the piano, but cannot in fact take two notes correctly without fumbling at random on the keys, and sings in a style something between that of a poor gypsy singer and a Parisian hairdresser.[13]

Turgenev makes periodic references to 'a self-taught genius' among the guests who is always playing waltzes. On one occasion he takes to the piano during lunch as one of the guests struggles to deal with a crab that has been brought to his table very much alive and is moving around on the plate:

> The self-taught genius, who had gone on striking notes during the experiments with the crab, dwelling on melancholy chords, on the ground that there was no knowing what influence music might have, played his invariable waltz, and, of course, was deemed worthy of the most flattering applause. Pricked on by rivalry, Count X, our incomparable dilettante, gave a little song of his own composition, cribbed wholesale from Offenbach. Its playful refrain to the words: '*Quel oeuf? Quel bouef?*' set almost all the ladies' heads swinging to right and to left; one went so far as to hum the tune lightly, and the irrepressible, inevitable word '*Charmant! Charmant!*' was fluttering on everyone's lips.[14]

Smoke also brings out the extent to which the spa concerts act as the highlight of the day in terms of drawing fashionable society:

> The blare of wind instruments floated up the avenue; it was the Prussian military band from Rastadt, in its weekly concert in the pavilion. Kapitolana Markovna got up. 'The music!' she said; 'the music *à la conversation!* We must go there. It's four o'clock now, isn't it? Will the fashionable world be there now?'
>
> 'Yes,' answered Potugin: 'This is the most fashionable time, and the music is excellent.'
>
> 'Well then, don't let us linger.'[15]

Turgenev himself was much involved in the musical salon Pauline Viardot created. He helped to organise the regular Sunday morning concerts in the 'Palace of Arts' and often blew the bellows of the pipe organ. Viardot set several of his poems to music and he helped her with other settings of Russian poems, three volumes of which were published. Between 1867 and 1869 she composed four short operettas for which he wrote the librettos, *Trop de Femmes, L'Ogre, Le Miroir,* and *Le Dernier Sorcier.* They were performed by her children and pupils in the Viardots' music room and in the miniature garden theatre Turgenev built in his garden. He took nonsinging roles and the invited audiences included the Grand Duchess of Baden and the king and queen of Prussia. Turgenev described his embarrassment when, as he lay on the floor in the character of the Pacha in *Trop de Femmes,* he observed 'the Crown Princess of Prussia looking at me with an ironical, and by no means flattering smile.'[16] *Le Dernier Sorcier* was professionally staged in Weimar in April 1869. Franz Liszt, who had a high view of the music, offered to orchestrate it but ran out of time and the task had to be completed by the conductor. Turgenev unsuccessfully tried to get the work performed in Russia but it was staged instead in Karlsruhe in 1870.

It was also because of the Viardots that Clara Schumann came to Baden-Baden with her seven children in April 1863. Following the death of her husband, Robert, in 1856, she had devoted herself almost manically to her recital work as a concert pianist, being perpetually on tour round Europe and spending virtually no time at her home in Berlin. This had a deleterious effect on her health and she spent a lonely melancholy month at Spa in Belgium seeking treatment for rheumatism. Pauline Viardot, who was an old friend, persuaded her to come to Baden-Baden to be near her and give the children a measure of stability. They set up home in a converted farmhouse about halfway along the Lichtentaler Allee. Described by Clara as 'a modest, but very nice little house' and nicknamed 'the dog kennel' by the children, it was, in fact, quite spacious, with a salon, five downstairs rooms, two kitchens, and an upper floor with enough bedrooms for all seven children. Its living rooms were big enough to accommodate three grand pianos. During the winter Clara went off on her concert tours around Europe, accompanied by her eldest daughter, Marie, and the younger children were farmed out as paying guests to friends, relatives, and private tutors. But from May to October the house in Baden-Baden provided an idyllic family home. Clara would breakfast with the children in the gazebo in the garden, devote the morning to work, take coffee and entertain guests in the afternoon, enjoy a long walk at 4 p.m. and organise musical parties after dinner in the evening. There were few times of the day when the house was silent and not filled with music or laughter. Clara's daughter Eugenie recalled the sound when her mother was practising, as she did for hours every morning:

> Scales rolled and swelled like a tidal sea, legato and staccato; in octaves, thirds, sixths, tenths and double thirds; sometimes in one hand only while the other hand played accompanying chords. Then arpeggios of all kinds, octaves, shakes, everything prestissimo and without the slightest break, exquisite modulations leading from key to key. The most wonderful feature of this practising was that although the principle on which it was based was always the same, it was new every day, and seemed drawn ever fresh from a mysterious wellspring. . . . [W]e often pressed Mamma to write down the sequence of an hour's exercises, but she always said it was impossible to retain exactly this kind of free fantasia.
>
> We never disturbed Mamma without good cause when she was at the piano, but we knew that we might come in at any time, and that she even liked it. She always gave us a kind glance whenever we entered the room. I used to wonder at the time that she could go on playing so unconcernedly while she talked to us of other things. While she played scales you would often read letters open on the desk in front of her.[17]

Clara Schumann craved company, becoming melancholy if she had too much peace and quiet, and delighted in mixing with the stimulating group of musicians, artists, and writers who descended on Baden-Baden every summer. Like Pauline Viardot, she regularly hosted musical soirées, although her guest list was considerably less exalted. The young Hungarian soprano Aglaja Orgeni, another regular visitor to Baden-Baden, described such an evening at No. 14 Lichtenthaler Allee on 6 June 1863: 'Frau Schumann played the Trio in D minor by Mendelssohn; that was wonderful—what an artist this woman is! Her energy, her power, her mastery of all technical difficulties, but above all that spirit, the enormous breath of life that imbues all her playing!' She was less enthusiastic about the other musicians attending the soirée, finding them 'more exclusive than one can imagine . . . true aristocrats, looking down on the maggots of mankind with pride and smugness'.[18] By 1867 Clara felt overwhelmed by the amount of entertaining that she was doing and resolved on a new way to pay back hospitality by giving a recital in her front room every Wednesday—'it will enable me to repay many social obligations which I cannot do by inviting people in return—too many people are coming here'.[19]

Clara Schumann and Pauline Viardot remained friends and gave a concert together every summer. However, Clara felt resentment and pique that Viardot moved in an altogether more exalted social circle, with Turgenev as her near neighbour and with grander parties than she could ever contemplate or afford as a single widow. After one of Viardot's official housewarmings at the end of October 1864, Clara wrote to her great friend Johannes Brahms: 'Madame Viardot consecrated her Palace of Arts (as she calls it) the other day, and to the first ceremony she invited high society (the Queen of Prussia etc.) when she naturally did not want me; and afterwards she had a reception for the populace for which I was considered good enough'.[20] Clara contributed a Beethoven sonata to a mixed entertainment, which ended with Viardot's 'tasteless' arrangement of the Bach-Gounod prelude for organ, harp, violins, and three women's voices 'bawling unisono'. Clara left the house 'bristling with indignation' and went off on her winter travels without saying goodbye to her old friend. She was all the more sore because of the splendid organ 'the Viardot woman', who could not play the pedals, had installed in her music room. 'Why can't I have such an organ? How sacred it would be to me', she wrote to Brahms. 'And if you came and played on it for me, what music for the gods we should have then! I have often wondered whether I ought not to go to America, where I should immediately earn enough to purchase such an organ'.[21]

Pauline Viardot may have held the more fashionable soirées with royal guests but it was Clara Schumann who was responsible for attracting Baden-Baden's most illustrious and regular musical visitor. Johannes Brahms spent every summer there between 1864 and 1872 and composed several major works during his stays. He had first met the Schumanns in 1853. Robert was his great hero and he visited him after his breakdown in 1854. Brahms developed a romantic passion for Clara, who was fourteen years his senior. The first time he came to Baden-Baden was for just three days in 1863 soon after she and the children had arrived. He lodged with a doctor in the Lichtentaler Allee. The following year at the end of July he made a surprise visit to Clara, who delayed a planned visit to Switzerland for ten days so she could see him. In mid-August he wrote to his father: 'Although Frau Schumann has gone to Switzerland, I am staying here for I enjoy it quite a lot'. He went on to ask for letters to him to be sent to her address despite the fact that 'I am staying elsewhere and in fact very charmingly, in a garden in Baden. Here one sees all kinds of people, the most beautiful surroundings and so it is bearable'.[22] In fact, after initially staying in an inn in Lichtental, he had found very comfortable and cheap lodgings in a villa near the Kurhaus that had been taken for the summer by Rubinstein, who left in August and placed it at Brahms's disposal for the rest of the season. Before she left, he and Clara performed his Sonata in F Minor for Two Pianos privately before Princess Anna, Landgräfin of Hesse. This piece, which he had reworked from a string quintet, had not received a particularly good reception at its initial performance in Vienna but it was greatly admired by the princess, to whom he was presented by Clara. Brahms called on her the following day and asked that the work might be dedicated to her. She enthusiastically agreed and on its publication the following year, further reworked as a piano quintet, it had her name on the title page. The princess reciprocated by giving Brahms one of her treasures, the autograph score of Mozart's G minor symphony.

Clara Schumann introduced Brahms to many of her circle and he found many musicians to play with in Baden-Baden, notably Joachim, with whom he was already a close friend. Brahms was also sucked into the Viardot circle and composed a short chorale serenade for Viardot's birthday, which he performed with some of her young female pupils outside her house early one morning. During his 1864 stay he spent much time with Ivan Turgenev. Over cigars they discussed the possibility of collaborating on an opera. Turgenev got as far as drafting six pages of a libretto set in an Alpine inn but the project evaporated. He also developed a close friendship with Hermann Levi, who had recently been appointed Kappelmeister at the court of the grand duke of Baden and was also conductor of the opera company of the nearby Karlsruhe Court Theatre, which regularly performed at the Baden-Baden Kurhaus during the season. Levi was much given to schoolboy pranks: he would hide in one of Clara Schumann's empty travelling trunks and suddenly burst into 'Freunde' from Beethoven's Choral

Symphony to startle Brahms. Later a leading Wagner conductor, who directed the first performances of *Parsifal* in 1882, he became one of Brahms's greatest friends and an enthusiastic promoter of his music. When Brahms recast his F minor sonata for two pianos into the Piano Quintet, Opus 34, he relied heavily on advice from Hermann Levi and Joseph Joachim. Clara also played a major role in persuading him that he had sacrificed too much in reducing the work to two pianos.

Apart from a brief visit to Göttingen, Brahms stayed on in Baden-Baden until October 1864. In September he composed his songs (Opus 32) and the first three movements of his String Sextet in G major (Opus 36). He also composed a cradle song, 'Geistliches Wiegenleid', to celebrate the birth of Joachim's first child in September. Based on the carol 'Resonent in Laudibus', known in Germany through the folk-song text, 'Joseph, lieber Joseph mein', it was later published as one of two *Gesänge* for contralto, piano, and viola.

The lengthy stay that Brahms made in Baden-Baden in 1864 showed that it was not just the presence of Clara Schumann that drew him to the Black Forest spa. As a northerner from Hamburg, he loved what he took to be its southern temperament and atmosphere. The waters were not important to him and there is no record that he ever drank or bathed in them. What attracted him was rather the scenery and the company. In May 1865 he took two rooms on the top floor of a house belonging to Frau Becker, the widow of a lawyer, at the edge of the village of Lichtental. He called it 'Das hübsche Haus auf dem Hügel' (the beautiful house on the hill). From the window of both his bedroom and his study, which he called the blue room because of its blue wallpaper, he looked out to pine-clad hills. He returned to these lodgings, which had the further advantage of being very cheap to rent, for most of his subsequent summer sojourns in Baden-Baden, developing a regular daily routine that hardly ever varied. He rose at four or five in the morning and after several cups of strong black coffee worked without stopping until midday. He then lunched out, either with Clara Schumann and her family or at an inn in town, usually Der Goldener Löwe (the Golden Lion) or Zum Bären (the Bear), and took a long walk through the woods in the afternoon. After taking coffee at 4:00, usually with Clara, with whom he would spend an hour or so in music making and conversation, he reviewed his morning's work and ruthlessly tore up the pages that did not satisfy him. Then invariably he was back at No. 14 Lichtenthaler Allee at 7:30 p.m. for

FIGURE 3.5. Brahms's lodgings in Lichtental, Baden-Baden (author's photograph).

dinner, where a place was always set for him at Clara's right hand. The rest of the evening was spent in making music with Clara and whichever friends she had gathered.

Brahms found the atmosphere of his little house on the hill at Lichtental highly conducive to composing. During his 1865 stay he wrote the last movement of the G major string sextet and the fugal finale of the Sonata in E Minor for Cello and Piano (Opus 38). He also began work on his Horn Trio in E-flat, Opus 40, having found the opening theme as he walked among the pines near his lodgings. Several years later he pointed out the exact spot where the theme had come to him to his friend Albert Dietrich. Apart from a brief journey to Basel to hear Bach's St Matthew Passion, he spent the whole summer of 1865 in Lichtental. In 1866 he did not arrive until August but found time to finish *Ein Deutsches Requiem*, except for the later, fifth movement added in Hamburg in 1868. On a September afternoon in Clara's house, he played and sang through the whole piece for guests including Levi and Allgeyer. Clara noted, 'I am most moved by the Requiem; it is full of thoughts at once tender and bold'.[23] He also played her his C minor quartet on the same occasion. He stayed on until November.

His 1867 visit was briefer and less productive. Brahms was moody, sullen, and infatuated with Clara's twenty-two-year-old daughter Julie. Clara herself found him so insufferable that she withdrew the usual dinner invitations. Despite the estrangement between them, however, she made the journey to Bremen to hear the first performance of *Ein Deutsches Requiem* on Good Friday 1868. When he returned to Baden-Baden in the summer of 1868, he was still infatuated with Julie and annoyed Clara by suggesting she should give up her concert tours around Europe. Once again the dinner invitations were withdrawn. Back in May 1869, he finished the *Liebeslieder* waltzes (Opus 52) and also the *Magelone Lieder* (Opus 33), written for the baritone Julius Stockhausen. Hearing from Clara that Julie had accepted a proposal of marriage from Count Vittorio de Marmorito, a distraught Brahms poured his grief and loneliness into the Alto Rhapsody (Opus 53), a setting of a poem by Goethe. A week after attending Julie's wedding he turned up at Clara's house in Lichtental and played the piece to her. She wrote in her journal 'It is long since I remember being so moved by a depth of pain in words and music. . . . This piece seems to me neither more nor less than the expression of his own heart's anguish. If only he would for once speak as tenderly'.[24] In fact, Brahms seems to have bounced back from his despair within a relatively short space of time. On 21 September Clara recorded in her daybook a delightful evening when, fortified with pineapple punch, he played Hungarian dances and Strauss waltzes. He stayed on in Lichtental until mid-October, apparently spending much of autumn flirting with a young Russian pianist.

The outbreak of the Franco-Prussian War in 1870 had a major impact on Baden-Baden. Many of the French visitors withdrew and the liberal cosmopolitan atmosphere disappeared. The banning of gambling in the new German Empire founded in 1871 led to the closure of the casino at the end of the 1872 season and heralded the end of the spa's reign as the summer resort of Europe's playboys and gamblers. The casino remained closed until 1933 when it was reopened by the Nazis to raise hard cash. The Viardots and Turgenev left the town in 1870, settling in Paris after a brief spell in London. Clara also thought seriously of leaving at the same time. Baden-Baden was perilously close to the Franco-Prussian border and she felt unsafe there. In the event, she stayed on for three years, hiding her valuables and choicest wines in the cellar. In September 1873, she moved to Berlin. 'I am leaving part of my life behind here', she wrote, and, indeed, she did not actually sell the house at No. 14 Lichtenthaler Allee until 1878 and returned for occasional visits to Baden-Baden until the mid 1880s.

Brahms continued coming to Lichtental through the 1870s. There were still musicians around with whom to play. He often visited the home of the cellist Bernhard Cossmann, who settled in Baden-Baden in 1870 and gave several performances there of his Cello Sonata in E Minor. Brahms spent the whole of the summer of 1871 in his cottage on the hill, staying from early May to mid-October, and writing the last two movements of the *Triumphleid* (Opus 55) his ultrapatriotic neo-Handelian paean for the Prussian victory against the French, and the *Schickalslied* (Song of Destiny). During this stay he gave piano lessons to the promising English pianist Florence May, who had come to Baden-Baden to study with Clara Schumann. Florence became very fond of Brahms, whom she found to be cheerful and kind, and went on to be his first English biographer. She was struck by his enthusiasm for long walks, which he took vigorously with one hand swinging a soft felt hat and the other behind his back, and by his fondness for cigars and cigarettes. He was back again over the summer of 1872, inscribing a birthday card for Clara with the second verse of his famous lullaby 'Guten abend, gut Nacht' which had originally been composed in 1868. There is a touching story that on this or an earlier birthday, he had taught the song to her children, who gave her a surprise performance after she had finished a long piano practice. With the closure of the casino, the Kurorchester was taken over by the town and became known from 1872 as the 'Städistches Kurorchester'. Brahms conducted it in his A major serenade and Schumann's piano concerto. The new orchestra received enthusiastic support from the influential music critic Richard Pohl, who lived in Baden from 1864 to 1896. Other guest conductors for its opening season were Hans von Bülow, later to emerge as a leading interpreter of Wagner, and Johann Strauss the younger. The two men sometimes jointly conducted the Kurorchester. A surviving programme for a concert in the Konversationhaus on 12 October 1872 combines works by Liszt and Wagner conducted by von Bülow with a medley of Strauss's works conducted by the composer.

Johann Strauss had first been contracted to play in Baden-Baden in July 1870 but his engagement was cancelled at short notice on the outbreak of the Franco-Prussian War. When he came in 1872 it was immediately after a triumphant if exhausting visit to the United States, where he gave three concerts in New York and conducted at sixteen concerts and three balls in Boston, one with an orchestra of 379 players. He arrived in Baden-Baden in mid-July and his biographer Ada Teetgen observes that 'in the course of the next few days Strauss was to be seen sauntering in the gardens of the Casino chatting in the liveliest fashion with one of his most ardent admirers, the Emperor Wilhelm I'.[25] The emperor, who was often in the audience for the waltz king's nightly concerts, is said to have had a particular penchant for 'Tales from the Vienna Woods' although it was the Blue Danube waltz that was most often played by the Kurorchester. The *Badeblatt* for 28 September reported that it was performed 'no less than fifteen times in fifteen concerts'.[26] Strauss stayed on in Baden-Baden until October, being in no hurry to return to Vienna, where cholera was raging. Towards the end of his time there he was decorated with the Order of the Red Eagle by the adjutant general of the Prussian Court and with the Knight's Cross of the Order of the Zähring Lions by the grand duke of Baden. He was not immune from the temptations of the casino in its last season of operation before closure and delighted the 50 players of the Kurorchester by inviting them on the occasion of a festive dinner to join him in emptying the barrels of a consignment of Viennese beer that he had ordered directly from one of the city's leading breweries.

The emperor was not Strauss's only fan. Hans von Bülow was another devotee of his concerts, writing to his mother of 'the charming magician Johann Strauss, whose compositions, conducted by himself with such grace and rhythmic precision, have given me one of the most stimulating of musical pleasures which I can remember having for a long time'.[27] Brahms walked the mile and a half into town from Lichtental every evening to hear Strauss conducting and he and von Bülow would sit drinking beer in the Kurpark listening to the waltzes wafting over from the music pavilion. Through von Bülow, Brahms met Strauss, and the three men took long afternoon promenades in the Kurpark. Brahms and Strauss in particular forged a close friendship during the summer of 1872. On the face of it theirs was an unlikely bond. Musically and temperamentally they were far apart. Yet they developed a great affinity and their friendship blossomed in Ischl through the 1880s and 1890s (see pages 134–37). Brahms, who loved dance music and especially the waltz, developed elaborate improvisations on Strauss waltzes and would often play them on the piano. He had an almost unreserved admiration for Strauss's mastery of technical skills and powers of orchestration. He wrote to von Bülow: 'he is one of the few colleagues I can hold in limitless respect', and to Paul Lindau, 'the man oozes music! He always comes up with something—in that he differs from the rest of us!'[28]

Brahms was back briefly in Baden-Baden in 1873, the year that Clara Schumann spent her last summer in her house in the Lichtentaler Allee. There he played her the finally completed String Quartets in C Minor and A Minor and the 'Rain Songs'. He next returned in 1876, conducting the Kurorchester in his Haydn Variations and Hungarian Dances and completing his First Symphony in C Minor (Opus 68), which on 10 October he played to Clara who was on one of her occasional brief visits back to her old haunts. Brahms returned again in September 1877, sorry to miss Strauss, who had conducted concerts of his work in March. He played through the First Symphony to von Bülow, who later that year conducted it in Hanover and Edinburgh. During this stay he also completed his Second Symphony in D Major (Opus 73), named the Lichtental. He did not return to Baden-Baden again until 1883 when he stayed briefly at the hotel Zum Bären (The Bear) and visited Clara, who was also back, on her birthday.

Brahms made two brief visits to Baden-Baden in the late 1880s. The first was in September 1887 to conduct his newly completed double concerto for violin and cello at a private performance in the Louis Quinze room of the Kurhaus. The solo parts were performed by Joachim and Hausmann and Clara was in the audience. His final visit was in September 1889, when he stayed again at his favourite hotel, Zum Bären. He was upset to find that three pine trees nearby had been cut down and vowed that he would never come back again. It was a sad note on which to part from a place that had provided him with so much inspiration and where, in the words of his pupil Florence May, 'all the circumstances of his surroundings were favourable to his creative activity'.[29] Brahms's favoured summer retreat was now Bad Ischl, while Clara Schumann had taken to spending a curative summer month each year in the Bohemian spa of Franzensbad. There was nearly one last reunion in the place where they had made so much music together. On 8 May 1896 he wrote to her saying that he had heard she intended to return to Baden-Baden: 'Please let me know when you are planning to go and for how long. I have always had a sort of longing for Baden-Baden any way and I would dearly like to take the opportunity to see the long-loved landscape—and friend!'[30] Nothing ever came of this visit, however. Clara was too ill to travel and she died on 20 May.

Baden-Baden's musical life continued to flourish through the late nineteenth and early twentieth centuries. A music festival in 1890 included a performance of Liszt's *Christus* and premieres of works by Borodin and Saint-Saëns. From 1892 to 1927 the Städistches Kurorchester was directed by Paul Hein, who considerably raised its musical standards and put it on a comparable footing with orchestras in much larger cities. From 1906 he organized musical festivals featuring Fritz Kreisler, Pablo Casals, and Ferruccio Busoni as soloists and guest conductors including Ernst von Schuch, Richard Strauss, Fritz Steinbach, and Max Reger. By 1919 the orchestra numbered fifty-three players. In that year Wagner's *Siegfried, Tristan und Isolde,* and *Der Fliegende Holländer* and Humperdink's *Hansel und Gretel* were all performed at the Kurhaustheater. Visiting opera companies that subsequently performed there included the Mannheim Nationaltheater under Kurt Fürtwangler, the Berlin Staatsoper under Bruno Walter, and the Metropolitan Opera of New York under Erich Kleiber and Artur Bodanzky. Pietro Mascagni conducted his *Cavalleria Rusticana* in Baden-Baden in 1925. Paul Hein's successors continued to uphold his high musical standards through the later 1920s and 1930s with the Deutsche Kammermusik and International Musikfest programmes having a special emphasis on contemporary music. Weill's *Kleine Mahagonny,* Hindemith's *Hin und Zurück,* and Milhaud's *L'enlèvement d'Europe* received their premieres in Baden-Baden in 1927, as did *Der Lindberghflug* by Brecht, Hindemith, and Weill in 1929.

The foundation of the South West Germany Radio Orchestra in 1946 further enhanced the musical importance of Baden-Baden. Since 1999 it has been known as the Südwestrundfunk Sinfonieorchester Baden-Baden und Freiburg. The Symphonie- und Kurorchester expanded its repertoire under conductors C. A. Vogt (1953–71) and H.-J. Wunderlich (1971–81). Visiting Baden-Baden in 1979 Joseph Wechsberg wrote somewhat disparagingly of 'the spa orchestra that performs from Easter to the end of September three times a day at the *Kurhaus* or in the gardens, weather permitting They play the same atrocious arrangement of Schubert's Unfinished Symphony that their predecessors played half a century ago'.[31] In fact, the orchestra's standards have risen considerably over the last three decades and the Baden-Baden Philharmonie as it is now known ranks as one of the

best in Germany. Wiener Stiefel, conductor from 1981 to 2007, moved away from daily performances in the Kurpark pavilion in front of the casino to less frequent but better rehearsed symphonic concerts, developed a close relationship with local music academies and established master classes for promising young players and conductors.

There are still many reminders of Baden-Baden's mid-nineteenth century belle époque, not least in the park at the start of the Lichtentaler Allee, where there are busts of Empress Augusta, Ivan Turgenev, and Pauline Viardot, the last always garlanded with red roses. Further along the Allee, in the dahlia gardens close to a pavilion erected by Edouard Bénazet, are busts of Clara Schumann and Johannes Brahms. The white-boarded house where Brahms stayed on the hill beyond Lichtental was saved from demolition in the 1960s and taken over by the Brahms Society of Baden-Baden in 1967. It is now a museum and although the view across the hills is obscured by new houses, the inside is largely unchanged. The two upstairs rooms where he lodged have been lovingly restored, with the study walls being painted blue as so many souvenir hunters tore down the original blue wallpaper. In the bedroom a bust of Clara Schumann stands on a chest. The ground floor rooms, formerly occupied by Frau Becker, are now made available to visiting scholars who can stay there and use the very comprehensive library. The society also runs a small festival every two years, when the works of Brahms and of contemporary composers are performed in a variety of locations around town including the Kurhaus, the Festspielhaus, and Brenner's Park Hotel. So is the memory of Baden-Baden's most distinguished and devoted musical visitor kept alive.

4

The Spas of Bohemia

One of the most significant concentrations of natural mineral springs in Europe is to be found in the northwest corner of Bohemia (now the Czech Republic) near the border with Germany. The principal spas here are Karlsbad, Marienbad, Franzensbad, and Teplitz (in Czech, Karlovy Vary, Mariánsnké Lázné, Františkovy Lázně, and Teplice v Cechách).

Karlsbad lies in the narrow pine-clad valley of the Tepl about 1,200 feet above sea level. In the words of a pioneering medical treatise on mineral springs, it is 'built on the crust of a vast common reservoir of hot mineral water, the Sprudel-Kressel. It stands on the lid of the kettle. The steam of this subterranean cauldron escapes through artificial apertures made in the rock, to prevent the natural boiler from bursting'.[1] Legend has it that the springs were discovered in 1347 when a fleeing deer led King Karl IV of Bohemia to them while he was out hunting. There are at least nineteen springs, varying in temperature between 48° and 162°F and having a strong concentration of sodium sulphate and sodium bicarbonate. The hottest, known as the Sprudel, spouts over 2,000 litres of water per minute from a depth of 2,000 metres, rising to a height of three feet from the ground and every few minutes suddenly leaping to a height of over twenty feet. The waters at Karlsbad are said to be particularly efficacious for disorders of the liver, jaundice, gallstones, gout, ulcers, and diabetes. The cure usually took from three to four weeks and involved drinking the waters early in the morning before breakfast, with an interval of a quarter of an hour between each glass, then an hour's walk and further doses of water at midday and between 4 p.m. and 6 p.m. This drinking cure was supplemented by baths at various establishments in the town. Karlsbad grew steadily in popularity through the sixteenth and seventeenth centuries, becoming known as Adelsbad, the aristocratic spa. Peter the Great took the cure in 1711 and 1712 and Goethe spent thirteen summers there between 1795 and 1823. A scholarly work by an English doctor in 1904 pronounced that

> of all the spas of Europe, Karlsbad may be regarded as the most important, if we have regard only to the activity of its mineral springs, and the gravity and seriousness of many of the maladies for which they are prescribed. It is one of the oldest as well as one of the most frequented of the German spas, and a vast concourse of invalids from every part of the world resort to it.[2]

Marienbad lies in a broader and higher valley with an elevation of 1,912 feet above sea level. The water from its forty mineral springs, which were apparently first discovered in 1528, is cold and contains a higher concentration of the aperient sodium sulphate and of other sodium salts (bicarbonate and chloride) than is found at Karlsbad. Water from the two main drinking springs, the Kreuzbrunnen and the Ferdinandsbrunnen, is piped to the Promenaden Platz in the centre of town. Like Karlsbad, Marienbad became a fashionable gathering place for the aristocracy and cultured classes of Europe, drawn in part by 'a great reputation for the reduction of corpulency and the treatment of cases of plethora and abdominal congestion in the overfed and sedentary'.[3] Its waters were also recommended for those suffering from jaundice, gallstones, and some cardiac conditions. The German poet Friedrich Schiller came in 1791 suffering from pneumonia and had to drink eighteen cups of water a day. As well as the drinking cure, Marienbad was also well known for its bathing treatments, which included mud baths, pine-cone baths, carbonic-acid-gas baths, and alkaline and chalybeate mineral baths.

Teplitz, the oldest of the Bohemian spas and also the most northerly, being closer to Dresden than to Prague, is situated in an open valley 750 feet above sea level. Its mildly alkaline thermal waters, which come out of the ground at a temperature of 115°F, are predominantly used for bathing and were channelled directly to a number of bathhouses, the most luxurious being the Kaiserbad. The twelve cold mineral springs at Franzensbad, discovered in 1502, have a higher iron content than those in the other Bohemian spas. They are used especially in treating women's conditions and in moor and mud baths, made with peat from the surrounding moorland.

The first composer of note to visit one of the Bohemian spas was Johann Sebastian Bach, who came to Karlsbad in May 1718 as one of six musicians in the entourage of Prince Leopold of Anhalt-Cöthen. It is not clear whether the prince brought so many musicians to exhibit himself as a patron of music or merely to alleviate the tedium of the cure that he was undertaking. Bach, who was the prince's *Kapellmeister*, accompanied him on a second visit to Karlsbad two years later. It ended tragically for the composer when he returned home to find that his wife had taken ill and died.

Beethoven spent the summers of 1811 and 1812 in Bohemian spas, forsaking his usual retreat of Baden apparently on doctor's orders. In 1811 Dr Malfatti advised him to spend two months taking the waters at Teplitz. In the event, he stayed a little over six weeks from the beginning of August until the middle of September. In between the demands of the daily regime of the cure, he found time for lonely rambles in the Schlossgarten and for composing the incidental music to two stage works by Kotzebue, *König Stephan* (Opus 117) and *Die Ruinen von Athens* (Opus 113). He also toyed with the idea of writing an opera based on a French melodrama but abandoned this project. It was during this stay that he met the lady who seems to have come closest to being the love of his life and whom he apparently had in mind when, walking in Baden in the summer of 1816, he told Cajetan Giannatasio del Rio, his nephew Karl's schoolmaster, that he had five years earlier made the acquaintance of someone 'a union with whom he would have considered the greatest happiness of his life.'[4]

There has been much speculation as to the identity of this lady. The leading contenders seem to be Amalie Sebald, a soloist from the Singakademie in Berlin with 'a fascinatingly lovely singing voice', and Rahel Levin, who had come to Teplitz from Prague for the season with the man she subsequently married, Varnhagen von Ense, a young officer in the Austrian Army. Beethoven certainly spent much time with both young women during his stay in Teplitz. He played the piano for

Rahel and inscribed an album for Amelie with his signature and the words 'Den Sie, wenn Sie auch wollten, doch nicht vergessen sollten' (whom, even if you would forget, you never should). Even more intriguing is the identity of the intended recipient of a letter that he wrote soon after arriving in Teplitz for his second visit in July 1812. Written in stages over two days, it pours out his passionate feelings for 'my Immortal Beloved' and seems at one and the same time to offer undying love and the possibility of a lifetime together and to signal a renunciation of any further attempt to marry or form a lasting relationship. This tortured and confused missive, the only one in all of Beethoven's surviving correspondence to use the affectionate form '*Du*' rather than '*Sie*', was never posted. References within it to the need to catch the early morning mail coach for K have been taken to suggest that the intended recipient was in Karlsbad at the time it was written. This seems to rule out Amelie Sebald, who was once again in Teplitz in the summer of 1812. It is also not clear that Rahel Levin was in Karlsbad then. This has led Beethoven's biographers to propose two other candidates for the 'Immortal Beloved': the twenty-two-year old Countess Almerie Esterházy, who certainly came to Karlsbad in July 1812, and Antoine Brentano, a member of a prominent Viennese family who married a Frankfurt merchant and seems to have been the recipient of the autograph manuscript of Beethoven's song 'An die Geliebte' (To the Beloved).

Whether the 'Immortal Beloved' to whom Beethoven wrote from Teplitz was the same lady whom he had first met there the previous year, and fondly recalled much later in Baden, we will never know. These two episodes do, however, point to the significant role that spas, and specifically the spas of Bohemia, played in his troubled love life. As well as having such an impact on Beethoven's emotional state, the 1812 visit to Teplitz also prompted one of his very few references to spa music. He informed Archduke Rudolph that he heard Turkish music there (according to Thayer this was military music with drums and cymbals) four times a day, 'the only musical report which I am able to make'.[5] Towards the end of July, apparently at the instigation of his new physician, Dr Jakob Staudenheim, he left Teplitz for Karlsbad, where he gave a charity concert with the Italian violinist Johann Polledro. After two weeks there he moved on to Franzensbad. A letter he wrote from there on 9 August suggests that he was not very enthusiastic about his enforced dash around the spas of Bohemia:

I have too much of several things, of bathing, idling and so forth. . . . [M]y doctor chases me from one spot to another to enable me finally to recover good health, i.e from Teplitz to Karlsbad, from Karlsbad to where I now am. . . . I must now refrain from writing any more and instead I must splash about again in the water. Hardly have I performed the duty of filling my inside with a large quantity of this water when I must have my outer surface washed down with it several times.[6]

Beethoven's peregrinations around the Bohemian spas were not over. After a month in Franzensbad, he was back in Karlsbad on 7 September and then returned to Teplitz on 16 September. He seems to have found the whole experience deeply unsatisfactory, writing from his bed on 17 September:

Nature too has her etiquette which must be observed. I am again using the baths at Teplitz; and I took it into my head early yesterday morning, in fact at daybreak, to go for a walk in the woods, although it was very foggy. Today I am doing penance for that *licentiam poeticam* and my Aesculapius [Dr Jakob Staudenheim] has led me round and round in a circle, seeing that after all the best cure is to be found at Teplitz. Those fellows have a poor idea of producing an effect; and I consider that in that respect we composers have undoubtedly outstripped them in our art.[7]

The cures taken by Beethoven in the Bohemian spas did little to improve his condition. He was forced to spend several days in bed and wrote gloomily to Amalie Sebald: 'sometimes I seem to be better, then again I seem to be jogging along in the old rut or even to be settling down to a prolonged indisposition. If only I could express my thoughts about my illness in as definite terms as I can express my thoughts in music, then I could soon help myself.'[8]

It was at this time that Beethoven first met Goethe, who was also travelling around the spas of Bohemia in the summer of 1812. Their first encounter took place at Teplitz on 19 July. They struck up an instant rapport and spent much of the following days walking together through the Kurpark. Their very different personalities showed up one afternoon when they encountered the Austrian empress and her suite. Goethe stood aside and bowed. Beethoven, by contrast, walked through the crowd, pressing down his hat and buttoning up his great coat. The two men resumed their acquaintance in Karlsbad in September. Beethoven later mistakenly thought that it was there that they had first met, telling Friedrich Rochlitz in 1822:

> It was in Karlsbad that I made his acquaintance—God only knows how long ago! At that time I was not altogether deaf, as I am now, though I heard with great difficulty. And what patience the great man had with me! He told me numerous little anecdotes and gave the most enjoyable details. How happy it all made me at the time. I would have died for him ten times over! Since that summer in Karlsbad, I read Goethe every day, that is, when I read at all.[9]

Frederic Chopin also seems to have come under the spell of the romantic atmosphere for which the Bohemian spas were particularly famed. He spent twenty-three days with his parents in Karlsbad in the summer of 1835, which were among the happiest of his life, principally because he fell in love there with Anna Mlokosiewicz, the daughter of a Polish general. He dedicated his Mazurkas in C Major and G Major (Opus 47 & 26) to her. While in Karlsbad, he also wrote his Waltz in A Major, Opus 34, No.1, known as the Tetschener Waltz because he inscribed it in the guest book at the nearby Tetschen Castle. The following summer he joined another Polish family, the Wodzinskis, with whose daughter, Maria, he had become infatuated, for four weeks in Marienbad. The house where he lodged, Bílá Labut (the White Swan) on the main street, Hlavní Trída, is now known as Dùm Chopin and houses the Tourist Office with a small museum dedicated to the composer on the third floor. Chopin had high hopes for this relationship but it was ended by Maria's mother. When his correspondence with Maria was found after his death, it had a note on top 'my grief'.

Louis Spohr stayed in Marienbad in 1833, composing a series of romantic violin waltzes entitled 'Memories of Marienbad' while there. Five years later he took a cure in Karlsbad following the death of his nineteen-year-old daughter, Therese. Franz Mozart also tried a cure in Karlsbad in 1844 when he became ill with a stomach ailment. He died there just a few days after his fifty-third birthday.

Richard Wagner, the most enthusiastic of all major nineteenth-century composers about the benefits of water cures, made several visits to Bohemian spas. The first was in 1835 when he went to Karlsbad, primarily in order to attend a performance of *La Dame Blanche* by the opera company playing there for the season. He had hoped to find 'the whole performance first class' but ruefully noted that 'not until much later did I fully realise how wretched was the quality of all these singers'.[10] His first visit specifically to take a cure was to Teplitz (or Töplitz to use his spelling) where he spent just over two weeks in the summer of 1842 with his wife, Minna, whom he hoped would benefit from its 'fine air and baths'.[11] They were joined by his mother, who took an annual cure there in an effort to relieve her gout. Wagner spent much of the time working on the score of *Tannhäuser*, which at this stage was entitled *Der Venusberg*. He returned to Teplitz the following summer, sending his wife on in advance, but did not gain much from the cure:

> I seized the opportunity of drinking the mineral waters, which I hoped might have a beneficial effect on the gastric troubles from which I had suffered ever since my vicissitudes in Paris. Unfortunately the attempted cure had a contrary effect, and when I complained of the painful irritation produced, I learned that my constitution was not adapted for water cures. In fact, on my morning promenade, and while drinking my water I had been observed to race through the shady alleys of the adjacent Thurn Gardens, and it was pointed out to me that such a cure could only be properly wrought by a leisurely calm and easy sauntering. It was also remarked that I usually carried about a fairly stout volume, and that, armed with this and my bottle of mineral water, I used to take rest in lonely places.[12]

The 'stout volume' carried by Wagner on his early morning drinking promenades was Grimm's *German Mythology*, which enchanted him with its legends and characters. He found the task of composing the music for *Venusberg* very difficult, noting that although he 'smashed all the strings' on the piano he had installed in his room at Teplitz, 'nothing satisfactory would emerge', and being much troubled by excitability and rushes of blood to the brain.[13]

In July 1845 Richard and Minna took their summer holiday in Marienbad, where they intended to take the cure. In order to follow 'the easy-going mode of life which is a necessary part of this somewhat trying treatment' he selected his books with care, taking the poems of Wolfram von Eschenbach and the anonymous epic *Lohengrin*. In fact, Wolfram's poem about Parsifal and the *Lohengrin* story excited him so much 'that I had the greatest difficulty in overcoming my desire to give up the rest I had been prescribed while partaking of the water of Marienbad'.[14] Ignoring his doctor's advice not to write down his ideas, by 3 August he had worked out a sketch of a new opera based on *Lohengrin*. He was also bubbling with ideas about setting the stories of the Meistersinger von Nurnberg that he had recently reread in Gervinus's history of German literature.

> Suddenly the whole of my Meistersinger comedy took shape so vividly before me that inasmuch as it was a particularly cheerful subject, and not in the least likely to over excite my nerves I felt I must write it out in spite of the doctor's orders. I therefore proceeded to do this and hoped it might free me from the thrall of the idea of *Lohengrin,* and this longing so overcame me that I could not wait for the prescribed hour for the bath, but when a few minutes elapsed, jumped out and, barely giving myself time to dress, ran home to write out what I had in mind. I repeated this for several days until the complete sketch of *Lohengrin* was on paper.
>
> The doctor then told me I had better give up taking the waters and baths, saying emphatically that I was quite unfit for such cures. My excitement had grown to such an extent that even my efforts to sleep as a rule ended only in nocturnal adventures.[15]

Although these early attempts were not auspicious, Wagner continued to take water cures, although he did not return to the Bohemian spas. In the spring of 1851 he was prescribed a course of sulphur baths for a curious rash that had spread over his whole body. Following several weeks of a bath every morning followed by a walk, the rash disappeared, although there were unpleasant side effects. He was much impressed by a book recommended by his close friend Theodor Uhlig, a musician with the Dresden Orchestra and enthusiast for hydrotherapy: 'Its bold repudiation of the entire science of medicine, with all its quackeries, combined with its advocacy of the simplest natural processes by means of a methodical use of strengthening and refreshing water, quickly won my fervent adherence'. The author, Rausse, argued that numerous poisons, including many medicines, could be expelled through the skin by a water cure.

> I naturally thought of the disagreeable sulphur baths I had taken during the spring, and to which I attributed my chronic and severe state of irritability. In so doing I was probably not far wrong. For a long while after this I did my best to expel this and all other poisons which I might have absorbed in the course of time, and by an exclusive water regimen restored my original healthy condition. Uhlig asserted that by persevering conscientiously in the water cure, he was perfectly confident of being able to renew his own bodily health entirely, and my own faith in it also grew daily.[16]

During the summer of 1851, on a walking holiday through Switzerland, Wagner was upset when Uhlig fell into a swollen mountain torrent they were crossing. However, his companion at once exclaimed that this was a very good way of carrying out the water cure, stripped off his clothes, and promenaded about 'in a state of nature' as the two men discussed 'the important problem of Beethoven's theme construction'.[17] Wagner himself tried the cure in a more orthodox form in September 1851 when, feeling particularly dejected, he booked himself into a hydropathic establishment at Albisbrunnen about three miles from his home in Zurich:

> The cure itself was superintended in the usual superficial way by a Dr Brunner, whom my wife, on one of her visits to the place, promptly christened the 'Water Jew' and whom she heartily detested. Early at five o'clock in the morning I was wrapped up and kept in a state of perspiration for several hours; after that I was plunged into an icy cold bath at a temperature of only four degrees; then I was made to take a brisk walk to restore my circulation in the chilly air of late autumn. In addition I was kept on a water diet; no wine, coffee, or tea was allowed; and this regime, in the dismal company of nothing but incurables, with dull evenings only enlivened by desperate attempts at games of

whist, and the prohibition of all intellectual occupation, resulted in irritability and overwrought nerves. I led this life for nine weeks, but I was determined not to give in until I felt that every kind of drug or poison I had ever absorbed into my system had been brought to the surface.[18]

Wagner thought of all the wine he had imbibed over many evening dinner parties 'and which must evaporate in profuse perspiration'. He persuaded his friend Karl Ritter to come and join him in the treatment but Ritter proved an unsatisfactory patient, denouncing the use of cold milk as 'indigestible and against the dictates of Nature' and discovering 'a wretched confectioner's shop in the neighbouring village, where he was caught buying cheap pastry on the sly'. Wagner, too, soon tired of his cure:

> My water cure and the hydropathic establishment became more and more distasteful to me; I longed for my work, and the desire to get back to it made me quite ill. I tried obstinately to conceal from myself that the object of my cure had entirely failed; indeed, it had really done me more harm than good, for although the evil secretions had not returned, my whole body seemed terribly emaciated. I consider that I had had quite enough of the cure, and comforted myself with the hope that I should derive benefit from it in the future.[19]

Despite this bad experience, Wagner remained an enthusiast for hydrotherapy, the principles of which he adopted as 'a new kind of religion'. He fulminated against alcohol 'as an evil and barbarous substitute for the ecstatic state of mind which love alone should produce'. Despite being increasingly pale and thin and finding it difficult to sleep, 'I still pretended that I had never been so well or so cheerful in my life, and I continued on the coldest winter mornings to take my cold baths, and plagued my wife to death by making her show me the way out with a lantern for the prescribed early morning walk'.[20]

Recurrent attacks of erysipelas (a febrile disease accompanied by inflammation of the skin) drove Wagner back to taking another water cure in 1856. He checked into a hydropathic establishment on Mont Salève near Geneva run by Dr Vaillant, who had himself been cured of paralysis in both legs at the hands of the pioneer hydrotherapist,

Vincent Priessnitz. Wagner found his treatment, 'which consisted in the most ingenious use of water at a moderate temperature' thoroughly calming and efficacious.[21] He was let off having to appear at the communal breakfast after the morning cure and allowed to sit drinking tea for two hours in his room while he read Walter Scott's novels. He initially took a volume of Byron's poems on his solitary strolls to look out over the Mont Blanc massif but he soon found that he did not need this distraction and left the book at home. At last he seemed able to switch off and not crave the stimulation and excitement of a new book or project. The only work he allowed himself on this cure was sketching plans for a new house. After two months he left Dr Vaillant's hydropathic establishment thoroughly refreshed and joined his wife, who had herself taken a sour-milk cure in his absence.

No other major musician was as doggedly persistent as Wagner in continuing to try water cures even when they did not seem to work. Other composers took the waters at the Bohemian spas but generally only made a single visit. Franz Liszt came as a patient to Karlsbad in 1853 and Paganini and Richard Strauss also went there. Anton Dvořák stayed in Marienbad in 1875 and in Karlsbad in 1893, where he conducted the European premiere of his *New World* Symphony. Gustav Mahler spent part of the summer of 1889 in Marienbad, and Johann Strauss stayed there with his family in 1890 and 1891. Brahms took his one and only spa cure in Karlsbad in September 1896. His initial impressions were favourable: 'I am grateful to my jaundice for having at last brought me to famous Karlsbad. I was at once greeted by glorious weather. What is more, I have an absolutely charming lodging'.[22] After three weeks of taking the cure, however, the report from his physician, Dr Grünberger, was not good. His liver was considerably swollen, with complete blockage of the gall passages and resulting jaundice and indigestion. Grünberger noted in his book a diagnosis of cancer of the liver. The truth was hidden from Brahms, who remained under the impression that he had jaundice, but he developed an increasing preoccupation with death—two of the chorales on which he based the organ preludes that he was working on through this last illness contained the text: 'O Welt, ich muss dich lassen' (O world, I must leave thee'). Brahms remained for a further three weeks in Karlsbad before returning to Vienna, where he died in April 1897.

The end of the nineteenth century saw the Bohemian spas enter their belle époque as resorts for the rich and famous. Marienbad had a particularly distinguished and faithful British clientele, headed by Edward VII, who went there twice as Prince of Wales and annually as king from 1903 to 1909. The Liberal statesman Henry Campbell Bannerman and his wife, Charlotte, took a six-week cure in Marienbad every year from 1872 to 1906. Other regular British visitors include the actress Lillie Langtry; Princess Louise, the daughter of Queen Victoria; and the politicians Lord Rosebery and David Lloyd George. Admiral Lord John Fisher spent twelve summers there. He was initially persuaded to try the cure there by an old lady friend, having despaired of ever finding a cure for his dysentery: 'I came across a lovely partner I used to waltz with, who begged me go to Marienbad. I did so, and in three weeks was in robust health. It was the Pool of Bethesda, and this waltzing angel put me into it, for it really was a miracle, and I never again had a recurrence of my illness'.[23]

The Bohemian spas continued to exert the amorous influence that Beethoven and Chopin had experienced on their visits. Marienbad had a particularly racy reputation, based partly on the supposed properties of its 'love spring'. As Prince of Wales, the future Edward VII spent much of his time there cavorting around the bushes with various young ladies, including Fraulein Pistl, a pretty hat seller. He regularly ordered a new hat, which she was required to deliver to him personally at his hotel. Henry Campbell Bannerman complained in 1899 that among the English visitors to Marienbad, 'quite half of the ladies either have already been, or are qualifying themselves for being, divorced; and a considerable number of the men are helping'. On a later visit he remarked that 'whether on account of the Prince's presence, or not, the English and American society here has contained an extraordinary number of tainted ladies—the decent people were almost in a minority and we thought of wearing our marriage certificates as a sort of order outside our coats'.[24]

Music remained an important accompaniment to the morning promenades when guests walked up and down the elegant colonnaded drinking halls sipping their prescribed morning dose of water through special vessels with spouts. The 1904 guide to spas noted that at Karlsbad 'the band plays at the Sprudel and the Muhlbrunnen springs from 6 to 8 a.m., and drinking begins at a very early hour' and at Marienbad 'the band begins to play at 6 a.m., either at the Kreuzbrunnen or the Ferdinandsbrunnen, situated at opposite ends of a long, covered colonnade, and at this hour drinking begins, and continues until 8 a.m.

At that time the band ceases playing, and the crowd of drinkers begins to disperse'.[25] In the evenings, there were operetta performances and concerts. Among the 'undemanding entertainments' that Henry Campbell Bannerman enjoyed at Marienbad were performances of *Die Fledermaus* and *Die Lustige Witwe*, Wagner concerts at the Bellevue, a dairy café at the edge of the forest and 'listening to Beethoven in the woods'.[26]

The Bohemian spas went into decline after the First World War but never lost their therapeutic reputation or their musical connections. With the coming of Communism to Czechoslovakia after the Second World War their clientele changed from liverish aristocrats to factory workers sent for a cure by their trade union. In Marienbad the great cast iron drinking hall was decorated with frescoes depicting Soviet cosmonauts and renamed the Maxim Gorky colonnade. But as Joseph Wechsberg noted after visiting Karlsbad in the early 1970s, although the springs were now named after Czech heroes rather than members of the imperial court, 'the repertory of the spa orchestra has not changed, ranging from Bizet's *L'Arlésienne* to Johann Strauss waltzes and Dvorak's Slavonic Dances. Attendance is said to fall off conspicuously when they play all-Russian progammes'.[27] When I visited Karlsbad, Marienbad, and Franzensbad in the mid-1980s the hotels' ballrooms were packed with rather portly and pasty-faced East Europeans dancing cheek to cheek. A *Times* journalist visiting Marienbad in 1988 gained much the same impression:

> In the former ballroom of the casino middle-aged men who understand the sartorial language of popular entertainment (butterscotch suits with black lapels, shirts with frilly fronts) are playing chugging versions of 'Volare' and 'O Sole Mio' on flimsy electric organs or metallic carmine guitars. And newly-met couples enjoying freshly-minted flings gambol with ever deserting inhibition till they dare dance *le slow*, cheek to worker's cheek, wiggling a little the way those reprogrammed into youth always will.[28]

5

Bad Ischl

Ischl, which nestles along the banks of the River Traun in the middle of the mountainous Salzkammergut (salt chamber) region of Upper Austria, was for long a small and unremarkable town in which most people made a living from forestry or salt mining. In 1820 Dr Joseph Götz, a local physician, discovered that adding water from the local hot sulphur springs to the brine baths taken by the workers in the salt mines helped to ease their rheumatism and skin complaints. He recommended them to Dr Wirer, physician to the imperial court, who publicised their therapeutic properties and commended them specifically to Sophie, wife of Archduke Franz Karl and daughter of King Maximilian of Bavaria, on whom hopes for the Habsburg succession rested but who seemed unable to bear children. In 1828, after suffering several miscarriages, she responded to Dr Wirer's suggestion that she try the salt baths at Ischl. Sophie loved the atmosphere of the place, which reminded her of the Bavarian mountains she knew as a girl. More to the point, eighteen months after her treatment, in August 1830, she gave birth to a healthy boy, Franz Josef, who would reign as Austrian emperor from 1848 to 1916. Following two further treatments, she gave birth to another two sons. The three brothers became known as the salt princes.

Franz Josef put Ischl put on the map, spending eighty-three of his eighty-six summers there. His parents, perhaps for obvious reasons, found the place enchanting and established it as their main summer base. They first took him there in July 1831 when he was just one to escape a cholera-ridden Vienna and he is said to have fallen in love with Ischl himself when he was three. Ascending to the throne at the age of eighteen, he established an annual ritual of bringing the court there every summer. He would arrive early in July when the hunting season started, forsaking his Vienna residences, the Hofburg and Schönbrunn Castle, and usually stayed until his birthday on 18 August. While in the Salzkammergut, he wore leather shorts, green jacket, thick woollen socks, mountaineer's boots, and a Tyrolean hat and devoted himself with an almost fanatical passion to hunting and shooting. Altogether, the emperor killed a total of 50,556 birds and animals during his summers at Ischl. His tally included 18,031 pheasants, 2,051 chamois, 1,442 wild boars, and 1,436 stags.

As well as succumbing to the lure of the chase, Franz Josef also found romance in Ischl. In August 1853 two Bavarian princesses, who were his cousins, were lined up for him by his domineering mother. She intended him to marry the older one, nineteen-year-old Helene, but he fell in love with her younger sister, fifteen-year-old Elisabeth, better known as 'Sisi'. At the court ball at the Hotel Austria on the Esplanade (now the town museum), it was Sisi with whom he insisted on dancing the cotillion. The following morning, his twenty-third birthday, it was quite clear that he was smitten, and his mother conceded defeat. The betrothal was made public at the end of Mass in the parish church. When Franz Josef and Sisi married the following year, his parents gave them the Kaiservilla with its magnificent wooded park on the outskirts of Ischl as a wedding present. For the next sixty-three years it served as his summer retreat.

With the patronage of Franz Josef and the presence of the imperial court from 1848 Ischl developed steadily through the nineteenth century as a major spa resort. In 1822 it attracted fewer than 50 summer *kurgäste*. By 1837 the number had risen to 1,400, by 1870 to 3,700, and by 1900 to 7,355, boosted by the coming of the railway in 1877, which reduced the journey time from Vienna from three days to six hours. As with other spas, Ischl attracted many more visitors who came not to take the cure but for a more hedonistic holiday. By 1900 the total number of summer guests had reached very nearly 17,000. At an early stage of the spa's development, in 1827, a 390-seat theatre (now the Lehár Cinema) was built in the Biedermeier style to house

the light musical comedies and operettas that became the principal entertainments offered to guests and established Ischl as a major centre
for touring performers. It regularly attracted well-known artistes
like Alexander Grimaldi (1850–1918), for 22 years the principal comic
singer in the Theater an den Wien in Vienna, and the soprano Pauline
Lucca. In 1875 the Kurpark was laid out and a magnificent Kurhaus
opened—as the Kongress und Theater Haus it is now the venue for
the annual Lehár summer festival of operetta. Equally important to
Ischl's burgeoning social and artistic life was the development of a
flourishing café culture. The Café Ramsauer, founded in 1826 in the
main square by the parish church, became a haunt of writers, singers,
and composers. Amongst its regular patrons were Alexander Grimaldi,
Johann Strauss, and Robert Stolz, who are commemorated today by
plaques on the wall. Café Walther, sited on the Esplanade along the
north bank of the Traun, where guests promenaded every morning
and afternoon, and the café established in the town centre in 1832 by
the Viennese confectioner Johann Zauner, became the other main
places for musical and literary figures to meet and gossip. In 1869
Café Zauner moved into the main shopping street, Pfargasse, where
it has remained ever since, with a reputation second only to Sachers
in Vienna as the leading café and konditorei in Austria.

FIGURE 5.1. Café Ramsauer, Ischl—a favourite haunt of writers, singers,
and composers (author's photograph).

Throughout Franz Josef's reign Ischl became a magnet for the crowned heads and high society of Europe and beyond. King Wilhelm I of Prussia, later emperor of Germany, came several times, as did the emperor of Brazil and the kings of Great Britain, Denmark, Rumania, Serbia, Greece, Bulgaria and Siam. With the imperial family and their royal guests came aristocrats, politicians, artists, composers, writers, and the inevitable hangers-on. Among the literary figures who were regular visitors were the poet, novelist, and painter Adalbert Stifter (1805–68) and the two leading nineteenth-century Austrian playwrights, Franz Grillparzer (1791–1872) and Eduard Bauernfeld (1802–90). Johann Nestroy (1801–62), who began his career as an opera singer and went on to write more than eighty comic plays, the best known of which was *Lumpazivagabundus* (1833), took a summer villa in the town for several years. Another visitor was Nikolaus Lenau (1802–50), the Hungarian-born poet who briefly emigrated to Ohio in 1832 but disliked the Americans for what he called 'their eternal English lisping of dollars' and returned to Europe. He spent several summers in Ischl in the late 1830s and early 1840s despite the fact that he disliked the almost incessant rain that often descended on the Salzkammergut. During one of his stays he complained that it rained for fourteen days without stopping.

Illicit romance and affairs with the singers and actresses performing for the summer season provided a further attraction for several of Ischl's distinguished male visitors. During one of his visits Lenau became totally infatuated with the Austrian contralto Caroline Unghar, best remembered as the soloist at the first performance of Beethoven's Ninth Symphony in 1824 who had turned the deaf composer round so that he could see the audience's applause and appreciation at the end of the work. The two had an intense affair and, indeed, became briefly engaged but it ended in tears and Lenau, who is regarded as modern Austria's greatest lyric poet and often compared to Byron, died a tragic and broken-hearted figure at the age of forty-eight. A chance encounter in 1865 between Otto von Bismarck and Pauline Lucca on the Esplanade outside the Hotel Kaiserin Elisabeth where he was staying with King Wilhelm of Prussia precipitated a major public scandal. After chatting to the distinguished guest about the difficult duties of being a courtier, the darling of the Ischl summer *kurgäste* added mischievously: 'Your Excellency, perhaps we could hold court together sometime too'. She then talked Bismarck into having their photograph taken together. Although it seems innocent enough today, with Pauline looking singularly uninterested and wearing a demure crinoline dress reaching down to her ankles, Bismarck's adoring gaze and the proximity of his knee to hers made the photograph a sensation and led his political opponents to mock the future Iron Chancellor's chaste reputation.

Franz Josef himself was not immune from extramarital amours in Ischl. It was where he pursued his relationship with the actress Katharina Schratt, an acknowledged beauty and leading lady of the Viennese stage. He had first been captivated by her appearances at the Burgtheater in Vienna in the early 1880s. In the summer of 1885 she accepted a seasonal engagement at Ischl. Franz Josef celebrated his birthday that year by taking his son, Crown Prince Rudolph, and his daughters Archduchess Gisela and Archduchess Marie Valerie to see her at the Kurhaustheater as Rosel in Ferdinand Raimund's musical play *Der Verschwender* (The Spendthrift), a tale of virtue triumphing over a husband's fecklessness. Sisi, who spent much time away from Ischl pursuing her own interests, encouraged her husband's attachment to Katharina and commissioned a portrait of the actress as a gift for him. In 1890 Katharina Schratt acquired her own house, the aptly named Villa Felicitas, on the Salzburg road on the outskirts of Ischl. Early most mornings Franz Josef walked or rode there on his own to breakfast with the actress.

Along with other creative artists, musicians were attracted to Ischl by the high society atmosphere and the prospect of securing commissions as much as for the clean air and delightful setting. Among the first major composers to stay there were Giacomo Meyerbeer (1791–1864), who came as a summer guest in 1840 and 1850 and Otto Nicolai (1810–49), best known for his opera, *Die Lustigen Weiber von Windsor* (The Merry Wives of Windsor). Imperial patronage brought Anton Bruckner to Ischl on a number of occasions. He was commissioned to write a Mass for the celebration of Franz Josef's birthday in 1864. However, he failed to get the work finished in time and although it is known as the *Ischler Messe*, the Mass in D Minor received its first performance in Linz. Bruckner came several times to play the organ at the parish church, notably on the occasion of the marriage of Franz Josef's youngest and favourite daughter, Marie Valerie, in 1890.

Johann Strauss the younger first came to Ischl in September 1855. The *Ischler Cur-Liste* records that he stayed at the Hotel Kaiserin

Elisabeth with an unidentified companion. He made frequent visits thereafter, finding that Ischl exerted a particular restorative charm. It was there that he went, possibly at the prompting of his third wife, Adèle, for the summer of 1892 to recover after his disastrous attempt at grand opera, *Ritter Pasman*, which closed after nine performances and much panning by the critics. From that year onwards Strauss spent the summer months in Ischl on his doctor's recommendation, staying in an imposing villa in the Kaltenbachstrasse, which he initially rented and later bought in partnership with his brother-in-law, Josef Simon, in 1897. He often worked at night standing at a high desk on the veranda and positively enjoyed the wet climate, writing to Alexander Girardi, who played the comic leads in several of his operettas, in September 1894:

> Only now does it become beautiful in Ischl. People disperse and according to what I hear, it's never going to stop raining. A splendid prospect for me! I love it when I can work in a pleasant house in stormy weather. . . . In a night of stormy weather I write twice as much as in the most beautiful summer night.[1]

In 1897 Strauss conducted the overture in a special performance of *Die Fledermaus* in honour of King Chulalongkorn of Siam, who was spending a week in Ischl as the guest of Franz Josef. Some time later, on the king's orders, he was invested with the Order of the White Elephant. On the eve of his departure from Vienna for his 1899 sojourn in Ischl, which he was planning to spend working on the score of his new ballet, *Aschenbrödel* (Cinderella), he developed a chill that turned into pneumonia. He never recovered and died on 3 June.

In the 1880s and 90s Ischl fulfilled the role that Baden-Baden had in the previous two decades as Johannes Brahms's favourite summer resort. Altogether, he spent ten summers there, including every one between 1889 and 1896. A major attraction for him was the presence of other musicians, notably Ignaz Brüll, who was his preferred partner for trying out new piano pieces for four hands. Brahms spent his first summer in Ischl in 1880, driven there partly by a desire to escape the attentions of his lady admirers at Pörtschach on Lake Worth where he had summered for the previous three years. Soon after his arrival he wrote, 'The fact that half Vienna is here doesn't spoil it for me. If half of Berlin or Leipzig were here, I'd probably run away, but half of

Vienna is very pretty and very easy to look at'.[2] During this stay he wrote substantial parts of both his Academic Festival Overture (Opus 80) and Tragic Overture (Opus 81). Unlike Strauss, he did not enjoy the cold and wet weather and developed an ear infection, which made him think that he was about to lose his hearing like Beethoven. He rushed back to Vienna in panic but the ear specialist he consulted there found no cause for concern. The following year, desiring to avoid a bad summer in Ischl, 'which I would not like to expose myself to again', he went to Pressbaum between Vienna and Linz.[3] However, he gave Ischl another chance in 1882 and enjoyed a productive summer there, completing his piano trio in C major (Opus 87) and writing his Quintet in F major (Opus 88) and the *Gesang der Parzen* for chorus and orchestra (Opus 89). Jan Swafford speculates that the ebullience of the Quintet was 'perhaps enhanced by the daily companionship of Ignaz Brüll and his tuneful music'.[4]

Brahms was intending to summer in Ischl again in 1883 but changed his plans at the last minute when he discovered that the young contralto Hermine Spies, whom he had met at a concert in Krefeld and with whom he had become totally infatuated, was going to spend the summer in the German spa of Wiesbaden. There was considerable disappointment in Ischl when word got around that he would not be coming. The proprietress of the Café Walther sent him a letter 'in the name of the heart-broken Esplanade' urging him to 'honour us with your visit again' and promising 'good coffee and plenty of newspapers'.[5] Brahms had become a well-known figure at the Café. The Viennese journalist Daniel Spitzer described him as usually sitting at an outdoor table about two in the afternoon, 'drinking coffee and smoking cigarettes, a very powerful, stocky fifty year old with blond hair, his flushed red cheeks framed by a grey beard'.[6]

Brahms was absent from Ischl for the next five years. Following his summer at Wiesbaden, where he wrote the whole of his Third Symphony in F Major (Opus 90), he took another last-minute decision in 1884 to forsake Ischl, this time in favour of the Austrian mountain village of Mürzzuschlag. 'Well, what a fellow he is!' Ignaz Brüll complained, 'he means to take rooms in Ischl for the summer, and then one morning he wakes up in Mürzzuschlag! I had been looking forward to our walks, our pleasant coffee parties and much besides—and most of all to playing new duets—and now all my hopes are turned to water—hence all this rain!'[7] Brahms returned to Mürzzuschlag in

1885 and spent the summers of 1886, 1887, and 1888 at Hofstetten on Lake Thun in Switzerland. However, the curiosity of the tourists there, and the laying out of a public promenade just beneath the windows of the house that he rented, drove him back to Ischl in 1889. Despite the unpredictable weather, he found the atmosphere suited him very well and he made Ischl his summer base for the remainder of his life, enjoying the companionship of Ignaz Brüll, Ludwig Bösendorfer, the piano maker, and Gustav Mahler, who visited him in 1894 and 1896 while cycling through the Salzkammergut. He was also much taken with the many attractive young female pianists who summered in Ischl. Visiting him there, the composer and conductor Gustav Jenner was somewhat surprised when following lunch, Brahms 'suddenly came up with the idea of visiting with me all the famous lady pianists spending the summer in Ischl—every year there were quite a number there. And so we went from house to house and were received with pleasure and astonishment everywhere'.[8]

Among the female visitors to Ischl to whom Brahms paid court were Ilona Eibenschütz, a piano pupil of Clara Schumann, and Adèle, Johann Strauss's third wife, whom he married in 1887 when he was 61 and she 31. Brahms remarked that both composers were 'in service at the Court of Adèle'—he for fugues, and Strauss for waltzes— and on one occasion he inscribed her fan with the opening bars of *The Blue Danube* signing it 'unfortunately not by Johannes Brahms'.[9] The friendship between the two composers forged in Baden-Baden blossomed in Ischl. Strauss gave lavish parties in his villa, to which Brahms was always invited even though he spent much of the evening insulting the guests. They often played cards together with Hans Richter (1843–1916), the leading Wagner exponent who conducted the premieres of Brahms's Second and Third Symphonies.

During his 1889 stay in Ischl, Brahms composed the three motets (Opus 110) and revised his Piano Trio in B Major (Opus 8). The following year, feeling that his creative powers were waning, he wrote the Quintet in G Major (Opus 111) and announced to all his friends that it would be his last work. He told his friend Fritz Simrock that on leaving Ischl that September, he had 'tossed a lot of torn-up manuscript paper into the Traun', abandoned his plans to write a fifth symphony, and decided at the age of fifty-seven to abandon composing altogether. In Ischl in 1891, he drew up his will, leaving his money to two charitable associations for needy musicians. In fact, he did go on composing but only when he was in Ischl. Of his last nine works, all but one were written there: the Clarinet Trio in A Minor (Opus 114) and the Clarinet Quintet in B Minor (Opus 115) in 1891; the piano pieces (Opus 116–19) in 1892 and 1893; the Clarinet Sonatas in F Minor and E-flat (Opus 120) in 1894; and eleven chorale preludes for organ (Opus 122) in 1896.

Brahms remained close to Clara Schumann. In 1894 he sent her a photograph taken on the porch of Strauss's villa in Ischl. Strauss, the older of the two men by eight years, looks dashing, dark-haired and slim, Brahms by contrast appears elderly, portly and grizzled. Increasingly, he dwelt on the deaths of friends and contemporaries. When he arrived in Ischl in early May 1896 he brought with him the manuscript of *Vier ernste Gesänge* (four serious songs) that he had drafted for low voice and piano. The texts were scriptural meditations on death, a subject he told friends was much on his mind. He was particularly concerned about Clara, who had suffered a stroke. News of her death reached him on 21 May. He hurriedly left Ischl for Frankfurt, thinking that the funeral would be there. He slept through his change of train at Wels and after spending the night at Linz Station, eventually reached Frankfurt only to find that the funeral was taking place in Bonn. After a journey of over forty hours he arrived exhausted in Bonn to find that although the burial had been delayed for him, the procession to the grave was already under way. He reached the cemetery in time to throw three handfuls of earth into Clara's grave. He returned to Ischl a few days later, where he worked on his eleven chorale preludes for organ, the last music that he wrote, and entertained Mahler. As the two men walked along the bank of the Traun, Brahms made his usual lament that music was going to the devil and would be finished for good after his death. Suddenly Mahler took his arm and pointed down at the river. 'What is it?' asked Brahms tetchily. 'Don't you see?' said Mahler, 'There goes the last wave'. 'That's all very fine', came the response, 'but maybe what matters is whether the wave goes into the sea or into a swamp'.[10]

As Mahler left Brahms's lodgings at the end of this visit, he glanced through the window and was struck by how elderly the figure looked who was wearily taking a sausage and a slice of bread from the stove for his lunch. In June Brahms's friends noticed a change in his complexion. A yellowing in the whites of his eyes suggested jaundice and they insisted that he see a doctor. Brahms, who had rarely visited a

FIGURE 5.2.
Brahms and Strauss
photographed together at
Strauss's Villa in Ischl, 1894
(author's collection).

doctor in his life, protested but agreed to consult Dr Hertzka, director
of the Cold-water Healing Institute in Ischl, who diagnosed jaundice
and told him to take a cure in Karlsbad. He was much relieved when
Professor Schrötter, an eminent Viennese medical authority who was
spending the summer near Ischl, told him that there was not the
slightest reason to go to Karlsbad. Schrötter later confided to Richard
Heuberger, composer of the operetta *Der Opernball*, that this was because Brahms's condition—later diagnosed as cancer—was too serious
to be helped by a spa cure: 'There's no Karlsbad for Brahms' illness!
It makes no difference where he spends his money'.[11] Brahms eventually did reluctantly take himself off to Karlsbad at the beginning
of September for his first and only spa cure (see page 123). Almost his
last action before leaving Ischl was to eat a large plate of goulash at
David Sonnenschein's Jewish restaurant. This was his favourite eating place. He was particularly fond of its highly spiced dishes like
Schalet, a Sabbath delicacy made of eggs and flour, prompting Daniel
Spitzer to remark that 'since he composed the splendid Hungarian
dances out of gratitude to the land of paprika, we now expect from
him a *schalet* eggs dance'.[12] Food was, indeed, one of the ailing composer's greatest pleasures. When he arrived at Attnang to change trains
for Ischl in May 1896, he found a sumptuous if somewhat unhealthy

lunch of very fatty roast pork and Salzburg dumplings, specially ordered in advance by Richard Heuberger, awaiting him at the station restaurant.

Brahms developed a set daily routine that changed little during his successive summers in Ischl. He lodged most of the time in simple rooms on the first floor of a house in Salzburgerstrasse on the northern outskirts of the town away from the main visitors' area.[13] From his windows he looked out over the River Ischl, a tributary of the Traun, and to the surrounding wooded hills where he walked most mornings as early as five o'clock. He spent the rest of the morning composing and finished work by half past eleven, when he made his way to Sonnenschein's restaurant in the rather damp basement of the Kaiserin Elisabeth Hotel. After eating a hearty plate of goulash with his friends at a table under the window dubbed 'The Patriarch's Table', Brahms joined the early afternoon promenade along the Esplanade beside the river. He always stopped at the Café Walther to drink black coffee, read the papers under the trees outside, and watch the tourists go by. It was to Walther's that visitors to Ischl went in order to see him. They were usually acknowledged, not least because his shortsightedness meant that he often bowed to people whom he did not know under the mistaken impression that they were his friends. In the early evening he moved on to a friend's house, often Johann Strauss's villa, to play cards and eat more.

The numerous descriptions of Brahms's behaviour left by those who encountered him in Ischl give a conflicting picture of his character. He was often gruff and reclusive. He gave his landlady, Frau Grüber, strict instructions that the doors of his rooms were to be permanently locked and no one allowed in when he was not there. Yet he also displayed touches of sociability and kindness. When starting out on one of his country walks, he would fill his pockets with sweetmeats and little pictures to distribute to the children who invariably followed him. He held the sweets high up and got the children to jump for them. Spitzer commented that 'in large gatherings he is very taciturn and just grunts the odd ironic comment; in intimate circles, however, he takes a lively part in the discussions and loves listening to and telling anecdotes and jokes'.[14]

Perhaps the most graphic descriptions of Brahms in Ischl come from the pen of his future biographer Max Kalbeck. On one occasion

Kalbeck mistook the composer, half running through the meadows towards him, for a peasant coming to shoo him away:

> Bare-headed and in shirt sleeves, no waistcoat, no shirt collar, he brandished his hat in one hand, with the other he dragged his cast-off coat in the grass behind him, and ran off quickly as though hunted by an unseen pursuer. Already from far off I heard him snorting and groaning. When he came nearer I saw how the sweat was streaming over his hot cheeks from the hair which hung about his face. His eyes were staring ahead into empty space and shone like those of a bird of prey: he appeared like one possessed.[15]

Kalbeck was struck by how often Brahms seemed to be in a dark and despairing mood. Passing the lodgings in Salzburgerstrasse, he heard piano music stopping and starting, with repeated phrases and then 'the strangest growling, whining and moaning, which at the height of the musical climax changed into a loud howl'. Kalbeck thought that Brahms must have acquired a dog but it was the composer himself, his face red and beard glistening with tears.[16]

As with Baden-Baden, the lure of Bad Ischl for Brahms was the rather paradoxical combination of the company that he found there and the seclusion that the remote mountain town provided. The atmosphere of the spa provided the sociability that his melancholy and lonely personality craved as well as the prospect of romantic dalliances. Although he did not share Strauss's enthusiasm for the sometimes incessant rain and storms, he came to accept the weather and even revelled in a heavy snowfall at the end of May 1895: 'the quite wonderful intermezzo of the loveliest of snow landscapes in the middle of summer'.[17] The saline and sulphuric waters seem to have had no appeal or fascination for him at all. The River Traun, however, did have its uses—and not just to promenade along and cast his discarded manuscripts into. Florence May, the young English pianist who came out to Ischl to sit at his feet and went on to become his English biographer, was worried that when she played the piano in her lodgings on the other side of the river, she might disturb him. However, her landlady assured her nothing could be heard: 'You can play quite without fear, *gnädiges Fräulein;* nothing is heard here—the water makes too much noise'.[18]

The ending of what might be called the Brahms era coincided with the beginnings of Ischl's golden age. In 1906 it was renamed Bad Ischl in recognition of its status as a health resort and one of the premiere spas of Europe. King Edward VII of the United Kingdom visited in 1905, 1907, and 1908, when he was given a sumptuous feast in the Kaiservilla. The first three decades of the twentieth century saw the resort boom, despite the trauma of the First World War, which began with the ultimatum signed and sent by Franz Josef from his Kaiservilla and ended with the collapse of the Austro-Hungarian Empire. The tally of summer *kurgäste* rose to 28,000 in 1907 and reached a peak of 35,000 in 1927. Socially and culturally, these were glittering times for Bad Ischl. Mark Twain and John Galsworthy were among the leading literary figures who patronised the resort alongside Austrian authors Arthur Schitzler (1862–1931), who came for over sixty years, and Hugo von Hofmannsthal (1874–1929). It was while staying for the summer at an inn at Lauffen, just outside Bad Ischl, that the German dramatist Oskar Blumenthal (1852–1917) gained inspiration for his play *Im Weissen Rössl*. He was much taken with the head waiter's wooing of the inn's proprietor, an attractive widow. This gave him the basis for the play, which he wrote with Gustav Kadelburg, in which the setting was transferred to nearby St Wolfgang, where a Gasthof named Weissen Rössl had existed for a long time. It premiered in Berlin in 1897 and was hugely successful, playing in Ischl soon afterwards. In 1926, another visit to Salzkammergut, this time by the theatre manager Erik Charell, led to an invitation to Robert Stolz, Ralph Benatzky, Bruno Granichstaedten, and Robert Gilbert to provide a score for *Im Weissen Rössl* (The White Horse Inn), and the creation of one of the most popular and enduring operettas of all time.

Several composers came to this part of the Salzkammergut in the 1900s. Franz Ramsauer wrote his opera *Hans Von Wildentsein* while staying in Ischl in 1901. Theodor Leschetitzky (1830–1915), the Polish pianist and composer, often took a villa in the town in which he wrote several piano pieces, including his 'Souvenir d'Ischl' waltz. Arnold Schönberg spent six summers in the 1900s in Gmunden on the shore of Lake Traun. In 1907 he and his wife, Mathilde, were joined there by the leading Austrian expressionist painter, Richard Gerstl. He taught Schönberg to paint and fell in love with Mathilde. The two pursued a torrid affair and went off to Vienna together, leaving Schönberg in the depths of despair as he struggled to compose his second quartet for strings. Threats of suicide brought Mathilde back to the marital home but plunged Gerstl into despair. He went into his studio, burned the entire contents including most of his drawings and then, in front of his studio mirror, hanged himself, and stabbed a knife through his heart. He was just twenty-five.[19] In 1908, having just finished his studies with Schönberg, Anton von Webern spent the summer as conductor of the operetta season in Bad Ischl.

Most significant of the musicians who came to Bad Ischl in the early decades of the twentieth century were the leading figures in the so-called silver age of Viennese operetta. Franz Lehár (1870–1948), Oscar Straus (1870–1954), Leo Fall (1873–1925), Robert Stolz (1880–1975), and Emmerich Kálmán (1882–1953), the five composers principally associated with this late flowering of the genre, which took it in a very different direction from the skittish, satirical bounce of Offenbach, Sullivan, and Johann Strauss, were all regular visitors. So were their less-well-known contemporaries, Rudi Gfaller (1882–1972), whose works included *Der Feurige Elias,* set on and around the Salzkammergut narrow-guage railway that plied between Salzburg and Ischl; Edmund Eysler (1874–1949), whose sixty works included *Die gold'ne Meisterin,* reputedly Hitler's favourite operetta; and Leo Ascher (1880–1942), who wrote more than thirty operettas between 1905 and 1932. A composer from an earlier generation, Carl Michael Ziehrer (1843–1922), who wrote twenty-three operettas and over six hundred dance tunes, took a summer villa in the town in 1897 and 1914. The principal operetta librettists of the period also spent their summers in Ischl, lured there by the presence of so many composers and the chance to pitch works at them. They included Alfred Willner (1859–1929), librettist for Puccini's *La Rondine* and for ten of Lehár's operettas; Victor Léon (1858–1940), librettist of *Die Lustige Witwe;* Fritz Beda-Löhner (1883–1942), who died in the Auschwitz concentration camp; and Alfred Grünwald (1884–1951) and Julius Bammer (1877–1943), joint librettists for Kálmán's *Grafin Mariza* (1926) and *Duchess of Chicago* (1929).

The proximity of this group of Vienna-based composers and librettists who decamped to Ischl for the summer months made for a rich interchange of ideas. It is difficult to establish what first drew them there. The Ischl Theatre had long been an important venue for operetta performances, and Franz Josef was an enthusiastic patron of the genre. There was undoubtedly a snowballing effect—when one or two composers started coming regularly, others followed, as did the small army of librettists eager for new commissions. By 1906, in the words of Bernard Grun, Ischl 'was already recognized as the official headquarters of the Viennese operetta. Authors and composers sat at work, theatre managers decided production dates, publishers paid advances and stars made their dispositions for the coming season'.[20] Much of this work was done at cafés and bars, notably in the Café Ramsauer and at Walther's on the Esplanade. It was of Ischl that Alfred Willner was surely thinking when he commented: 'Nothing is easier than making an operetta—you just borrow a story and go to a café'.[21] In fact, competition was fierce between librettists, and the term *'Operettenbörse'* (Operetta Exchange) was coined to describe the atmosphere in Ischl as they vied with each other to come up with suitable texts and sell their ideas to composers.

Of all the figures associated with the silver age of Viennese operetta, it was the acknowledged master of the genre, Franz Lehár, who had the longest and closest connection with Bad Ischl. He first seems to have come in August 1902 to complete his orchestrations for *Wiener Frauen* and *Der Rastelbinder*.[22] He returned for several more summer stays during the 1900s, working among other things on the score of *Die Lustige Witwe*. There is a (possibly apocryphal) story that during his 1903 visit he was driving through Ischl in a one-horse cab when he saw a lady and her young daughter, whom he knew slightly. With his usual courtesy, he offered to drive them back to their lodgings on the outskirts of town and then walk back to his own rented villa nearby. After dropping them off and dismissing the cab, they were astonished when he suddenly cried out, 'Where is she? Lost! I've left her in the cab' and dashed back along the road. He had left the half finished score of *Die Lustige Witwe* in the cab. Maria von Peteani, the young girl who witnessed this rare incident of absentmindedness on the part of the normally meticulous former regimental bandmaster, went on to become Lehár's principal biographer.

Another young lady visitor made a significant impression on Franz Lehár during one of his early summer sojourns in Ischl. The story has it that he first caught sight of Sophie Meth, a Viennese beauty who had entered into a loveless marriage to escape the boredom of her petit bourgeois parental home, from the window of his lodging in Salzburgerstrasse while she was staying in the house opposite. He was captivated by her and made no secret of his feelings. Initially flattered by the attentions of the thirty-six-year old composer, who was already being pursued by many women, Sophie came to reciprocate his feelings and divorced her first husband to become his lifelong companion, although it was not until 1924 that they married. Lehár stayed in several different lodgings during these early summers in Ischl, of which his favourite was the Rosenvilla set back from the Esplanade. The pavilion in the garden is said to have been the model for the one in which Camille and Valencienne hide away together in the second act of *Die Lustige Witwe*. It was in the Rosenvilla that his beloved mother died in August 1906 the night after he had conducted a performance of *Die Lustige Witwe* in the Ischl Theatre attended by Emperor Franz Josef. The list of those who stayed in this romantic Biedermeier villa, now known as the Rosenstöckl and still available for letting over the summer, testifies to the close relationship between spas and music making in the nineteenth and early twentieth centuries. Giacomo Meyerbeer, Theodor Leschetitzky, and Joseph Joachim all stayed there before Lehár, and he recommended it to Emmerich Kálmán, who spent 'three lovely summers amidst the roses' before moving to the Villa Sarsteiner in the street now named after him. Later the librettist Bela Jenbach and the opera composer Julius Bittner lodged there. At least three major musical scores were largely written in the Rosenvilla: Meyerbeer's *Dinorah*, Lehár's *Der Graf von Luxembourg,* and Kálmán's *Die Csardasfürstin*. It is surely no coincidence that they all belong to that genre of operetta I have suggested is the quintessential spa music.

In 1912, using the profits from *Die Lustige Witwe,* Lehár bought a substantial villa on the south bank of the river Traun opposite the Hotel Kaiserin Elisabeth. This became his favourite place of work for the rest of his life, although he also maintained a large house in Vienna. The Lehár Villa is now open to the public and preserved exactly as it was when he died there in 1948. The interior has a dark, heavy, bourgeois feel and the rooms are crammed with antiques, objets d'art, and old master paintings. Especially striking are the number of crucifixes, icons, statues of saints, and other pieces of religious art. Lehár keenly guarded his privacy when he was composing, usually at night, in his top-floor study furnished with a simple desk and a large Steinway piano. He locked a pair of wrought-iron gates half way up the staircase so that he could not be disturbed and insisted that his wife sleep in an adjoining house, an arrangement that also pertained in Vienna.

FIGURE 5.3. The Lehár villa on the bank of the River Traun, Ischl (author's photograph).

It was undoubtedly the presence of Lehár that brought so many librettists to Ischl every summer. An interesting example of the workings of the *Operettenbörse* is provided in the recollections of Alfred Willner, for long the composer's favourite librettist. One 'sultry, almost suffocating' afternoon in July 1913 he was summoned to the table at the Café Walther where Brahms had often sat to be told that unless he came up with a libretto by the following morning, Lehár would go to Unterach, a nearby village, where Victor Léon was staying. Desperate for a story line, Willner wandered the streets of Ischl and went into the church to pray for inspiration. Then he returned to his rooms, resolving to pass the night in solitary meditation. As he sat alone gazing on the dark mountain peaks, an idea came to him at last: a libretto based on the story of a pair of lovers who climb a peak together to escape the turmoil and frustrations of the world below. The next morning he went to the composer's villa and suggested that an entire act could be devoted to the two characters alone above the world. Lehár was enthusiastic and thus was born *Endlich Allein* (Alone at Last), which he later declared his favourite work. The work was premiered in 1914 and substantially revised in 1930, when it was renamed *Schön ist die Welt* after its best-known song.

Lehár composed the greater part of his last twelve operettas during his summer residences in his riverside villa in Ischl. He told a friend in 1939 that while for mere technical labour and orchestration, the metropolitan climate of Vienna would suffice, he always created the overall concept of an operetta and composed the melodies in Ischl: 'I have written thirty stage works so far, yet I must confess I always had the best ideas in Ischl. This must be due to the air there'.[23] The water played a part as well—not the sulphur and salt springs nor, as for Strauss, the incessant rain but rather the ever-present murmur of the swiftly flowing Traun, which he would often listen to from the balcony of his villa at night as he sought inspiration. During the day, he often crossed over the river to play cards with Viktor Zauner, who in 1927 took over and renovated the Café Walther to create a new branch of Zauner's on the Esplanade. Whenever Lehár lost a game, he did not pay his debts but wrote some bars of music on a piece of paper or one of the café's famous wafers and handed them to the proprietor saying, 'This will be worth much more to you than the money I owe'. Zauner seems to have accepted this unusual form of payment and to this day, one of the bestsellers at the Esplanade café and konditorei is the *Lehár schnitte,* a rectangular chocolate cake with the opening bar of the song 'Schön ist die Welt' iced on the top.

It was thanks to Lehár that Ischl acquired another of its most famous summer residents, the tenor Richard Tauber. In 1921 Lehár heard the singer in a production of his *Zigeunerliebe* in Salzburg. He was captivated by his voice and Tauber was invited to Ischl a few days later where the composer played through numbers from his latest score, *Frasquita.* It was the first of many sessions in the drawing room of Lehár's villa where Tauber would be introduced to songs written specifically with him in mind, including the immortal 'Gern hab'ich die Frau'n geküsst' (Girls were made to love and kiss) from *Paganini* and 'Dein ist mein ganzes Herz' (You are my heart's delight), the autographed manuscript of which is now on display in the room where Tauber first heard it. In August 1924 the Ischl *Operettenbörse* swung into action again when, over lunch at the Hotel Post, Heinz Saltenburg, manager of the Deutsche Künstlertheater in Berlin, learned from Tauber, who by now had his own villa just a hundred yards or so along the banks of the Traun from Lehár's, about *Paganini.* The two men went round to Lehár's villa where Tauber sang 'Gern hab'ich die Frau'n geküsst'. Saltenburg immediately drew up a contract that, in the words

FIGURE 5.4. The *Lehár schnitte* sold at Zauner's decorated with the opening bars of 'Schön ist die Welt' (author's photograph).

of Grun, 'opened the way for Lehár's second career, provided the practical basis for the Lehár-Tauber association and brought the Vienesse operetta to its final blossoming'.[24] For the rest of his career, Lehár devoted himself to writing soaring, Pucciniesque, bittersweet operettas with Tauber specifically in mind as the romantic lead. In the summer of 1933 Tauber went to the composer's drawing room to learn about his role as Octavio in *Giuditta*, the last and most operatic of all Lehár's works. After sitting with the authors of the libretto until four o'clock, he paused on the bridge over the Traun outside Lehár's villa and declared that the work should be performed in the Vienna State Opera—as, indeed, it was in January 1934.

Bad Ischl remained a mecca for operetta composers and librettists through much of the 1930s and right up to the dark days of the Anschluss and the Nazi annexation of Austria. The camaraderie and competitiveness of the *Operettenbörse* refashioned the genre of operetta, blending the nineteenth-century waltz style of Strauss and Lanner with the twentieth century rhythms of tango, Charleston, fox-trot, and jazz. As before, it was not so much the mountain air and thermal waters that provided inspiration as the smoke-filled cafés and bars. When the stars of the operetta world felt the need of a cure, they forsook Ischl in favour of somewhere more serious or grand. Tauber was taken to Pistyan in western Slovakia for sulphur baths, mud packs, and electrotherapy when he was stricken with severe and very painful arthritis in 1929, and Lehar repaired to Baden-Baden to celebrate his sixtieth birthday the following year. It was over cigars, beers, coffee, and cakes at Zauner's, Café Ramsauer, and the salon of the Gasthof Goldener Ochs that plots, libretti, and musical numbers were discussed and hammered out, deals done, gossip exchanged, and inspiration gained. The effects of this somewhat sybaritic and unhealthy lifestyle—in many ways the antithesis of the strict and austere spa regime—are evident in the surviving photographs and drawings from this era. A picture on the wall of the Café Ramsauer shows the rather portly and pasty figures of Lehár; Leo Fall, best-known for his work *Madame Pompadour;* and Oscar Straus, remembered for *Ein Walzertraum* and *Der Tapferesoldat* (The Chocolate Soldier), sitting on a bench smoking cigars. A cartoon of Lehár and Straus with Leo Ascher and Edmund Eysler on the Esplanade in the early 1930s gives a similar impression. Those sitting at the outdoor tables at Zauner's café on a summer afternoon must often have included Fritz Beda-Löhner and Franz Lehár poring over *Das Land des Lächelns, Schön ist die Welt,* or *Giuditta,* and Albert Grünwald and Julius Brammer working with Oscar Straus on *Der Letze Walzer* or with Kálmán on *Grafin Mariza* and the *Duchess of Chicago.* At least one of the most active members of the Ischl *Operettenbörse* did not have far to go for these meetings. A plaque on the wall of a house just a few yards along the Esplanade from Zauner's records that 'in this house the operetta librettist Albert Grünwald did his best work from 1922 to 1937'.

Many of the operetta composers and librettists left Austria for Britain or the United States before the outbreak of the Second World War, but Lehár and his Jewish wife remained. They took up residence in Ischl in 1943 and it was there, in the spring of 1945, that they received news that their house in Vienna had been sacked by Russian troops. At the end of April, in the week of Lehár's seventy-fifth birthday, Bad Ischl was liberated by U.S. troops. A GI later recalled knocking on the door of his villa: 'the door was opened by an old gentleman, short in height, with a deathly white face which showed no sign of bitterness but a smile of welcome. He took us into the drawing-room and asked us politely to take a seat. Then he walked to the piano without saying anything; his eyes stared into the distance and his hands trembled'.[25] Later in 1945 the Lehárs withdrew to Switzerland, largely because of Sophie's poor health. She died there in 1947 and Franz returned in July 1948 to spend the last months of his life in his beloved villa in Ischl. As the ailing composer lay on his small bed surrounded

FIGURE 5.5. Cartoon of Franz Lehár, Oscar Straus, Leo Ascher, and Edmond Eysler on the Esplanade, Bad Ischl (author's collection).

by icons, images of the Virgin, and crucifixes, crowds thronged the Lehárkai in national costume and bands marched past to salute him. He died on 24 October 1948. His body, dressed in white tie, tails, and patent-leather shoes, lay in state for a week in the parish church before he was buried alongside Sophie and his mother in the town cemetery.

Although several of the most prominent figures associated with the silver age of Viennese operetta, including Kálmán and Tauber, never returned to Austria and preferred to stay on in the United Kingdom or the United States, some did come back to Ischl. Robert Stolz and his fifth wife, Einzi, were the first civilian travellers allowed to fly back from the Unites States to Austria after the war ended. In 1948 they settled in Bad Ischl, where Stolz continued writing and conducted numerous concerts and operettas. Oscar Straus also settled permanently in Bad Ischl in 1948, after twenty years living abroad. In 1961 a summer operetta festival was established, using the Kongress und Theater Haus as the venue. Each year there is a fully staged production

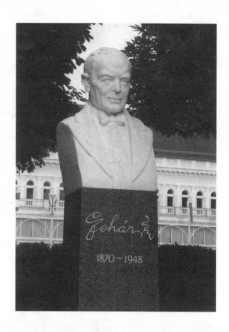

FIGURE 5.6.
Statue of Franz Lehár in front of
the Kongress und Theater Haus,
Bad Ischl (author's photograph).

of a work by Lehár and one by another composer. For many years the
musical director was Eduard Macku. The square around the theatre
has recently been named after him. Other composers associated with
Ischl have also been remembered in street names: Brahmsstrasse,
Anton Bruckner Strasse, Kálmánstrasse, Lehárkai, and Oscar Straus
Kai. There is no doubt at all who is kingpin among the town's musical luminaries. Brahms's bust is tucked away in a small square behind
the museum and Kálmán's in a permanently shaded side alley in the
Kurpark. Lehár has pride of place in front of the Kongress und Theater Haus, where the restaurant also bears his name, as does the town's
cinema, his villa, and those best-selling *schnitte* at Zauner's.

6

Buxton

Known as England's 'mountain spa' and standing on the edge of the Derbyshire Peak District a thousand feet above sea level, Buxton is the only place in the British Isles apart from Bath with natural thermal waters. They are forced up from a fault line through layers of carboniferous limestone to emerge in nine springs with a constant temperature of 82°F (27.5°C). Mildly saline, they have traces of a number of minerals and also significant quantities of nitrogen gas.

The waters here were undoubtedly known and used in the Iron Age but as with so many spas the Romans put the place on the map. They called it Aquae Arnemetiae, probably after a Celtic deity, Arnemetia, whose name may have derived from the word *Nemeton*, meaning a sacred grove. Coins found among the remains of the Roman baths suggest that they were in continuous use between 50 and 400 AD. There is evidence of pilgrims coming during the Middle Ages to take the waters at a well dedicated to St Anne, but it was not until the sixteenth century that Buxton's fame as a place to take the waters really developed. Mary Queen of Scots found the waters efficacious for alleviating recurring pain in her side. The first known medical treatise on Buxton's water, written by a local doctor, John Jones, in 1572, extolled the benefits of both bathing in and drinking it for 'women that by reason of overmuch moisture, or contrary distemperature bee unapt to conceive and weake men that be unfruitful'. It went on to commend the water as being 'profitable for such as have the consumption of the lungs . . . very good for the inflammation of the liver. . . . [I]t stayeth wasting of man's seede, the Hemoroydes, and Pyles, it soone amendeth . . . for them that be short winded it much availeth . . . the greene sickness it perfectly cureth'.[1]

Buxton continued to develop as a spa throughout the seventeenth and eighteenth centuries. Visiting it around 1720 Daniel Defoe commented on the purity of the air and contrasted it favourably with the more low-lying and close city of Bath 'which may be said to stink like a general common sewer'. A treatise published in 1734 by a Sheffield doctor, Thomas Short, recommended the water for a wide variety of complaints:

> Upon the whole, Buxton water being warm, highly impregnated with a mineral stream, vapour or spirit, containing a most subtle and impalpable sulphur, and being the product of limestone; it is therefore rarefying, heating, relaxing, thinning, sweetening, and a little drying, hence it is signally beneficial, and surprisingly successful in the gout, rheumatism, scorbutic and arthritic pains, wandering or fixt pains inveterate or recent; cramps, convulsions, dry asthmas without the fever or quick pulse, bilious colic, want of appetite and indigestion from intemperance, harddrinking etc; contractions, stiffness and lameness therefrom in any part, barrenness from a constriction and indilatibility of the fallopian tubes and uterus, ringworms, scab, itch, and for scouring sand, sludge and gravel out of the kidneys.[2]

The local landowners, the dukes of Devonshire, did much to improve Buxton and put it on a par with Bath. In the 1780s the fifth duke had a new complex of natural baths built, including separate private and communal baths for ladies and gentlemen and a special bath 'for the indiscriminate use of the poor'. An imposing crescent was laid out on the site of the Roman baths containing an assembly room and ballroom. It was here, and in the main hotel known as the Hall, that music making began. An anonymous mid-eighteenth-century poem enjoined those taking the cure to remain:

> Till health restored forbids your longer stay;
> And the brisk fiddle speeds you on your way.

Dress balls were held in the Assembly Room on Wednesdays and less formal undress dances on Mondays and Fridays. As at Bath, a master of ceremonies laid down rules of entry and a code of conduct and an annual subscription preserved social exclusivity. A reference to the Hall Hotel in 1778 mentions music being played in the corridors during mealtimes with diners being expected to give a gratuity to the musicians.

By the early nineteenth century Buxton was booming. New thermal baths were opened in 1818 with the water heated to 95°F. The standard regime of drinking and bathing was supplemented by walks along the riverside and more bracing excursions on the surrounding moors and hills as well as visits to picturesque places of interest in the Peak District. Almost as much was made of the mountain air of Buxton as of its waters. An early Victorian guidebook enthused that 'the invalid may inhale the pure and invigorating air of the highlands, and the spicy fragrance, carried on the wings of the wind and diffused throughout the entire valley, which exhales from the heather and many a virgin flower adorning the mountain's brow'.[3] Buxton was seen as providing an altogether more invigorating atmosphere than Bath, although it tried to keep up culturally with its southern rival by opening a new promenade and music room in the Crescent in 1828. On a visit around 1840 as part of his tour of English spas, the London doctor A. B. Granville found it dull compared with the Continental spas. He felt that Buxton needed a Kur-Saal or Promenade-room so that people could take the waters under cover and with some style and formality. He was also critical of the way that water was dispensed from the well: 'A nearly decrepit old woman, seated before the scanty stream, with her shrivelled hands distributes it to the applicants as they approach her. Now it is one of the great attractions of the German spas that smart female attendants are provided, ever ready to supply the limpid and sparkling water in crystal or china beakers, which almost every visitor carries with him.'[4]

Dr Granville was put off bathing at Buxton by the fact that the surface of the water 'exhibited a gathering of scum' and by 'the class of persons who kept coming in' to the free baths:

> When I saw the pot-bellied farmer of sixty, half palsied, and the lame artisan with his black and calloused hands, and the many who suffered from cutaneous disorders—all plunging together,

or one after the other, in quick succession—some of whom would set about scrubbing up from their hardened cuticles the congregated perspiration of ages, with a hand brush kept *pro bono publico* on the margin of the bath;—I say, when I beheld all these things, I confess my courage failed me, despite of my constant desire to try on myself, and ascertain by my own feelings, the effects of the various mineral waters.[5]

For much of the nineteenth century the main musical entertainment in the spa was provided by a uniformed band financed by the duke of Devonshire which played in the music room or around the Crescent for two hours every morning and two hours every evening as people took the waters and promenaded. The music had a soothing effect on at least two female visitors. During a seven-week stay with her aunt, who was seeking treatment for rheumatism, in 1824, Anne Lister noted in her diary that the band sometimes provoked sad memories and on another occasion led her to muse on an old love affair. For Mary Cruso, who came to Buxton for the summer of 1836 with her maid, Olive, in an effort to cure the acute gout and rheumatism for which she had already unsuccessfully tried leeches, poultices of camomile leaves, cooling powders, fomentations, and colchicum, the band provided some distraction in what was otherwise a fairly miserable stay:

> 28th June. Got up this morning, my pains and aches not charmed away. The band was playing in the Crescent when I went down. After Olive settled me on the sofa, I fell into a painful reverie: the melancholy airs, the lame and the halt, the old and the young, without looks of animation or sounds of cheerfulness passing round and round the arcade appeared as if struck by the wand of an enchanter who had doomed them to perpetual motion in one spot. When the music ceased the enchantment was over and the noble cold looking Crescent was left to solitude and to me as I saw no one but myself at any of the windows.[6]

Dr Granville too found the band one of the few distractions in Buxton's otherwise dull cultural life. In order to gain an impression of the spa 'at that hour of the day when the gayest scene of social life mingles with the natural beauties of Buxton', he took up a midmorning vantage point at the top of the landscaped mound overlooking the Crescent. The wide gravel walks below were crowded with men and women either standing or walking backwards and forwards: 'They were listening to the Duke's band, which plays (though not every day) between eleven and twelve o'clock, and which seemed to be composed of young lads dressed in a French grey uniform jacket and caps'.[7] A description of the band in the early 1850s suggests they were later kitted out in blue uniforms 'ornamented with a plenitude of small silver buttons'. The bandsmen played in a circle facing inwards and standing around a portable wooden bandstand with an umbrella-like roof.

Accounts for 1858 reveal that the band had ten members, several doubling on wind instruments and strings:

Mr Irving—clarinet and harp (bandmaster)
Mr Johnson—French horn and violin
Mr Perkins—clarinet
Mr Smith—bassoon and double bass
Mr Piddock—trombone
Mr Pearson—orpheclide
Mr Sutton—clarinet
Mr Pidcock—flute
Mr Percival—flute
Mr Goodwin—drum

A somewhat undistinguished rhyme from this era records:

Of the Buxton old band, old Goodwin was drummer,
They always were thirsty, both winter and summer;
They have played many a time in our old cot!
And never in this world was there a merrier lot![8]

The 1858 accounts reveal that £318.3s.8d was spent on the band's wages (which amounted to £31 every two weeks), music, and the repair of instruments. The duke himself subscribed £200, with hotels, inns, and boarding houses contributing £26.1s.2d and local shops very reluctantly paying a voluntary rate that brought in £58.15s. It is clear from these figures that the band ran at a substantial loss. In 1870 the seventh duke of Devonshire resolved on a major new initiative in an effort to relieve himself and his heirs of the burden of supporting it. He gave twelve acres of land bordering the River Wyre to a new Buxton Improvements Company. The conveyance was made without charge on condition that the land would be enclosed and landscaped to form pleasure gardens and a suitable building erected to shelter the band when it was playing in inclement weather. The company would charge an admission fee, which would be used to pay the band.

The pleasure gardens were laid out in 1871 and a fine pavilion erected to the design of Edward Milner, who had worked for Joseph Paxton during the planning and construction of the Crystal Palace in London for the Great Exhibition of 1851. The influence of the Crystal Palace is clearly evident in the design and structure of the Buxton Pavilion, a central hall flanked by conservatories, substantially constructed of glass and cast iron with local touches like a row of ducal coronets on the roof and stags' heads, from the coat of arms of the Cavendish family, on the interior ironwork.

Although there was considerable local opposition to shutting off the riverside gardens and levying an admission fee beyond the range of many local people, the establishment of the Pavilion as a place for regular morning and evening concerts proved hugely popular with visitors, whose numbers were enhanced by the coming of the railway from both London and Manchester in 1866 and the rapidly developing popularity of hydrotherapy cures. The band concerts proved so popular that in 1876 a new domed octagonal concert hall was built next to the Pavilion, measuring a hundred feet across and sixty-eight feet from floor to the apex of the dome. The opening ceremony involved three brass bands playing throughout the day and an evening orchestral concert featuring works by Mendelssohn, Verdi, Rossini, and Johann Strauss. It ended with the grand march from Wagner's *Lohengrin* and a final fireworks display with more brass band music. Seating a thousand people, and equipped with a large pipe organ on its stage, the concert hall, now known as the Octagon, greatly enhanced Buxton's musical life.

By the late 1870s the concert hall, Pavilion, and the pavilion gardens that surrounded them, augmented by a further twelve acres of pleasure gardens and a skating rink, were the centre of Buxton's social and cultural life. Admission to the gardens, which were accessed through a turnstile, cost 4d until 5 p.m. and 6d for the evening. A weekly ticket could be obtained for 2s 6d, a monthly ticket for 7s, and a yearly ticket

FIGURE 6.1. The concert hall built in Buxton in 1876 and now known as
the Octagon (author's photograph).

FIGURE 6.2. The Pavilion and Octagon, Buxton (author's photograph).

for 10s 6d with a special family rate of 25s. There was a further charge for bringing a bath chair into the gardens and for admission to the reading room adjoining the Pavilion. On the strength of these charges, the Buxton Improvements Company was able to employ a twenty-five-piece orchestra, which played either inside the concert hall, or outside on the broad walk in front of the Pavilion, depending on the weather, every morning from 11 to 1 p.m. and every evening from 7 to 9 throughout the season, which lasted from early June to late October. In addition, there were piano recitals in the concert hall every afternoon from 3:15 to 4:30 p.m. Edward Bradbury, who made a 'pilgrimage to the Peak' in 1879, left a vivid description of an evening concert and fireworks display:

> A carriage took us along the Duke's Drive in the cool and fragrant evening air with the sunset fire in the sky. Afterwards we found ourselves again in the delightfully seductive grounds of the Pavilion, where the orchestra was playing one of Godfrey's Schottisches, while icy and frigid duennas worked themselves into a fierce heat with their fans, or stabbed reputations with their knitting needles. At dusk there were fireworks. Quite a Crystal Palace display of pyrotechny. The crowd, which was composed of gentility that would regard it as 'awfully bad form, don't you know' to applaud at a theatre, actually cried 'Oh!' in affected wonder at the rockets as they lit up the dusky trees and flew upward. Sometimes a flying firework fell among the spectators, and revealed young Manchester in a fit of amorous abstraction, stealing within his own the soft white hand of Miss Stockport. Sometimes a sudden flash of light from a run-a-way squib or a cracker on the loose, showed somebody's sister allowing her brother's friend to span her waist with his arm. At last the music died away; the fireworks faded, and spluttered and died; the cold moon blanched the trees and silvered the waterfall; and a bugle bade us retire.[9]

The Buxton Pavilion Orchestra played for forty years, from 1872 to 1912. During this period, it had eight conductors. The first was Julian Adams, who had already conducted in London, Paris, Edinburgh, and Dublin. In common with other spa musicians, the members doubled as both orchestral and military band players. The repertoire was extensive. A correspondent to the *Buxton Advertiser* in September 1894 noted that during an eight-week stay in the town, he had heard music by 170 different composers. The most popular by far was Emile Waldteufel, the French composer of light classical pieces, 58 of whose waltzes and gallops were played, followed by Sullivan with 48 pieces, Wagner with 32, Rossini with 30, Suppé with 28, Auber with 26, and Gounod and F. Godfrey with 23 each. Next came Meyerbeer (21), Mendelssohn (20), Weber (19), Gungl (16), Stephen Adams (14), Verdi and Faust (12), Balfe (11), Audran, Handel, and Eilenberg (10), and Beethoven, Mozart, Schubert, Collier, and Michiels with 9 each. Despite the strong showing of Wagner in this list, the correspondent ventured to suggest that more could be done 'for the Wagner school' and that 'Wagner is very inadequately represented by *Tannhauser, Lohengrin*, and *Rienzl*'. He also expressed his longing to hear the Pavilion orchestra 'render some of Beethoven's grand symphonies'.[10]

A typical day's programme for 8 September 1897 confirms the popularity of Sullivan and Wagner. The morning concert included Auber's overture 'Crown Diamonds', Langer's *Grossmülterchen*, the Valse from Sullivan's ballet *Victoria and Merrie England*, selections from *Ruddigore*, the march from *Tannhauser*, and a suite of English dances by Cowen. The evening concert featured the *Bohemian Girl* overture by Balfe, a selection from *Rigoletto*, the overture to *William Tell*, Handel's Largo performed with the organ and a concluding selection from *The Geisha*. It ended, as all evening performances did, with orchestra and organ joining forces for the National Anthem. An editorial in the *Buxton Advertiser* at the end of the 1897 season, which lasted from 7 June to 23 October, noted that the orchestra, which at full strength numbered thirty-one players plus the organist and accompanist, had performed well over 400 pieces in the course of its twice-daily concerts, quite apart from numerous selections when constituted as a military band. The conductor, Charles Godfrey, who only directed at Buxton for two seasons, was praised for his programmes and his fine musicianship. He had resisted requests to make one evening a week a 'classical night', preferring to 'try and introduce items of good quality here and there in every programme'. Among the new works which had gone down particularly well were Sullivan's ballet suite *Victoria and Merrie England* and overture *In Memoriam*, Elgar's *Imperial March*, and Massenet's *Scènes Pittoresques*. The final concert of the season culminated with a performance of Haydn's *Farewell*

Symphony. The paper noted that the winter band would now take over in the Central Hall of the Pavilion with the full orchestra returning at the end of May.[11]

The dawning of the twentieth century saw Buxton reach its zenith as a spa. A pump room had been built in 1894, which provided some of the comforts that Granville had found lacking, and by 1900 there were fifteen grand hotels in the town as well as a large number of hydropathic establishments, specialising in the water cure pioneered by Vincenz Priessnitz at Grafenbürg. New forms of treatment were introduced from the Continent, including the Sitz bath, which immersed the lower trunk and thighs, recommended for ailments of the genitals and haemorrhoids, the surge bath, separate arm, leg, and head baths, mustard baths, fango mud baths, and ear, nose, and throat baths. Those with cardiac conditions were prescribed graduated hill-walking exercises and sessions in the effervescent and saline Nauheim baths, while sufferers from syphilis were subjected to mercury injections and sulphur baths in the Aachen treatment. Among those taking a cure at Buxton in 1899 was W. S. Gilbert, who was ordered there because of his gout. He was doubtless pleased to hear so many of the melodies from the Savoy operas being played around the spa.

The music became more elaborate with the Pavilion orchestra, now around thirty-five strong, being supplemented by solo vocalists. A grand midweek concert at the end of July 1899 featured two female soloists whose performances of Cowen's 'In the Chimney Corner' and Blumenthal's 'Sunshine and Rain' were both encored. It also included the premiere performance of Bernard de Lisle's 'Song of the Sea', a symphonic poem suggested by the words of Oliver Wendell Holmes and composed expressly for the pavilion orchestra, and works for solo cello (Popper's 'Romance') and solo violin (the andante from Mendelssohn's violin concerto). The following Saturday evening's popular concert featured a solo cornet playing Adams's 'The Holy City' and a baritone soloist, Mr Bantock Pierpoint, whose rendering of 'Ho! Jolly Jenkin' from Sullivan's *Ivanhoe* 'brought forth a storm of applause, in response to which Mr Pierpoint sang it all over again'. The continuing popularity of Wagner is confirmed by the fact that both concerts featured items from *Tannhäuser*—the overture and the grand march respectively—with the prelude to act 3 of *Lohengrin* additionally being played in the evening concert. The Sunday afternoon organ recital the following day included works by Haydn, Mozart, Handel, Gounod, and Mendelssohn.

Many of the musicians who played in the Buxton Pavilion Orchestra through the summer season were recruited from the Manchester-based Hallé Orchestra and the Glasgow-based Scottish Orchestra. Neither of these orchestras offered all-year-round employment, and their players were only too pleased to spend summer in the Derbyshire hills. The violinist Horace Fellowes was recruited from the Scottish Orchestra to lead the spa orchestra for four seasons between 1898 and 1901. Looking back on his first season, he was impressed by the calibre of his fellow players:

> Here were such fine players as Robert Murchie of Greenock, the famous flautist, principal of the Queen's Hall Orchestra, and the equally brilliant clarinettist, Henry Mortimer, Principal of the Hallé Orchestra. In this Buxton orchestra one had to be double-handed, as the orchestral players had to take part in the military band which played in the open in the mornings, weather permitting. Looking back, it seems to me now that this must have been a brilliant summer, as in the season of nearly five months there were few mornings when the military band did not play. Certainly it was fine on that first morning when, with a clarinet in my hand, I took my place as one of the two third clarinettists, in the Garden Pavilion Bandstand. I was in a state of fear and trembling, and with reason: I had had only one week's tuition on this instrument. However, the first part of the programme passed without mishap on my part, though at the interval the conductor, Edward de Jong (a famous flautist) remarked to me: 'I hope you play the violin better than you do the clarinet.'[12]

Like many another visitor, Fellowes found the atmosphere of a spa in summer conducive to romance: 'I met and became deeply enamoured of a charming young lady'. After a few outings, she invited him home to meet her parents. Unfortunately, the young musician did not make a good impression on the girl's father, 'a retired army colonel with a ferocious scowl', who told her 'I'm having no damned fiddler in the family'. When his wife expostulated that 'Mr Fellowes is not a fiddler but a rising young violinist', he replied, 'Doesn't matter—it's the same thing'. Fellowes notes somewhat ruefully in his autobiography: 'This conversation was reported to me later by a rather tearful young lady, and that was the end of our romance'.[13]

The 1900s were almost certainly the heyday of music making in Buxton. Patrons were not without their complaints but they were often directed at the audience rather than the orchestra. A correspondent to the *Buxton Herald* complained that 'several of the most delicate passages in Miss Nora Clench's magnificent solo, *'Airs Russes'*, were completely spoiled to those in the back part of the hall by the sacrilegious tramping of late arrivals in search of seats' and commented that he and others 'felt strongly inclined to get up and smite the intruders', whom, he was reliably informed, 'were parvenus—the bad imitators of gentility whose time had been too much occupied in making money to permit of them devoting any of it to the acquisition of manners'.[14] Another correspondent complained that the winter concerts in 1908 had been ruined by the roller-skating craze, which had transformed the concert hall from 'a hitherto welcome retreat for intellectual entertainment into a roaring pandemonium'. The skaters in the adjoining hall 'don't care a fig for the laudable efforts of the musicians to make themselves intelligible above the continual racket of roller skates on a wooden floor'. Skaters had even invaded the concert hall itself during the second movement of a Beethoven symphony. A lady in the audience 'endeavoured to persuade a few precocious girls on skates to quit the concert hall' but to no avail.[15] Noting these and other complaints, the *Buxton Herald* quoted an article from the national *Daily News*:

> Regulations for the comfort and convenience of music lovers ought to be enforced at all concert halls. A number of people attend merely to kill time, or to talk to friends about domestic concerns, or because it is fashionable to patronise a concert. These folk are seen at their worst in such inland watering places as Harrogate and Buxton, which possess fine halls for musical purposes and good orchestras. Their preference seems to be to enter or leave the room during a solo passage, and to do so as noisily as possible.[16]

The Sunday evening sacred concerts proved another object of criticism. A visitor from Cambridge in 1909 complained that they scarcely differed from the weekday concerts apart from having no dance music and that the only sacred item in them was 'God Save the Queen'. A regular attender at the concerts sprung to their defence, suggesting that excerpts from Mendelssohn, Beethoven, Schubert, Handel, Haydn,

Grieg, Wagner, Tchaikovsky, Thomé, Sibelius, and Sullivan were quite sacred enough and that if this visitor pined for a church service, then that is what he should attend. The complainant retorted with a proposed programme for a properly sacred concert:

> In rather less than four weeks I have heard the glorious *Tannhaüser* overture about that number of times. That piece, which never palls on me, is, I think, not only noble in character but religious in intention, and it stands most fittingly in the Sunday programme. But if only to avoid repetition, why not some Sunday give Handel's noble *Samson* overture with its lovely minuet? Again, I heard Handel's *Largo* twice on week-days. Why not give it on Sundays? Or, for change, with vocal help, Gounod's *Ave* or *Nazareth*? Further, as you have a fine organ and a highly competent organist, why not give occasion-ally one of Handel's grand organ concertos? Once more, in my four weeks' stay, Beethoven's name did not appear in the Sun-day programme. Let Gungl and Sibelius give place to the mighty master. Let us some Sunday evening—you have all the players required—have at least some movements of the immortal septet or give us the Pastoral Symphony with its hymn of gratitude to the Almighty.[17]

Like other spa bands, the Buxton Pavilion Orchestra provided a valuable training experience for young musicians. Among the distin-guished instrumentalists who cut their performing teeth there was the bassoonist Archie Camden. In 1906, aged eighteen and having al-ready been engaged for the winter season as fourth bassoon with the Hallé Orchestra, he was contracted to play for the summer as second bassoon at Buxton. For this particular season the pavilion orchestra numbered thirty-eight players, made up of six first and three second violins, three cellos, double basses, flutes, cornets and trombones, two violas, clarinets, bassoons and horns, one oboe and euphonium, two drums, and two organists/accompanists. Camden's contract stipulated that the dress for morning concerts was 'tall hat and frock coat'. Duly attired, he appeared for his first concert on 1 July:

> On arriving at the outdoor bandstand I found several play-ers already there, dressed in light suits and straw hats. I was greeted with howls of laughter and asked why I was wearing

those extraordinary clothes. I was confused and replied that my contract had stipulated this get-up. When the laughter had subsided I was told that the company was using very old contract forms for the 'extras' and must have forgotten to cross out on mine the paragraph relating to clothes.

Archie Camden played for several seasons at Buxton and found the experience very valuable. As much of the repertoire was new to him, it provided good sight-reading practice. With concerts from 10:30 to 12:15 p.m. in the mornings and from 8 p.m. in the evenings, the afternoons were free, and many of the orchestra members played cricket, with matches against local schools arranged on Wednesdays and Saturdays.

> They were happy days and I gradually became more at home in the orchestra and picked up a great many valuable tips. I learned, for example, how to find my way through the mysteries of music for lancers or quadrilles—and, even more important, the way through a Viennese waltz. The complicated form of these waltzes was the undoing of many a young and inexperienced player, with the constant 'repeats', the doubling back to an earlier 'repeat' sign, the tapping by the conductor for coda, and the little signs which the conductor gives to indicate whether repeats are to be made, or if one of the many little movements is to be cut out because of time.[18]

In 1903 Buxton acquired another important accoutrement associated with Continental spas with the opening of the Opera House designed by Frank Matcham and built onto the end of the Pavilion, to which it was linked by winter gardens. Its first season opened with a sacred concert on Sunday, 1 May, and then an opening week of two plays, *Mrs Willoughby's Kiss* and *My Miliner's Bill*, with songs interspersed in the drama. The opening season also included two musical comedies, *The Rose of the Riviera* by F. Osmond Carr and *Somebody's Sweetheart* by Edward Morris, a Hallé Orchesta concert, and a week's appearance by the D'Oyly Carte Large Repertoire Company performing Gilbert and Sullivan's *Yeomen of the Guard, Mikado, Gondoliers,* and *HMS Pinafore*. Groups performing in the Opera House in its early days included the Cavaliere F. Castellano English and Ital

FIGURE 6.3. The Opera House, Buxton (author's photograph).

ian Grand Opera Company, the Empire Grand Opera Company, the E. St Alban's Opera Company, Carl Rosa, and the D'Oyly Carte. The most frequently performed operas were *Faust, Il Trovatore, Cav & Pag, Rigoletto, Carmen, Madame Butterfly,* and *Maritana*.

The Opera House had its own orchestra, which played every afternoon in the Pavilion music hall between 3:30 p.m. and 5 p.m., except when there was a matinée performance. With organ recitals from 2:30 p.m. to 3:30 p.m. every afternoon and the regular orchestra playing every day in summer from 11 a.m. to 1 p.m. and 7:45 p.m. to 9:45 p.m., it was possible to enjoy seven and a half hours of live music in and around the Pavilion every day. In addition to the Pavilion and Opera House orchestras, two hotels employed resident bands during the season. In winter a reduced fourteen-strong Pavilion orchestra played every day from 11:30 a.m. to 1 p.m. and from 7:30 p.m. to 9 p.m..

The printed daily programme for 11 September 1907 shows the range of music performed in Buxton during the season. The fine weather programme began with an open air morning band concert including the ubiquituous *Tannhauser* overture, a Chopin polonaise, and Auber's *Fra Diavolo* overture. The wet weather alternative offered a string orchestra performing Strauss waltzes, extracts from Suppé's *Bocaccio,* and a movement from Haydn's *Surprise* Symphony. The afternoon piano recital included Mendelssohn's *Songs without Words* and the afternoon concert by the Bijou Opera House Band marches, waltzes, and gallops. The open-air band concert in the evening featured works by Cellier, Weber, and Lecocq while the alternative wet weather programme in the Pavilion included Suppé, Edward German, and Sullivan.

The Borough Guide to Buxton for 1910 proudly listed 'good music' alongside stately buildings, pleasant gardens, well-kept walks and drives, clean streets, high hills, baths and bath-chairs, and mineral waters as the distinguishing characteristics of the mountain spa. However, at a meeting of the Buxton Gardens Company (as the Improvements Company had become known) in March 1911 the chairman reported on a poor season the previous year, and there were complaints about the cost of the orchestra—eight pounds a day, or forty-six pounds a week—and the repertoire which 'was too severely classical, and being so there must necessarily be a great deal of repetition. People got sick of it'.[19] As at Bath, comparisons were made with seaside resorts like Llandudno and Bournemouth, which were turning in a handsome profit for their shareholders. In vain did some brave voices point out that both these resorts employed bigger orchestras and that the answer was not to reduce the Buxton band but increase it.

Following another lacklustre season in 1912 the decision was taken that henceforth there would be no resident orchestra. Instead military and other bands would be hired to play for a period of one or two weeks at a time. Prices were raised to sixpence for single admission to a summer evening concerts, five shillings for a weekly ticket, and twenty-one shillings for an annual season ticket. The bands were first class, including the Gordon Highlanders, the Royal Horse Guards, and the Royal Artillery, and there were guest appearances by such exotic groups as the Famous Grecian Ladies' Orchestra and Herr Wurm's Celebrated White Viennese Orchestra. However, many longtime visitors complained about the disappearance of the resident orchestra, and this nostalgic lament by a female correspondent to the *Buxton Advertiser* was typical:

> Her memory turns back and lingers lovingly on mornings
> of glorious sunshine when, as the visitor made her way along
> Broad Walk, the strains of the stirring march indicated to her
> ear that the morning's programme was being discoursed in the

open-air. Then would the notes of *Leonora,* or *The Lost Chord,* or it might be *Kathleen Mavourneen,* float out sweetly and clearly into the morning air intimating to the initiated that Mr Fred Goddard was rendering one of his inimitable cornet solos. . . . Pleasantly-passed drowsy afternoons, to the accompaniment of organ or piano . . . and then the evenings—who that has loved the Buxton of former years can forget the charm of those crisp starlit nights, when one stepped out of the cool keen air into the warm gaily-lit Pavilion?[20]

Buxton's fortunes went into a steady decline following the First World War. An orchestra was reinstated but with far fewer players than in the halcyon days of the Edwardian era. In 1919 George Cathie, former leader of the seaside orchestra in Eastbourne, took over as conductor. Despite having just fifteen players, the orchestra played a repertoire including several symphonies, among them Haydn's *Clock* and Mendelssohn's *Italian* as well as lighter pieces by contemporary composers such as Albert Ketelbey and Percy Grainger. The Buxton orchestra continued to provide a valuable training ground for future solo instrumentalists: Leon Goossens was its oboist for a short time. In 1927, due to continuing financial loss, the Buxton Gardens Company sold out to Buxton Corporation for approximately thirty thousand pounds. Buxton Municipal Orchestra was formed the following year with Horace Fellowes as its conductor. He remained until 1937, often directing the orchestra with his violin bow and joining in when required. There were regular Strauss nights and the orchestra broadcast live on the BBC on Thursday evenings.

The Opera House kept going through the 1920s, but financial difficulties and changing popular tastes led to its becoming a cinema in 1932. It continued in this role until 1976, occasionally hosting live events, including a recital by Paul Robeson in 1934, a series of annual theatre festivals from 1937, and Christmas pantomimes. The Octagon, as the former music hall was now known, became a popular venue for big bands such as those of Ted Heath and Humphrey Lyttleton, and the Beatles appeared there in 1962 and 1963. Although the Buxton orchestra was revived after the Second World War, with such distinguished conductors as Vilem Tausky and Charles Haberreiter, who had worked in Vienna with Franz Léhar, it was soon reduced to a core of just nine players: three violins, cello, bass, clarinet, trumpet, trombone, and drums. Increasingly, it became a dance band. From the late 1940s to the early 1960s the Pavilion ballroom was one of the premiere dance venues in Northwest England. A quintet played twice daily in the Pavilion café through the 1950s, but by the 1960s all that was left of Buxton's former musical glories was a lone organist, Miss Esmé Hand, who played in the lounge bar.

There was a brief renaissance in Buxton's musical life in the early 1960s when a week-long International Festival of Music brought the full Hallé Orchestra under Sir John Barbirolli to the town. It only lasted for a few years, however, and by the early 1970s a threat hung over the whole Pavilion complex. The Octagon was very nearly pulled down in 1971. The following year saw the closing of Buxton's natural baths and the effective end of its life as a working spa, although some treatments continued in the baths of the Devonshire Royal Hospital. A significant turnaround in the fortunes of the town came in the late 1970s with the refurbishment of the Opera House, which reopened in all its former gilt-laden glory in 1979. In the same year the International Buxton Arts Festival was inaugurated. It opened on 30 July with a performance of Donizetti's *Lucia di Lammermoor*. The leading lady, Monica Pick-Hieronimi, had been struck with a flu virus that morning. A call was put through to the American soprano Deborah Cook, who was in Munich. She gave her measurements over the phone so that the costume could be altered for her, jumped on a plane to Dusseldorf, and from there caught another flight to Manchester, arriving in Buxton less than two hours before curtain-up.

Since then, the Buxton Festival has gone from strength to strength, specialising in the performance of recent and rarely staged operas. In 1982 it gave the first British staging of Kodaly's *Háry János* as part of a highly successful Kodaly festival. It now runs through most of July and usually features seven operas. The 2002 selection was particularly daring: Cavalli's *Erismena*, Edward Rushton's *The Young Man with the Carnation*, Walton's *The Bear*, Nigel Osborne's *The Electrification of the Soviet Union*, Nicola LeFanu's *The Green Children*, Puccini's *Suor Angelica*, and Offenbach's *La Périchole*. There is always a children's opera and also recitals, opera workshops, and concerts as well as a series of literary events and talks by well-known authors.[21]

In 1994 Ian and Neil Smith, father and son Gilbert and Sullivan enthusiasts, brought to Buxton an international festival of the Savoy Operas. It has grown in size every year and now occupies three weeks every August, bringing amateur Gilbert and Sullivan societies from across the British Isles, the United States, Canada, and South Africa for one-night performances in the Opera House. On weekends there are professional performances from the recently reformed Carl Rosa Company and a specially created Gilbert and Sullivan Opera Company. Fringe events, singalongs, workshops, and rehearsals fill the Octagon and other parts of the Pavilion complex with the sound of singing policemen, pirates, fairies, and bridesmaids, constituting a veritable Savoyard heaven for addicts from around the world.[22]

7

Saratoga Springs

Saratoga Springs is the only town I know that has a grand piano in the waiting room of its railway station. It provides an appropriate if slightly out-of-tune introduction to the rich musical life of this elegant resort, developed in the nineteenth century to bring the cultural and therapeutic ambience of European spas to upstate New York. During a ninety-minute wait for the misnamed and long delayed Ethan Allan Express to New York, I sat down and played through some of the folk tunes in the only music book provided. Perhaps Amtrak could be prevailed on to provide a more comprehensive selection of sheet music and so enable long-suffering passengers to recapture the atmosphere of the spa's golden days. Judging by the comments of those who regularly use the line, there is often time enough to rehearse and perform several musical numbers before a long-awaited train actually arrives.

This most European-like of all North American spas has provided the setting for both an operetta and a musical. The operetta, *Pauline or the Belle of Saratoga,* written by Hart Pease Danks in 1874, recounts the lives and loves of a group of guests taking the waters over a summer season. The 1959 musical, *Saratoga,* based on Edna Ferber's novel *Saratoga Trunk,* with book by Morton da Costa, lyrics by Johnny Mercer, and music by Harold Arlen, tells the story of a young beauty, Clio Dulaine, who comes from New Orleans to Saratoga in the 1880s.

Maybe the scores of both works could be kept alongside the grand piano in the Amtrak waiting room together with a folder containing some of the many tunes inspired by and dedicated to the spa in its heyday. They include two Saratoga gallops (composed respectively by Gustave Blessner in 1841 and G. D. Wilson in 1866); the Saratoga Polka (Charles Grobe, 1844); the Saratoga Gallopade (W. C. Glyn, 1844); the Saratoga Mazurka (Adolphe Kurs, 1846); the Saratoga Congress Waltz Polka (Francis Rziha, 1848); the Saratoga Lake Waltz (Frederick Grambs, 1850); the Saratoga Schottische (Johann Munch, 1851); 'Just Arrived in Saratoga', a Grecian Bend Schottische (E. Mack, 1868); 'Just One Saratoga', a march and two-step (Charles Tyler, 1910); the Saraspa Waltz, 'dedicated to Saratoga Springs, Queen of spas' (Helene de Le Boeuf, 1927); and the Saratoga Trunk Blues (Lawrence McAllen, 1941).

This list, which is by no means exhaustive, clearly shows the character of the music written and performed in Saratoga Springs during its belle époque as a resort of the rich and well connected between 1840 and 1940. It was predominantly light dance music, played at the balls and 'hops' held in the huge hotels and the daytime concerts in the bandstands, pavilions, and drinking halls in the spa parks surrounding the springs. More serious music featured in the evening promenade concerts, and especially the very popular Sunday evening sacred concerts. What visitors to Saratoga craved, however, were tunes that were easy on the ear and liltingly seductive to distract them from the grim business of taking the highly carbonated and strong-tasting waters and to accompany the hedonistic pleasures of gambling, flirting, and showing off in what became known as the Queen of Spas.

Saratoga Springs was developed as a spa in the early nineteenth century in conscious imitation of the watering places of England and Continental Europe. Native American Indians had long known of the therapeutic powers of the naturally carbonated and mineral-rich waters in the thickly wooded region near the southeastern edge of the Adirondack Mountains bordered by the Hudson and Mohawk Rivers. A possibly apocryphal story tells of Sir William Johnson, the superintendent for Indian affairs in North America for the British Crown, being taken by Iroquois around 1770 to what later became known as the High Rock Spring in the hope of curing a severe and long-standing ailment. The waters proved so efficacious that he told all his friends about them and their fame spread. In the aftermath of the American

Revolution a number of settlers erected wooden cabins near the springs. George Washington tried the waters in 1783 and was so impressed that he attempted to buy land nearby. In 1790 Elkanah Watson, visiting Saratoga from nearby Albany, felt confident enough to assert that 'from its natural position and the great virtues of these waters, it must in some future day become eventually the Bath of America'.[1] The first serious analysis of the waters, published three years later by Valentine Seaman, a New York physician, found them to be particularly rich in iron, sodium, and other vital minerals and recommended that they be taken internally and bathed in as a treatment for numerous ailments.

Gideon Putnam, who settled in the area in 1789 intending to make a career out of forestry, was the first to see the potential of developing a spa in a place that was equidistant between New York, Boston, and Montreal. In 1802 he built a lodging house near the newly discovered Congress Spring. Named Putnam's Tavern (later the Union Hall), it was the resort's first hotel and quickly expanded as more springs were discovered, tubed, and housed in drinking pavilions or bathhouses. Before his death in 1812 Putnam had begun to lay out parks and develop a broad main thoroughfare planted with elm trees to link the main springs. Known as Broadway, it remains the city's central artery today. The burgeoning spa was further developed and promoted by Dr John Clarke, who had opened the first soda fountain in New York in 1819. He came to Saratoga Springs in 1823 and set about landscaping the area around one of the most popular springs, clearing away trees and bushes and draining the swampy ground to create what became known as Congress Park. He also bottled the water and marketed it so effectively that it became the most widely known mineral water in North America.

By the 1820s Saratoga Springs was emerging as the preeminent watering place in the United States, and people were coming in significant number for cures prescribed by doctors based on both drinking and bathing in the waters from the various springs. As with European spas, although its supposed therapeutic benefits initially drew visitors, Saratoga rapidly attracted a fashionable clientele who were more interested in seeking pleasure than in improving their health. As early as 1809 a visitor noted that 'where one person now applies there to repair a disordered constitution, twenty go, in the gaiety of health, to sport a sound one, against the enervating influence of revelry and riot'.[2]

Jacques Milbert, a Frenchman who came to Saratoga Springs in 1816, observed that 'time passes with a series of gay affairs; in the morning everyone drinks the water religiously; at night they make fun of it'.[3] Visiting from Massachusetts in 1827, Elihu Hoyt expected to 'find everybody here on the sick list—but it is far from being the case. Seven tenths of the visitors come here probably in good sound health, for amusement, and for the sake of spending a week or two among the fashionable to see and to be seen'.[4]

The opening of a railroad to Schenectady in 1833 allowed New Yorkers to travel relatively easily to Saratoga by taking a steamship up the Hudson River and completing the journey by rail. This development greatly increased the number of visitors and boosted the fortunes of the three main hotels in the town—the Union Hall on the site of Putnam's original tavern; the Congress Hall, which Putnam had begun building shortly before his death in 1812 on a key site near the Congress Spring; and the United States, which opened farther along Broadway in 1824. These three hotels became the principal venues for music making throughout Saratoga's golden age as a spa. Initially, the music on offer was relatively modest and depended principally on the talents of guests. Jacques Milbert noted during his stay at the Union Hall in 1816 that after supper 'several ladies take turns at the piano and, despite a noisy obligato of arrivals, departures and animated discussions, they pursue their sonatas unperturbed and receive the applause of the whole gathering'.[5] Gradually a more professional element was introduced into the musical entertainments. In 1822 Alexander Coventry, visiting from Massachusetts, attended a vocal recital by an English lady 'middle sized, with agreeable features' and rated her rendition of eight songs, including 'Robin Adair' and 'Charlie Is My Darling', 'the finest specimen of singing that ever I heard: every word was very distinct'.[6] By the time of Elihu Hoyt's stay in Saratoga in 1827 there were 'fashionable balls, stated concerts and all descriptions of amusements, which are calculated to take up the time and spend the money in our pockets'.[7]

A key step in the professionalisation of music making in Saratoga Springs occurred in 1821 when the proprietor of the Congress Hall engaged Frank Johnson, often regarded as the first native-born North American musician and composer, to provide a resident group of musicians through the summer season. In subsequent publicity the Congress Hall claimed to be the first hotel in America to employ a resident band and to adopt a regular programme of dances and balls. Johnson's all-black band played there from June to September every year except one between 1821 and 1843. It was also hired by Dr John Clarke in 1826 to play during the day in Congress Park, so establishing a tradition of daily spa concerts that continued for more than a hundred years.

Johnson was in many ways the most interesting musician to have a significant association with Saratoga Springs. Born in Philadelphia in 1792, he came to fame as a bugle virtuoso and was trumpeter of the First Troop of the Philadelphia City Cavalry before establishing his own all-black band in the city. Generally recognized as America's first full-time professional dance band leader, he particularly championed and developed the cotillion, a brisk quadrille-like dance involving frequent changes of partner. His band, which sometimes described themselves as 'The American Minstrels, self taught men of color', led the inaugural cavalcades for three U.S. presidents, James Monroe, John Quincy Adams, and Andrew Jackson, and was also in much demand outside North America. A highly successful British tour in 1837 included a command performance before the newly crowned Queen Victoria, for whom Johnson wrote a 'Victoria Galop'. The following year he visited Vienna, where he met Johann Strauss the elder. Johnson is credited with introducing Strauss waltzes to North America. Later, he introduced the polka, which he apparently learned from a retired officer of the Hungarian Army named Korpornay, who came to Saratoga in 1844 to take the waters. Johnson put the new dance into his regular evening programme at the Congress Hall, much to the alarm of a journalist from the *New York Herald* who was staying there for the summer season and reported to his readers: 'The indecency of the polka as danced at Saratoga Springs stands out in bold relief from anything we have ever witnessed among the refined and cultivated tone of European cities. It even outstrips the most disgraceful exhibitions of the lowest haunts of Paris and London'.[8]

Frank Johnson established a pattern of music making, based around daytime open-air concerts and evening dance music that continued in Saratoga Springs until well into the twentieth century. He imported the European concept of the Promenade concert, created by Philippe Musard in Paris, and aimed to provide a selection of 'music from all the recent operas, together with waltzes, gallopades, marches, quicksteps, etc.' for hotel guests and those taking the waters or strolling through

Congress Park. By bringing his Philadelphia-based band to Saratoga every summer, he pioneered a tradition of westward and northward musical migration that brought many East Coast–based orchestras to the resort. He helped to establish the distinctive Saratoga tradition of 'hops', slightly less formal alternatives to balls. The distinction between the two was perhaps best summed up by Samuel Dawson, a West Point cadet who visited Saratoga Springs in 1837 and wrote to a friend: 'We sup at six; promenade and then at eight the dancing commences and continues until twelve or one. They have three balls a week and three hops which are the same thing only the ladies do not dress as well'.[9] Hops, in fact, seem to have been a Saratogan invention and Johnson did his bit to contribute towards their success by turning out a steady stream of marches and quadrilles as well as his beloved cotillions, most of them written during his summer sojourns at Saratoga. In this respect, too, he established a model for future dance band and orchestra leaders, several of whom found their compositional muse stimulated by the atmosphere of the spa.

Perhaps Johnson's most important achievement was to establish music as one of the main attractions of Saratoga, rated second only to the beneficial effects of the waters in guidebooks and visitors' accounts. His publicity material boasted:

> The whole world could be seen at Saratoga, the cynosure of the nation's resort society; the politicians and the dandies; cabinet ministers and ministers of the Gospel; office holders and office seekers; the humbuggers and the humbugged; fortune hunters and anxious mothers and lovely daughters and Johnson serenaded them all.[10]

Johnson's introduction of the polka may have caused more of a frisson, but it is as the man who introduced the Viennese waltz to North America that he surely deserves to be remembered most in terms of his contribution to spa music. It is highly appropriate that this most characteristic musical expression of the culture of European spas in their golden age should have entered the United States by way of its premiere watering place. The centrality of the waltz in Saratoga's musical life, and its importance to the hugely important pastime of flirting, is attested in the poem, 'Pray, What Do They Do at the Springs?'

which was written in the 1840s by John Saxe and set to music in 1860 by C. M. Tremaine as 'The Song of Saratoga':

Now they stroll in the beautiful walks,
Or loll in the shade of the trees;
Where many a whisper is heard
That never is told by the breeze;
And hands are commingled with hands,
Regardless of conjugal rings;
And they flirt, and they flirt, and they flirt,-
And that's what they do at the Springs!

The drawing-rooms now are ablaze,
And music is shrieking away;
Terpsichore governs the hour,
And fashion was never so gay!
An arm round a tapering waist,
How closely and fondly it clings!
So they waltz,and they waltz, and they waltz,-
And that's what they do at the Springs![11]

By the middle of the nineteenth century Saratoga was attracting an increasingly aristocratic and wealthy clientele. It was also acting as a magnet for those who wanted to mingle with the great and famous, as described by James Buckingham in 1841:

Hundreds who in their own towns could not find admission into the circles of fashionable society came to Saratoga where, at Congress Hall or in the United States, by the modest payment of $2 a day, they may be seated at the same table, and often side by side, with the first families of the country, promenade on the same piazza, lounge on the sofas in the same drawing room, and dance in the same quadrille with the most fashionable beaux and belles of the land'.[12]

The popular appeal of Saratoga was further increased by the opening of the first gambling house in 1861. A purpose-built casino was built in Congress Park in 1871 and a racecourse opened in 1874, both becoming important venues for music making. Gambling was to become even more important than the waters in drawing visitors to the town but for many the main draw remained the possibility of mixing with the social elite. A journalist from *The Times* observed in 1887: 'The crowd goes mainly because the crowd is there, and this makes the crush so great upon the Hotel piazzas and drawing rooms. . . . [D]ays are devoted to ease and amusement, and the nights to mirth and pleasure. . . . [T]he place is almost perpetually en fete'.[13]

As in the European spas, music provided a much-appreciated accompaniment and distraction for those engaged in the serious business of taking the waters. A band played in Congress Park for two hours from 7:30 a.m. while drinkers imbibed two or three cups of mineral water before breakfast at either the Congress or Columbian Springs. Another band played at the same time for those who preferred to take the Alka-Selzer–like waters in Hathorn Park. Even more dedicated adherents to the cure were up at 4 a.m. for their first bath, but they were not serenaded by music at that hour, unlike those following a similarly strict regime at a European spa. 'At Kissingen', a comparative study made in 1887 of the daily routine at Saratoga and the main European spas, noted, 'the band passes under the windows at full blast at 5am, calling the Cur-guest to his morning devotions at the shrine of Hygeia and her healing springs.'[14] If those taking the waters at Saratoga missed out on early morning music, however, they were given plenty later in the day, although not quite as much as at Kissingen, where 'a baker's dozen of brass bands may be heard at the same moment by any ear for music on any afternoon of August'. There were further daily concerts in Congress Park from 4 p.m. and 5 p.m. and from 8 p.m. to 10 p.m. For the evening concerts the band often played from a pavilion constructed in the lake in Congress Park in the 1860s. Most of the open-air concerts were provided by military bands. The Seventy-seventh Regimental Band, made up of Civil War veterans, was much in demand in the 1860s and 1870s, with Doring's Ninth Regimental Band proving the main attraction for the next three decades. The admission charge was fifteen cents for the morning and afternoon concerts and twenty-five cents in the evenings.

On Saturday evenings there were Promenade concerts following the tradition started by Frank Johnson. Sunday was the only day of the week when there were not morning and afternoon concerts in Congress Park. There was, however, a sacred concert every Sunday evening

for which the band was often joined by a vocal group singing planta-
tion songs and such perennial favourites as Barnby's 'Sweet and Low',
Webster's 'Sweet Bye and Bye', Gounod's *Ave Maria*, and Rossini's
Stabat Mater, which appeared again and again on the programme by
popular request. The atmosphere of these events is captured by a
pious poem published in the *Daily Saratogian* in August 1876 and
entitled 'A Sabbath Evening at Congress Spring Park':

Hark! I hear soft music breathing,
Swiftly o'er the lakelet there-
'Tis Rossini's grand bequeathing;
List! It charms the very air!
Stabat Mater 'Lord how blessed
are thy mercies' unto me.
Though unworthy, poor, distressed,
Blessed in beauteous harmony.[15]

Aside from Congress Park, the main venues for concerts were the
hotels. By 1870 Saratoga Springs had more than thirty hotels and
eighty boarding houses providing accommodation for well over 10,000
visitors, who more than doubled the resident population of 7,516 in
the summer months. The big three hotels, which between them could
accommodate 5,000 guests, significantly expanded around this time.
The Union Hall was rebuilt in 1860 and further extended and improved in 1872 when it became known as the Grand Union. The Congress Hall was rebuilt in 1868 after burning down two years earlier,
and the United States was rebuilt in 1874 also having been destroyed
by fire. The scale of these three hotels was enormous. The Grand
Union had 850 rooms with sleeping accommodation for 1,200 guests
and a dining hall that could seat 1,500. The United States had over 900
guest rooms, which could sleep 2,000, a parlour of over 4,000 square
feet, and a dining room of over 10,000 square feet. All three main hotels had colonnaded piazzas or loggias extending the length of their
front and rear facades. These vast verandahs, two or three storeys high
and equipped with wicker chairs and rockers, opened at the front on
to Broadway and at the rear on to the hotels' private gardens and
parks. The United States Hotel had half a mile of verandahs with over
1,000 rocking chairs overlooking six acres of ground. These loggias
were the venues for morning, afternoon, and evening concerts by

resident orchestras, which drew considerable crowds, made up both of hotel guests and others who paid a modest entry charge to mingle with the rich and famous.

The hotels made much of their orchestras in their publicity material. A brochure for the Grand Union Hotel in 1894 pointed out that

> At all hours of the day the piazza is the favourite resort of the hotel guests, who here may linger in *dolce far niente,* in solitary enjoyment, or join in pleasant converse with the groups of gay gossipers who are wont to gather there, or better still, to listen to the sweet strains of the hotel orchestra—not a mere band of music-makers, but a gathering of trained artists, playing selections of highest merit, and conducted by a director of national reputation. . . . The scene at one of these concerts, where exquisite summer toilets for the ladies is the unwritten law of the occasion, is most attractive. Here feminine beauty is seen in its most gracious character. Allied to the delights of the music and the attractive entourage the result is truly unique and most charming, and dwells in the memory of visitors among the most pleasant recollections of Saratoga.[16]

Programmes for the morning and evening concerts were the most prominent item in the Grand Union's sixteen-page *Programme du Jour,* taking precedence over the lists of that day's arrivals at the hotel and other entertainments on offer. The United States Hotel printed the programmes for its morning and evening concerts on stiff card adorned with a coloured picture of a peacock. The reverse side provided a list of arrivals at the hotel that day—the majority coming from New York with some from Chicago, Boston, and Detroit—and details of the local springs, golf courses, places of interest and amusement, and suggested bicycle trips. Programmes for the daily concerts at the three biggest hotels were also printed in the *Daily Saratogian.*

The loggia concerts, which took place at 10:30 a.m., 3:30 p.m., and 8 p.m., followed a broadly similar pattern. They generally began with a march, followed by an overture, a waltz, a selection from an opera or operetta, a dance, and a medley of popular airs, sometimes interspersed with a cornet or violin solo. By the 1890s they often finished with a cakewalk, an item that was especially popular—a penciled note on the programme for an evening concert at the United States Hotel

FIGURE 7.1. Victor Herbert conducting the orchestra at the Grand Union Hotel, Saratoga Springs, c. 1905 (George S. Bolster Collection, Historical Society of Saratoga Springs).

FIGURE 7.2. A seven-piece orchestra playing on the loggia of the Grand Union Hotel, Saratoga Springs, c. 1905 (George S. Bolster Collection, Historical Society of Saratoga Springs).

on 6 July 1899 implores: 'Ask for Cake Shuffle'. The repertoire was drawn from the same light classical favourites that provided the staple fare of the kurhaus orchestras in the European spas—a typical concert in the mid-1870s included a Suppé overture, a Strauss waltz, a selection from Wagner's *Tannhäuser,* and a Schubert serenade. By the turn of the century the selection had become somewhat more eclectic and broad-ranging to accommodate changing tastes. A Monday morning concert in 1902 at the Grand Union Hotel included Delibes's *Intermezzo,* Dvořák's Slavic dances, and a selection from Wagner's *Lohengrin* and finished with a cakewalk, 'Creole Bella'.

As in Congress Park, the hotels offered special Sunday evening concerts, although they were not exclusively of sacred music—one in the United States Hotel in September 1902 included Adams's 'Holy City' as a cornet solo, the quartet from *Rigoletto,* a selection from *Faust,* the March 'Athalia' by Mendelssohn, the concert waltz *'Amereuse'* by Berger, and the overture *Stradalla* by von Flotow. Sacred items frequently cropped up in midweek concerts, inspiring these uplifting reflections from the correspondent of a New York newspaper in 1884:

> At the evening concert at the Grand Union on Wednesday one of the numbers was that grand old hymn, 'Nearer My God to Thee'. As the familiar strains went out upon the still night air, there was a hush throughout the piazza's length and the sound of a falling pin could be heard. As the last note died away, the vast assemblage broke forth into a storm of applause that would not be stilled until Lothian had repeated the air. What a boon to poor suffering humanity are those sweet, simple airs whose melody steals away down into the great hard heart of the world, making life so much better and sweeter.[17]

As well as performing up to three times a day on the loggias, the hotel orchestras also played later in the evening for hops and balls. All the major hotels in Saratoga had dancing masters with whom guests spent long hours learning the often very complex dances. There were three grand balls a week during the season, one at each of the big three hotels, with hops on the other nights. As well as its important role in introducing the Strauss waltz and the polka to North America, Saratoga has a further claim to fame as the birthplace of the 'Grecian bend', a popular ballroom walk 'developed to balance the fashionable appendage of the bustle'. Perhaps the success of this slow and stately dance also owed something to the gargantuan meals served in the hotels, which must have rendered many guests incapable of anything more vigorous. The luncheon menu at the United States Hotel ran to eight courses: soup or beef tea; fried smelts with tomato sauce; Salisbury steak, lobster or scrambled eggs and tomatoes; ribs of beef or leg of mutton with potatoes, peas, and stewed corn or cold meats with extensive salads; a choice of eight desserts including cup custard, blueberry pie, and hot gingerbread; pineapple sherbet; preserved fruit, ginger or stewed prunes; and finally cheese with milk or wafer crackers followed by tea, coffee, cocoa, milk, or buttermilk.

A contract to play in one of the resident hotel orchestras in Saratoga provided attractive summer employment for East Coast musicians. The season usually began on 4 July and lasted until the second week of September. The standard of players was generally high. At one time the United States Hotel had musicians from the Boston Symphony Orchestra. In 1890 much excitement was caused, especially among the spa's young male visitors, when an all-female orchestra from Boston took up residence at the Balmoral Hotel, a mountaintop resort just a few miles from Saratoga. Its ten members were all under the age of twenty and clad in striking white and gold dresses. Many players and conductors came back to Saratoga year after year. Professor C. W. Stubs led the orchestra at the United States Hotel from the early 1870s until the early 1900s. Napier Lothian, another Bostonian, led the Grand Union orchestra from 1880 to 1895, being succeeded by John Lund, who conducted a twenty-seven-piece orchestra made up largely of players from Pittsburgh.

The most celebrated of the orchestra leaders during Saratoga's belle époque was the operetta composer Victor Herbert. He first came to the Grand Union Hotel in 1892 as principal cellist in Lund's band. Lund spent much of his time in the casino and quite often left Herbert to conduct during subsequent seasons. Herbert formally took over as leader of the Grand Union orchestra in 1902 and for the next ten years brought fifty-four players from the Pittsburgh Symphony Orchestra to play at 10 a.m. and 8 p.m. daily on the hotel piazza and provide music for balls and hops, by now dominated by waltzes and two-steps. His concerts, for which a fifteen-dollar season ticket admitted two people for the duration of the season, rivalled the gaming tables at the casino as the main draw for those either going on to or returning from the races. Although he included pieces by Wagner, Strauss, Gounod, Massenet, Bizet, Saint-Saëns, Liszt, Beethoven, Mendelssohn, Puccini, and Berlioz, his repertoire was dominated by lighter fare, as a typical daily programme from his first season demonstrates:

Morning
Overture If I were king Adams
Little waltz Eilenberg
Waltz: My Ideal Schaffer
Selections from *Tannhäuser* Wagner
Hearts and Flowers Tobani
Oasis Lange
Rag melodies Mackle
Afternoon
Suite from Peer Gynt Grieg
Yesterthoughts Herbert
Punchinello Herbert
Fantasie Cavalleria Rusticana Mascagni
Two Hungarian Dances Brahms

Herbert's evening concerts in particular were among the highlights of the Saratoga social scene, and woe betide those who disrupted them:

No American resort ever has had anything which would quite compare to his evening concert. The stand was under the huge elms in the garden of the Grand Union. Bejewelled ladies and white tied men crowded the piazza and the cottages to listen. Farther away, where the shadows reached, would be even greater numbers of those who had neither jewels nor white ties.

If anyone ventured to pass by while the orchestra was playing, Victor Herbert would stop all music until they were by him. One wasn't apt to make that mistake again. I think I enjoyed it most when the coloured lights were played on the fountains in the courts in the evening for then the whole place seemed enchanted.[18]

On one occasion, a particularly grande dame swept out of the Grand Union piazza in her Paris taffeta silk gown and diamonds in the midst of the Blue Danube waltz. Herbert stopped the orchestra in midbar and waited in silence until she took her seat. Unlike many who habituated Saratoga in the season, the Irish Wagner, as the Dublin-born and Stuttgart-trained musician was known, was no snob. He spent most afternoons at the races, often losing considerable sums to the bookmakers—it was said that he was the best-paid musician ever in Saratoga but took the least money home. After his concerts he would repair to the Grand Union Café and down several Pilzners in the company of fellow musicians, horsemen, actors, merchants, and whoever happened to be around.

Herbert found the atmosphere of Saratoga congenial for composing. He wrote the scores of several of his operettas there, including *Madamoiselle Modiste* and *Eileen*. Evening walks under the elms in the gardens of the Grand Union inspired his song 'Under the Elms, or Souvenir de Saratoga' and, at least according to one story, directly brought out about his best-known composition, which was inspired by overhearing the soft repeated request of one lover to another 'kiss me again'. Another slightly less romantic version of the genesis of his 1905 song 'Kiss Me Again' suggests that he could not sleep on a hot summer night after conducting a concert and was plagued by a tune that went round and round in his head. He got up, jotted it down in outline, crawled back to bed, and fell asleep.[19]

Victor Herbert was by no means the only composer who found inspiration from the atmosphere of Saratoga during the summer. Dr W. J. Wetmore composed 'Bright Face at the Door', the Mad River Polka, 'The Streets of New York', and 'Departing Sons of the Soldiers' in the Grand Union Hotel garden during a stay to take the mineral waters. Other pieces written by summer visitors to Saratoga during their stay include 'Castles in the Air' by Boullantine, 'Child of the Regiment' by Glover, 'Song of all Songs' by Stephen Foster, and 'If You Love Me, Say So', 'I'm Down in the Double Quick', and 'Never Court but One' by L. L. Parr.

The daily programme of music in the Congress Park and in the hotels was supplemented by special festivals and more occasional events. Throughout the 1870s, for example, annual musical conventions directed by Professor L. O. Emerson featured professional musicians and singers from Boston and offered local choirs instruction in the art of 'rendering difficult pieces of sacred music' such as Rossini's *Stabat Mater* and Mendelssohn's Forty-second Psalm. Matinée concerts brought the Boston professionals and newly drilled local amateurs together to display their talents, and evening concerts began with the singing of 'some specimen hymns of common church music'.[20] There were also numerous one-off charity concerts, ranging from a chamber music recital in August 1853 for the relief of those suffering from pestilence in New Orleans to a vocal recital in 1895 in the blue parlour of the United States Hotel in which Mrs E. Berry Wall, 'among the social arbiters of her day in New York society', sang Gounod's *Ave Maria* to violin accompaniment for the benefit of the Home of the Good Shepherd.

The opening of a 5,000-seat Convention Hall in 1893 put Saratoga firmly on the circuit for internationally acclaimed solo singers. Enrico Caruso, John McCormack, and Caeseratta Jones, the African American soprano whose voice resembled that of Adelina Patti and who became known as 'Black Patti', were frequent and popular visitors. Chauncey Allcott, the Irish-born tenor famous for 'When Irish Eyes Are Smiling', 'My Wild Irish Rose' and 'Mother Machree', regularly came to Saratoga for the golf and horse racing and had a summer home in the town. Another singer who later set up a summer home nearby was Marcella Sembrich, diva at the Metropolitan Opera in the 1920s and 1930s. Her summer estate on Lake George is now an opera museum.

Saratoga was also the setting for the discovery of two significant late-nineteenth and early-twentieth-century North American singers. Emma Albani, who sang around the world, made her debut there in 1863 as an eleven-year-old singing in a gala fair to raise funds for St. Peter's Catholic Church. Her French-Canadian parents had moved to Saratoga Springs the previous year. A rich lady from Albany who heard Albani persuaded her father that she should have operatic training and personally paid for her to study in Milan. Albani made her debut in Messina in 1870 in *La Sonnambula* and was a soloist in the world's great opera houses for the next four decades, giving her farewell performance at London's Albert Hall in 1911. Harry Thacker Burleigh, the black singer who became particularly famous for his arrangement of the spiritual 'Deep River', was discovered while a boy soloist at the Bethesda Episcopal Church in Saratoga in the early 1880s. At the time he was working as a wine waiter at the United States Hotel. His singing at the afternoon church services particularly impressed Mrs Frances MacDowell, a guest at the hotel, whose son Edward was making his way as a composer. She paid for him to study at the National Conservatory of Music in New York, where he became a close friend of Anton Dvořák. Burleigh went on to become a highly successful baritone soloist, often featuring Edward MacDowell's song 'To a Wild Rose' in his recitals alongside the spirituals for which he was especially renowned.

Music making in Saratoga Springs, centred on concerts in Congress Park and the three big hotels, went on well into the twentieth century. Letters from band leaders tendering for the 1914 season provide an interesting insight into both the economics and repertoire of the Congress Park concerts. George Dowing, band master of Dowing's Military Band, offered to provide eighteen 'first class musicians' to play one two-hour concert every Sunday evening and three concerts each weekday (one and a half hours in the morning, one and a half hours in the afternoon, and two hours in the evening) for $388 per week with the proviso that 'should your committee decided to do without afternoon concerts in the racing season, I will allow your committee $50 per week during that time'.[21] A slightly more expensive tender came from William Noller, who offered an eighteen-piece band 'thoroughly rehearsed and completely equipped with entire new uniforms' for $470 per week. On a grander scale, Edmund Tiersch offered a band of twenty-two musicians for $840 per week plus transportation costs from New York to Saratoga. He was also prepared to provide an eighteen-piece orchestra for $665 per week and he provided specimen programmes. For the Sunday evening concert he proposed:

Hymn: Nearer My God to Thee
First part (religious):
1 Hallelujah from the Messiah (Handel)
2 Overture to *Tannhäuser*, Wagner
3 *Inflamatus* from *Stabat Mater*, Rossini—cornet solo
4 Cloister scene from *Kamennoitstrow*, Rubinstein
5 Funeral march, Chopin
Second part:
6 Overture The Chimes of the Eremite, Maillard
7 Paraphrase on 'Home, Sweet Home', Nehl
8 Waltz—'Tales from the Vienna Woods', Strauss
9 Selection from *Mademoiselle Modiste*, Herbert
10 March: Entrance of the Gladiators, Fucie

Despite this enticing programme, and Tiersch's promise that 'each musician is an artist picked out from the wind section of the New York Symphony Orchestra', the committee responsible for administering the entertainments in Congress Park, doubtless mindful of economy, awarded the contract for the season starting on 4 July 1914, as they had for many years, to Dowing's Military Band.[22]

Even before the outbreak of the First World War Saratoga's fortunes were beginning to wane. Fewer members of the East Coast social elite were attracted to the idea of taking the waters, and the increasing use of motor cars meant that those with means took to touring rather than staying in one place throughout the summer. The Congress Hall Hotel closed its doors and was demolished in 1913, an early victim of changing customs and worsening economic conditions. The rich and leisured clientele that had contributed so much to Saratoga's distinctive atmosphere and social prestige, and enabled its rich musical life, was being replaced by a more impoverished group of visitors who came for a shorter time, stayed in cheap boarding houses, and were more focused on medicinal than cultural matters. In 1910 New York State took over ownership and management of the springs, which had been seriously overexploited by private companies extracting carbon dioxide gas for fizzy-drinks manufacture and soda fountains across the United States. Saratoga's medical profile was considerably boosted by the arrival in 1912 of Dr Simon Baruch, professor of hydrotherapy at Columbia University, who came with ambitious plans to build it up as a serious rival to Continental spas offering hydrotherapy and other treatments. It was also helped by the growing number of Jewish immigrants into the United States who came to Saratoga in the 1920s and early 1930s, seeking the nearest that they could find in their new homeland to the therapeutic benefits and atmosphere of the spas of central Europe. To cater to them huge new bathhouses were built in the State Spa Reservation to the south of the town—the Washington in 1920 and the Lincoln in 1930, which proudly proclaimed itself to be the largest bathhouse in the world, with a capacity to offer 4,500 treatments a day.

Although these developments switched the focus of spa-related activities away from the downtown area to the vast parkland of the reservation, music making of both traditional and new kinds still flourished in some of the old venues through the 1930s, although less and less in the grand hotels, which were feeling the effects of the recession.

Jazz and marching bands went on playing at the racetrack until the 1930s. There was still music in the casino—Bing Crosby was a favourite guest artist there and joined the troupe of singers who acquired a summer home in Saratoga. The Congress Park concerts continued to attract substantial audiences. In 1932 a survey revealed an average of 488 people at the evening concerts—the highest attendance being 1,000 recorded on 14 August. The afternoon concerts attracted an average audience of 213.

Meanwhile, an important new venture put Saratoga in the van of the movement to promote and support twentieth-century contemporary American music. It was centred at Yaddo, a large mansion on a 400-acre estate next to the racecourse, which was made available in 1926 as a retreat centre for creative artists thanks to the generous bequest by its first owners, Katrina and Spencer Trask. The idea was that writers, composers, and artists would stay in the house for between two and six weeks in the summer and be left in peace to pursue their work. Aaron Copland, who came to Yaddo in 1930 and composed part of his piano variations during his stay there, felt that it was the perfect place to host an American festival of contemporary music which would bring together composers, players, and critics and raise the profile and the status of what he felt to be a seriously neglected part of the nation's cultural life.

The first Yaddo Festival of Music, held in April 1932, gave American premieres to thirteen works. They included Charles Ives's Seven Songs, Oscar Levant's Sonatina for Piano, Roger Sessions's Sonata for Piano, Virgil Thomson's *Stabat Mater*, and six works specially written for the festival: George Antheil's Sonatina for Piano, Marc Blitzstein's Serenade for String Quartet, Paul Bowles's Six Songs, Henry Grant's Suite for Flute and Piano, Israel Citkdwitz's String Quartet, and Vivian Fine's four polyphonic piano pieces. Reactions to the festival were mixed. For Copland, it 'proved to be the first of a series of efforts towards the improvement of the economic and artistic status of the American composer', while critic Alfred Meyer declared 'American music need no longer step aside for Europe'.[23] Oscar Levant, however, did not enjoy his time at Yaddo:

> Added to my constitutional aversion to the country was the annoyance I had built up during the five-hour train trip, alone, from New York to Saratoga. I had no eye for the attractions of

the mansion. . . . [B]efore the concert we all sat down to dinner in an atmosphere whose preciosity exceeded anything in my experience. The air was full of jeer for every thing and everyone outside the closed shop of those present.[24]

The Yaddo festivals, of which there were nine total between 1932 and 1952, provided many composers with valuable showcases for new work. The 1940 festival was broadcast on the NBC radio network and among the works premiered were Charles Ives's Second String Quartet in 1946 and his Third Symphony in 1949. Altogether, 137 composers had works performed at the festivals. Longer summer stays at Yaddo also proved popular and fruitful for several leading twentieth-century American composers. Copland returned several times. Blitzstein stayed in 1931 to work on his opera *The Cradle Will Rock*, in 1939 to compose his opera *No for an Answer,* and in 1952 to work on his opera *Regina.* Leonard Bernstein came in 1952 to work on a one-act opera and symphonic piece and Virgil Thomson finished his opera *Lord Byron* there in 1971.

Another new venue for music making was provided in 1935 with the opening of an extensive new complex of public buildings in the Saratoga Spa State Park. Built in a rather gloomy neoclassical style, heavy with pillars and porticos, they were among the public works supported by Franklin Roosevelt's New Deal to alleviate the effects of the Great Depression. Roosevelt had taken a key interest in the development of Saratoga as a major spa treatment centre since being governor of New York State in 1929 and took the waters there himself. The new complex included a bathhouse named after him, a research centre named after Simon Baruch, and a new hotel named after Gideon Putnam. In keeping with the complex's municipal crematorium style of architecture and forbidding setting surrounded by dark and looming pine trees, the emphasis was severely and seriously medicinal, with far fewer of the diversions and distractions, including musical ones, that had been provided for earlier generations taking the waters in the town centre. However, there was some music making in the Spa State Park. In the huge new drinking hall, the Hall of Springs, an orchestra played on the balcony while below three circular yellow marble fountains spouted water from the Geyser, Coeso, and Hathorn Springs, recommended respectively for mild digestive aid, strong laxative, and vigorous digestive aid. The fountains were, in fact, purely there for show. They were so far from the source of their respective springs that their water had lost much of its carbonation and visitors actually drank bottled water in the hall. The nearby Spa Little Theatre, which was built in 1934 as a lecture hall for medical students working at the Baruch Research Laboratories, later became an important musical venue, hosting Lake George Opera and the Saratoga Chamber Music festival. In 1946 it was the main venue for the Saratoga Spa Music Festival, which premiered forty-three concert works, including twenty-four written specially for the occasion, played by members of the New York Philharmonic Orchestra under Charles Adler.

Despite the efforts to give Saratoga a new lease on life as a modern European-style medicinal spa, it continued to decline through the 1940s and 1950s. The big hotels, in particular, suffered from the departure of the rich and the socialites and the advent of a more utilitarian and modest clientele. The United States was demolished in 1946 and the Grand Union suffered the same fate seven years later. In 1960, however, a new star appeared in Saratoga's musical firmament, which has continued to shine brightly ever since. A small café on Phila Street in the centre of town opened by Lena and Bill Spencer opened its doors to singer-songwriters at the forefront of the burgeoning folk music scene. The unknown Bob Dylan came there on his first tour, Don Maclean first played 'American Pie' on the tiny stage in the cramped upper floor café, and Pete Seeger and Arlo Guthrie were early visitors before they were widely known. Café Lena proudly claims to be the oldest continually operating folk music venue in United States. Fans still pack its tables to drink mugs of coffee, tea, or chocolate, eat cookies, and listen to the visiting artists who perform on most weekday evenings.

Undoubtedly the most important event in the recent history of music making in Saratoga Springs was the opening of the Saratoga Performing Arts Center (SPAC) in a romantic rural setting at the heart of the Spa State Park. The fan-shaped, open-sided amphitheatre seats just over five thousand and provides an unobstructed view for another twenty thousand seated on the lawns behind. SPAC opened on 8 July 1966 with a performance of *A Midsummer Night's Dream* by the New York City Ballet. On 4 August the Philadelphia Symphony Orchestra under Eugene Ormandy made its debut with Beethoven's overture from *Die Weihe des Hauses*, which had, appropriately, been written in the European spa of Baden bei Wien. Both companies made SPAC their summer base, the New York City Ballet generally performing there through July and the Philadelphia Symphony Orchestra in August. Other orchestras had come close to choosing Saratoga Springs as their summer base. The Boston Philharmonic seriously considered it in the 1920s before settling on Tanglewood. Those behind the creation of SPAC had originally hoped to secure the New York Philharmonic, and its conductor, Leonard Bernstein, was keen to come to Saratoga but was pushed into summer commitments at Central Park. What proved decisive in securing the Philadelphia Orchestra was the fact that it had recently signed a contract guaranteeing its players employment fifty-two weeks of the year, the first U.S. symphony orchestra to do so. The Saratoga residency provided the ideal way of guaranteeing performances through the summer. Ormandy had a hand in designing the auditorium and even the natural magic of Saratoga's mineral waters was subordinated to his musical demands. When he complained that the sound of a waterfall was coming too loudly through the open sided building, the spa park authorities obliged by ordering it to be dammed up.

The New York City Opera first performed at SPAC in 1986 wth a double bill of *Carmen* and *Candide* and joined the City Ballet and the Phildelphia Orchestra in making it their regular summer base. Their 1993 double bill of *Carmen* and the *Mikado* drew a total audience of 14,396. A high successful jazz festival in 1977 was repeated in 1984 and has been an annual event ever since. Another important addition to the musical and cultural life of the Spa State Park came in 1986 when the Washington Baths, which had closed due to declining patronage in 1978, were reopened as the only museum in the United States dedicated to dance. The National Museum of Dance, which became a programme of SPAC in 1990, has had exhibits on all kinds of dance and paid homage to such diverse talents as Isadora Duncan, Fred Astaire, Martha Graham, and Bill 'Bojangles' Robinson. It is very much an interactive museum—in one room you are invited to put on tap shoes and try tap dancing to recorded music. It is also very much a living display. In 1992 three studios were built immediately behind the museum, which function as teaching and rehearsal rooms and are also used for displays and events. When I was there they were packed with aspiring ballet dancers and mothers sewing ballet dresses in preparation for displays. A Sunday afternoon presentation by the American Dance Legacy Institute on black dance in the 1950s included much rare early television footage of black music and dancing.

Saratoga Springs continues to attract musicians and to inspire songwriters and composers. In 1974 it hosted the first American national Song-Writing Competition which attracted more than sixty thousand entries. The winning song in the professional category was 'Lonely Together' by Rod McBrien and Estelle Levitt of New York City and in the amateur section 'Charmer' by Tim Moore of Woodstock. In 1983 the calculation was made (on what basis I have no idea) that the tunes on more than fifty thousand record albums circulating in the United States were written by musicians residing in Saratoga Springs. How many of them actually mentioned the place does not seem to have been computed. There is at least one relatively recent song that takes its place in the long tradition of those that have serenaded the Queen of Spas. Written in 1995 by Tony Oliveto, an advertising copywriter, it is entitled 'Saratoga Is More than a Day at the Races' and begins: 'Saratoga is Rock and Roll and jazz with soul'.

Like its European counterparts, Saratoga still breathes a wonderful fin de siècle air. The vast hotel loggias and elm-shaded gardens of the grand hotels may have gone, the crinolines and frock coats may be no more, but somehow the echoes of Johnson's cotillions, Viennese waltzes and polkas, and Herbert's gentle, romantic melodies linger on, just as they did more than eighty years ago when Robert Hillyer, professor of English at Harvard, was already looking back wistfully in his poem 'Rosewood' to an age that had gone:

The square piano knew
The summers when the Danube still
Was blue at Saratoga Springs.
The sprightly dance that pattered on its strings
Set hoop skirts and moustaches in motion
When glances were the language of devotion.
Or on a rainy afternoon
That separated crinoline from June
Upon the misty air
Inside the fragrance of the 'Maiden's Prayer'.
That when the nights grew cold and autumn came
It saw the gentleman and dame
With proper offspring, youth and maid

Join in a decorous charade.
Now in the tinkle of its musty strings
A quavering voice awakes and sings
Of how the Danube once was new
And beautiful and blue
At Saratoga Springs.[25]

Who knows—maybe it is that piano which is now in the Amtrak waiting room?

8

Coda: Spa Music Today

Music making still flourishes in all the major spas featured in this book. Many of them are enjoying a renaissance as an increasing emphasis on health and well-being and the cult of the body beautiful leads more and more people to steam baths and jacuzzis if not always to sulphurous and chalybeate springs. Meanwhile a whole new genre of spa music has developed to provide a suitably relaxed atmosphere for those undergoing contemporary treatments and chilling out in hot tubs and saunas.

In Bath, treatments and bathing in the thermal waters were reintroduced in 2006 with the long-awaited opening of the New Royal Bath, complete with open-air rooftop pool, and the refurbishment of the old Cross Bath to create Thermae Bath Spa.

Those wishing to drink the waters may do so at the Pump Room, where they are dispensed from a fountain. A cursory sip is more than enough for most visitors, who find greater solace from sitting down at one of the elegant tables and munching their way through a Georgian Elevenses (toasted Bath bun with lemon zest butter, hot chocolate with whipped cream, and a glass of Bath spa water) or Beau Nash Brunch (orange juice, eggs Benedict, with locally baked ham or wilted spinach, toast and preserves, and a pot of tea or coffee). Here they are serenaded by the Pump Room Trio, which plays every morning throughout the year and every afternoon through the summer season with a repertoire ranging from Mozart trios, Telemann and Handel sonatas, via Lehár, Strauss, Gilbert and Sullivan, Rodgers and Hammerstein, Jerome Kern, Cole Porter, and Ira Gershwin to the Beatles, Abba, and Lloyd Webber. In a conscious link with the past, the works of Carl Abel, the German musician who regularly came to Bath in the eighteenth century, are still on the programme. Robert Hyman, the American-born Juilliard graduate who currently leads the trio, reckons that its current repertoire is around two thousand pieces. Nothing is rehearsed and new pieces are simply dropped into the programme of the highly trained and experienced players. Two violinists box and cox with a cellist and pianist to make up the trio. Each player is individually contracted by the local council and is responsible for finding a substitute when necessary.

Music at lunchtime and on winter afternoons in the Pump Room is provided by pianists employed directly by the company that has the franchise to run the catering there. The Pump Room also hosts around forty evening concerts a year, including those by the Bath Recital Artistes Trust, which provide an opportunity for young musicians to perform chamber music. Stephen Clews, administrator of the Roman Baths complex, reckons that the Steinway piano, acquired for the Pump Room in 2004 and tuned every week, must be the most heavily used instrument in Britain, being played for six hours a day for 363 days a

FIGURE 8.1. The Pump Room Trio, Bath (author's photograph).

year as well as at the evening concerts. The piano was paid for by a trust established by Mrs Rosenberger, a Jewish refugee who fled from Germany to Bath with her husband in the 1930s and wished to give the city back something for the kindness its people had shown her.

The Pump Room, the Abbey, and the Upper Assembly Rooms, substantially reconstructed after they were bombed during the Second World War, continue to be major venues for music making in Bath alongside newer ones like the Forum, a converted cinema. The Bath International Music Festival, which runs through the last two weeks of May every year, encompasses a wide variety of styles from classical and folk music in the Pump Room and the Assembly Rooms, through choral music, brass bands, and school orchestras in the Abbey, to jazz in the Forum and the Pavilion. Artistes appearing in the festival in 2007, when the director was the pianist Joanna MacGregor, included the Borodin Quartet, LSO Brass, Imogen Cooper, Emma Kirkby, Nicola Benedetti, and Jools Scott, who provided live music to accompany early evening suppers in the Pump Room and yet more pounding for the Steinway.

Baden bei Wien continues to host an operetta festival every summer. A company of around seventy-five, supported by the federal and regional government, perform two works in the Sommerarena between late June and mid-September—in 2008 Lehár's *Schon ist die Welt* and Zeller's *Der Vogelhändler*. The twenty-four-piece spa orchestra gives thrice-weekly afternoon *kurkonzerte,* performing in a little pavilion in the Kurpark in the summer and in the Haus der Kunst in the winter. A typical programme includes two or three Strauss waltzes or polkas, a Lehár overture, a movement from a classical symphony (when I was there in 2008 these included Haydn's *London* Symphony and Schubert's Fifth), and a Komzak march or gallop to give a stirring conclusion. The annual rose festival in June includes evening concerts in the Rosarium, where there are more than twenty thousand rose bushes in bloom. I spent an enchanting evening there watching ballet dancers performing in front of the Orangerie to the accompaniment, inevitably, of Strauss's 'Roses from the South' played by a Japanese violinist studying at Vienna who later gave a haunting performance of Massenet's Meditation on Thais under a huge fir tree in front of a gargoyle spouting thermal water.

The International Schubert Institute has its headquarters at Baden and organises training courses for lieder interpretation. There is also

FIGURE 8.2A. The Summer Arena, Baden bei Wien (author's photograph).

FIGURE 8.2B. An afternoon orchestral concert in the Kurpark, Baden bei Wien (author's photograph).

an annual Beethoven festival in September with performances in historic locations associated with the composer, including Beethoven Haus in Rathausgasse, the courtyard of the Grand Hotel Sauerhof, and Bellevue Square, above the Beethoven Temple in the Kurpark, where 'Moonlight Sonata' concerts are also given in July and August. From October to April the Stadttheater houses operettas and musicals. The 2007–8 season featured Johann Strauss's *Casanova*, Oskar Nedbal's *Polenblut*, Franz Schubert's *Das Dreimäderlhaus*, Cole Porter's *High Society*, and Andrew Lloyd Webber's *Evita*. Regular chamber concerts in the Beethoven Haus feature the five-pedal walnut piano built by Konrad Grafs. Baden's town church, dedicated to St Stephen, remains an important centre of church music with one of the best choirs in Austria. The magnificent two-manual baroque organ on which Anton Stoll played is still in use and has recently been renovated. Those attending Sunday morning Mass are often treated, as I was, to performances of Mozart's *Ave Verum Corpus* and either the Schubert or Lachner four-hand fugue (see page 80), played by the church's two organists, Professor Margit Fussi and Susanna Pfann.

Music is still an important element in the entertainment provided at Baden-Baden for *kurgäste* and the increasing number of visitors who come for conventions, horse racing, and vacations. The Baden-Badener Philharmonie Orchester, which celebrated its 150th birthday in 2004 and has been conducted since 2007 by Pavel Baleff, increasingly concentrates on major symphony concerts, while still performing between one and three afternoons a week during the summer in the music pavilion opposite the Kurhaus and casino. I attended an afternoon *Promenadenkonzert* on the theme of student life. The programme included Franz von Suppé's overture to *Flotte Bursche*, which incorporates the student anthem 'Gaudeamus Igitur', a selection from Karl Millöcker's *Der Bettelstudent* (written in Baden bei Wien), Emil Waldteufel's *Estudiantina* waltz, Johann Strauss's *Studenten Polka* and Josef Strauss's *Auf Ferienreisen* and *Mein Lebenslauf ist Lieb und Lust*.

The Philharmonie plays in the Lichtentaler Allee and at other outdoor venues in the summer and also gives regular Sunday morning concerts through the season in the Weinbrenner Saal, long used as the concert room of the Kurhaus. The one I attended included Stravinsky's *Pulcrinella* Suite, Vieuxtemps's Violin Concerto No. 5, and Mendelssohn's Scottish Symphony, each work conducted by a young conductor from a different country as part of a master class. The orchestra is much involved with training young musicians. String players come each summer to Baden-Baden in a scheme that was originally instituted by Carl Flesch before the Second World War.

The new Festspeilhaus, opened in 1998 and the second largest concert hall in Europe, hosts an extensive programme of opera and concerts—highlights in 2008 included Beethoven's *Fidelio* conducted by Claudio Abbado, Wagner's *Tannhäuser*, and Gerswhin's *Porgy and Bess*, and among the soloists appearing that year were Nigel Kennedy, Cecilia Bartoli, and Alfred Brendel. The Südwestrundfunk Sinfonie-orchester also contributes considerably to the musical life of Baden-Baden. There is still much lighter music making going on as well. On summer afternoons where there is not a *Promenadenkonzert* a trio plays jazz and old-time dance music, encouraging enthusiastic dancing in the area in front of the Kurhaus. There are regular Sunday afternoon tea dances inside the Kurhaus throughout the summer and the casino hosts Broadway dinner shows featuring songs from musicals.

There is no longer any live music in Baden-Baden's two main thermal baths which are still well patronized. Bathing in the splendidly old-fashioned Friedrichsbad, an all-naked affair involving fourteen carefully timed different stages, with hot rooms, steam rooms, baths of varying temperatures, and a scrub down and soap massage, is a serious business undertaken largely in silence. The ultramodern Caracalla Spa complex, which offers bathing and hot tubs of every variety, is a much noisier affair accompanied by piped music. Those who want to take the waters at the Trinkhalle, now the Tourist Information Office, must do so without the encouragement of the wind band that once serenaded morning and evening sippers and dippers.

Since the fall of communism, the former Bohemian spas have reinvented themselves to cater to the booming market in health and wellness vacation packages and are now among the leading tourist destinations in the Czech Republic. They have not lost their musical traditions. Bands still sometimes play outside the vast colonnaded drinking hall in Karlsbad (or Karlovy Vary as it is known in Czech) as those taking the cure parade up and down sipping the hot fizzy water from porcelain cups with long spouts that resemble small inverted watering cans. The former spa orchestra in Teplitz (Teplice), which was reestablished in 1948, has since 1979 been a full-scale symphony orchestra, known as the Severoèeská Philharmonic. In 1986 it found a new home in the purpose-built Kulturní Dùm Concert Hall and in 1997 it recorded all of Schubert's symphonies to celebrate the two hundredth anniversary of his birth. In Marienbad (Mariánsnké Lázné) the Frederyk Chopin Society has run an eight-day festival every August since 1959. It includes symphony concerts and recitals and incorporates an international piano competition designed to identify and encourage up-and-coming Chopin interpreters. Since 1986 one of the town's major tourist attractions has been the singing fountain by the drinking colonnade. From May to October, the computer-controlled fountain, which has more than 250 water jets, plays a daily programme of recorded music every other hour, from 7 a.m. to 9 p.m.. Music by recent Czech composers is interspersed with classical favourites that would have been familiar to those who frequented the spas of Bohemia a hundred or more years ago.

Bad Ischl still caters to traditional *kurgäste* as well as modern tourists. It is the only place I have ever visited where the street map handed out routinely at the Tourist Office has on its reverse side a detailed list of doctors specialising in every conceivable medical complaint. It also remains deeply proud and conscious of its imperial connections. A *Kaisermesse* is still held every year in the parish church on 18 August, the birthday of Emperor Franz Josef, and a branch of the Habsburg family continues to occupy a wing of the Kaiservilla. The Lehár festival, held every summer in the Kongress und Theater Haus, presents two operetta productions, one often innovative and the other traditional, both sumptuously staged and superbly sung. Sadly, there are not as many *kurkonzerten* as there used to be. When I first came to Ischl in the early 1980s they took place almost every day both in the morning and the afternoon. Now there is just one a week with full orchestra. On other days the kur-quartett plays either in the morning in front of the restored Trinkhalle, which now hosts the Tourist Information Office, or in the afternoon at Zauner's Café on the Esplanade. It is at Zauner's while working one's way through a huge ice cream or chocolate cake and listening to the melodies of Strauss, Lehár, Kalmann, and Stolz that the atmosphere of Bad Ischl in its golden age can best be recaptured.

Buxton is the most Continental-like of all the British spas and will be even more so if and when ambitious plans to reestablish a grand hotel and spa complex in the Crescent come to fruition. Music is once again flourishing as part of the town's general cultural regeneration.

FIGURE 8.3. The Kur-quartett playing at Zauner's Café on the Esplanade, Bad Ischl (author's photograph).

As well as providing the main venue for the International Festival and Gilbert and Sullivan Festival during July and August, the Opera House hosts touring opera companies, musicals, and concert performances throughout the year. There is a particular emphasis on recreating the nostalgic atmosphere of the interwar years, and an Ivor Novello Festival is held at the end of August. The pavilion gardens have recently been extensively improved and the bandstand, built in 1998 as a memorial to local conductor Don Redfern, is regularly occupied by brass bands on summer weekend afternoons. A new concert venue has recently been added with the opening of the great dome of the former Devonshire Royal Hospital as the Buxton campus of the University of Derby in 2006.

There is still plenty of live music making in Saratoga Springs every summer. A recent flyer lists sixteen venues for live music and events ranging from a Baroque Festival at the Spa Little Theatre and free band concerts at Congress Park to jazz in the cafe at the Gideon Putnam Hotel. The annual programme at the Saratoga Performing Arts Center continues to feature Lake George Opera and the New York City Ballet during July. In August the first three days of every week are given over to a chamber music festival while the Philadelphia Orchestra plays nightly from Thursday to Saturday under its current conductor, Charles Dutoit. In 2004 a Viennese season at SPAC brought back to Saratoga the quintessentially European spa music of the Strausses, Lehár, Stolz, and Kalman as well as compositions by Mozart, Schubert, Haydn, Mahler, and Beethoven. Café Lena continues to host singer-songwriters performing astringent satirical numbers. There is evident nostalgia for the spa's heyday and an increasing movement to recreate its musical and cultural ambience. The Canfield Casino in Congress Park regularly hosts fully costumed Victorian balls with an opening grand march, cotillions, quadrilles, and gallops danced to period music provided by a trio of violin, viola, and piano. The posters advertising these events make clear that 'vintage, military, period-style or formal attire is requested and Victorian custom dictates the wearing of gloves by all dancers'. The participants I observed making their way to one such ball in 2005 seemed to have taken these strictures very seriously and observed them to the letter.

It was while in Saratoga Springs that I first encountered a whole new kind of water music, specially composed and recorded for the booming modern spa industry. While taking a series of treatments at the Crystal Spa, a typical contemporary spa complex housed in the Grand Union Motel on Broadway opposite the old Lincoln Mineral Baths, I was fascinated by the ambient background music, a mixture of panpipes, keyboard, synthesiser, and birdsong. I learned that it came from a hundred CDs loaded in an automatic stacking system and played in a random sequence, with the volume control being differently adjusted for each part of the spa, very low in the sauna and higher in the treatment rooms, baths, and whirlpools. Some of the music being played was recognisably classical. One of the CDs in use, like all the others specially produced for the spa market, entitled 'Solitudes' and described on its cover as 'an enchanting union of classical melodies to nurture a state of deep relaxation' included extracts from Mozart's *Marriage of Figaro* and Clarinet Concerto, Bizet's *Carmen*, Albinoni's Oboe Concerto, Beethoven's *Emperor* Concerto, Schubert's *Ave Maria*, and Chopin's piano concertos. Many other modern CDs for relaxation and spa use similarly feature classical pieces that would have been familiar to guests at European and North American watering places in their nineteenth- and early-twentieth-century glory days. As I write this, I am listening to one such—a disc in Sharon O'Connor's Menu and Music series entitled *Spa* which features piano pieces by Chopin, Debussy, and Ravel including such 'watery' works as 'Reflets dans L'Eau'.

Much of the recorded music played in modern spas, however, has a very different provenance. It comes from contemporary composers working specifically in this genre. Kimberly Williams, who has worked as a massage therapist at the Crystal Spa in Saratoga Springs, is responsible for two CDs, *Sanctuary* and *The Fifth Season*, designed for general relaxation and meditation as well as for use in spas. They are among the products marketed by Primal Waters, a company that 'provides innovative digital media products that facilitate relaxation and meditation'. She has also written the soundtrack for *Lessons from Water*, a film which suggests that humans have much to learn from the behaviour and qualities of water.[1]

The ever-expanding catalogue of music designed for use in spas includes much that is nature-related, notably birdsong, ocean waves, and the sounds of dolphins and whales. Among musical instruments, flutes, panpipes, harps, guitars, and percussion predominate. The North American companies specialising in recording and selling compilation CDs for spas include the aptly named Spa-la-la, which promotes a 'mixture of classical, New Age and sound healing collections designed for deep relaxation, aromatherapy, wellness, massage, yoga and meditation'.[2] Founded in 2002 by Laura Nasham, who studied flute performance at the University of Toronto, it is described as 'Canada's Number One creator of sensuous, soothing music for different kinds of spa therapies'. Its many CDs make much use of flute melodies, played by Laura Nasham and often accompanied by vibraphone and chimes, and also feature 'romantic solo piano', strings, and full orchestra.[3] At Peace Media, another company specialising in this genre, offers separate collections of predominantly acoustic music for massage spas, healing spas, and spa lounges. Individual spas produce compilations of commercially recorded spa music for their own use and to sell to their clients. Kohler Waters, which runs spas in Kohler, Wisconsin, Burr Ridge, Chicago, and St Andrews in Scotland, markets *A Musical Journey through Water*, with tracks entitled 'Spirit of the Healing Waters', 'Midnight Ocean Reflection', and 'Secret Lake' as well as 'Meeting Mozart'.

Some modern spas make more radical use of music for therapeutic purposes. Alex Rentz, a German-born therapist working in the El Monte Sagrado Living Resort and Spa in Taos, New Mexico, is an expert in acutonics, a sound and vibrational therapy based on the use of tuning forks. Gary Walther, editor of *Luxury Spa Finder* magazine, gives this graphic description of the treatment:

He begins by striking a gong to create a 'sound space' and placing an om vibration beside my ears. Then comes the tuning. At one point I have a tuning fork at the base of my skull and another at the base of my spine to balance the magnetism of my back. At another point Rentz, who has the intensity of an orchestra kettle drummer waiting to play his three notes, strikes two forks and swirls them above me. To balance my front and back, he holds the Mars and Venus forks at my abdomen and coccyx. He concludes by striking a Tibetan gong and swinging it to-and-fro like a priest with a censer.[4]

Guests at Sanibel Harbour Resort and Spa, Fort Myers, Florida, can have their entire body bathed in sound waves and massaged by vibrations through a session in a BETAR bed (Bio Energetic Transduction Aided Resonance), which reads the electromagnetic field produced by the body and produces an appropriate sound level to soothe away imbalance and stress. The spa's publicity material promises that 'guests who experience this treatment float away on a bed of sound for the ultimate in relaxation'. Several spas, including the Ojai Valley Inn and Spa in California and the Fairmont Banff Springs Hotel in British Columbia, have vibrating sound systems in their swimming pools to provide sonic baths. Others, such as Miraval in Arizona and New Age Health Resort in Upstate New York, offer drumming classes as a way of relieving stress and tension.[5] Music therapy more widely features on the menus of several spas and health resorts and is increasingly being used in hospitals and clinics for those with conditions ranging from cancer to depression. This kind of modern water music is not just confined to the new spas that have sprung up around the world over the last twenty years or so. It has also infiltrated much more traditional establishments. The Friedrichsbad in Baden-Baden has an ultramodern 'Blue Room' consisting entirely of fibreglass beds contoured to fit the human body and fitted with loudspeakers emitting electronic echoes and vibrations.

It is all a long way from the music that has been the main subject of this book. As the purpose and nature of spa treatments change, inevitably so too does the kind of music that accompanies them. There is less call now for the stirring cadences of the waltzes and marches that helped past generations of spa goers through their early morning drinking and bathing sessions. Nowadays the emphasis in spas is more on pampering and relaxing. There is less need to cheer guests up than to calm down those with overstressed lives. For this purpose the piano pieces and chamber works that Beethoven and Brahms wrote in Baden, Baden-Baden, and Bad Ischl are played on the sound systems in massage rooms and spa lounges alongside the panpipes, birdsong, and acoustic vibrations. The operettas of Offenbach, Strauss, Lehár, and their contemporaries that I have defined as the quintessential spa music do not feature on modern CD spa compilations. Their live performance, however, is the highlight of the summer festivals in several European spas and their waltzes and marches remain the core of the kurorchester repertoire. Long may they continue to weave their escapist magic and occasionally bitter-sweet enchantment.

Encore

Since finishing this book I have experienced a further connection between spas and music, which I feel is worth recording. In June 2009 I was among a small but select group of enthusiasts who gathered in Bad Schwalbach in Germany to establish *Der Deutschen Sullivan Gesellschaft,* a society dedicated to promoting the appreciation and performance of the music of Sir Arthur Sullivan in the German-speaking world. We met on a wet Saturday afternoon in the *Oper-akademie,* which is housed in part of the spa's *Moorbadehaus* where baths and massages using the local peat and mud are still given. In the evening soloists from the Opera Academy gave a concert in the *Kur-haus* of extracts from Sullivan's works, including *The Mikado, The Yeomen of the Guard,* and *The Beauty Stone.* The composer himself spent a day and a night at Bad Schwalbach in a whistle-stop tour of Germany in August 1881, which also took in nearby Wiesbaden and Bad Ems. This fact, and the existence of the Opera Academy, has prompted Meinhard Saremba, who is behind this new venture, to explore whether Bad Schwalbach might become the home of a festival dedicated to Sullivan and other English composers. If it does, then yet another link will be forged between spas and operetta and there will be one more watering place where the sound of that most characteristic kind of spa music will be heard once again.

Notes

Preface

1. Alev Lytle Croutier, *Taking the Waters* (New York: Abbeville Press, 1992), 127.

Introduction

1. John R. Williams, *The Life of Goethe* (Oxford: Blackwell, 1998), 23.

2. John Mainwaring, *Memoirs of the Life of the Late G.F. Handel* (London, 1760), 121–23.

3. Richard Wagner, *My Life* (London: Constable, 1911), 575.

4. Bernard Grun, *Gold and Silver: The Life and Times of Franz Lehár* (London: W. H. Allen, 1970), 29.

5. Archie Camden, *Blow by Blow: The Memoirs of a Musical Rogue and Vagabond* (London: Thames, 1982), 37.

6. Both of these quotations are from Croutier, *Taking the Waters*, 110, 111.

7. Geir Kjetsaa, *Fyodor Dostoyevsky—A Writer's Life*, trans. Siri Hustvedt and David McDuff (London: Macmillan, 1988), 305.

8. John Wilson, *CB: A Life of Sir Henry Campbell-Bannerman* (London: Constable, 1973), 141.

9. S. L. Bensusan, *Some German Spas* (London: Noel Douglas, 1925), 158.

10. Ibid., 134.

11. Quoted in *Villes d'Eaux en France* (Paris: Institut Francais d'Architecture, 1985), 95.

12. Ibid., 150.

13. John Cunningham, ed., *Four Hundred Years of the Wells* (Royal Tunbridge Wells Civic Society, Historical Monograph No. 5, 2005), 20.

14. Ned Ward, 'A Step to Bath' quoted in Peter J. Neville Havins, *The Spas of England* (London: Robert Hale, 1976), 146.

15. Arthur Moss and Evalyn Marvel, *Cancan and Barcarolle: The Life and Times of Jacques Offenbach* (Westport, Conn.: Greenwood Press, 1975 reprint), 171. I owe the other anecdotes about Offenbach to A. Faris, *Jacques Offenbach* (London: Faber & Faber, 1980).

16. Moss and Marvel, *Cancan and Barcarolle*, 204.

17. Quoted in Arthur Jacobs, *Arthur Sullivan, a Victorian Musician* 2nd edn. (Aldershot, Hants: Scolar Press, 1992), 337.

18. Quotations from Sullivan's diaries from microfilm reels made available by the Beinecke Rare Book and Manuscript Library, Yale University.

19. Thomas Mann, *The Magic Mountain*, trans. H. T. Lowe-Porter (New York: Vintage, 1999), 114.

20. Ibid., 318.

21. Ibid., 636.

22. Ibid., 639, 640.

23. Guy de Maupassant, *Mont Oriol*, trans. Marjorie Laurie (Chappaqua, N.Y.: Turtle Point Press, n.d.), 9.

24 Ibid., 25–26.

25. Ibid., 254.

26. Ibid., 55–56.

27. John Thomas Smith, *A Book for a Rainy Day* (London: Richard Bentley, 1905), 139–40.

28. Karen Ralls-MacLeod, *Music and the Celtic Otherworld* (Edinburgh: Edinburgh University Press, 2000), 74, 87.

29. Article in *La Revue Musicale*, December 1938, 20, quoted in notes by Roger Nichols to *Jeux d'Eaux* (London: Edition Peters, 1994). I owe this reference to Tessa Mayhew, who also played this piece for me particularly beautifully.

30. Ronald Hingley, *Dostoyevsky: His Life and Work* (London: Paul Elek, 1978), 186.

31. Mann, *The Magic Mountain*, 637.

32. *Villes d'Eaux*, 97.

33. W. MacQueen-Pope and D. L. Murray, *Fortune's Favourite: The Life and Times of Franz Lehar* (London: Hutchinson, 1953), 127; Richard Traubner, *Operetta, a Theatrical History* (London: Gollancz, 1984), 1.

34. Traubner, *Operetta*, 36.

35. Wilson, *CB*, 141.

1. *Bath*

1. F. O. Morshead, ed., *Everybody's Pepys* (London: Bell, 1926), 488–89.

2. Ned Ward, *A Step to Bath* (London, 1700), 15.

3. Daniel Defoe, *A Tour Through England and Wales* (London: Everyman Edition, 1927), 2:34.

4. Quoted in Thomas Hinde, *Tales from the Pump Room: Eight Hundred Years of Bath, the Place, Its People, and Its Gossip* (London: Victor Gollancz, 1988), 62.

5. Oliver Goldsmith, *The Life of Richard Nash*, 2nd ed. (London, 1762), 48.

6. Francis Fleming, *The Life and Adventures of Timothy Ginnadrake* (Bath, 1771), 3:23.

7. Ibid., 3:23.

8. Ibid., 3:24, 25.

9. Ibid., 3:25.

10. Goldsmith, *Life of Richard Nash*, 29.

11. John Wood, *A Description of Bath* (1765, Kingsmead Reprints, 1969), 270.

12. Tobias Smollett, *Humphry Clinker* (London: George Bell, 1895), 42.

13. Philip Thicknesse, *The New Prose Guide for the Year* (London, 1778), 33.

14. Kenneth E. James, 'Concert Life in Eighteenth Century Bath' (PhD thesis, University of London, 1988), 53.

15. *Bath Journal*, 4 November 1757.

16. Otto Erich Deutsch, 'From Michael Kelly's "Reminiscences," London, 1826' in *Mozart: A Documentary Biography* (London: Simon & Schuster, 1990), 530.

17. James, 'Concert Life', 49.

18. *Bath Weekly Chronicle*, 15 April 1778.

19. Charles Dibden, *The Musical Tour of Mr Dibden* (Sheffield, 1778), 24.

20. Ibid., 35.

21. *Bath Chronicle*, 15 December 1774.

22. Cunningham, *400 Years of the Wells*, 64.

23. Jane Austen, *Persuasion* (London: Folio Society, 1961), 174.

24. Ibid., 178.

25. *White's Music Warehouse Catalogue*, n.d., Special Collections, University of St Andrews.

26. Augustus B. Granville, *Spas of England* (1841, reprint Adams and Dart, Bath, 1971), 2:395.

27. Ibid., 2:398, 395.

28. Pump Room Band Account Book, Bath and North East Somerset Record Office, ac. no. 0169/2/1.

29. Bath Archaeological Trust, extracts from Corporation papers relating to the spa, 17 October 1876.

30. Ibid., 8 March 1892.

31. Ibid.

32. Contracts, Bath and North East Somerset Record Office, ac. no. 0169/3/1.

33. Correspondence on concerts, Bath and North East Somerset Record Office, ac. no. 0169/1/1.

34. Contracts, Bath and North East Somerset Record Office, ac. no. 0169/3/1.

35. Kenneth Young, *Music's Great Days in the Spas and Watering Places* (London: Macmillan, 1968), 72.

2. *Baden bei Wien*

1. Alfred Einstein, *Gluck,* trans. Eric Blom (London: J. M. Dent, 1936), 181.

2. Emily Anderson, ed., *The Letters of Mozart and His Family* (London: Macmillan, 1938), 3:1387.

3. Ibid.

4. Ibid., 3:1399.

5. Ibid., 3:1410.

6. Ibid., 3:1413.

7. Ibid., 3:1416.

8. Ibid., 3:1418.

9. Ibid., 3:1425.

10. Ibid., 3:1433.

11. Ibid., 3:1438.

12. Ibid., 3:1442.

13. Wolfgang Hildesheimer, *Mozart*, trans. Marion Faber (London: J. M. Dent, 1985), 260.

14. Letter to Luigi Polzelli, 20 June 1793, quoted in R. Hughes, *Haydn* (London: J. M. Dent, 1962), 87.

15. H. C. Robbins Landon, *Haydn: The Years of the Creation* (London: Thames & Hudson, 1977), 497.

16. Ibid., 543.

17. Theodor Frimmel, 'Beethoven im Kurort Baden bei Wien', *Neues Beethoven Jahrbuch* (1930), 46.

18. Elliot Forbes, ed., *Thayer's Life of Beethoven*, by Alexander Wheelock Thayer (Princeton: Princeton University Press, 1967), 1:284.

19. Martin Cooper, *Beethoven: The Last Decade, 1817–1827* (London: Oxford University Press, 1970) 30. Remarkable as it may seem, many of Beethoven's doctors agreed in seeing a connection between his deafness and his abdominal problems and colitis. Cooper's book contains, as an appendix, an interesting assessment of Beethoven's medical history by Edward Larkin.

20. Emily Anderson, ed., *The Letters of Beethoven* (London: Macmillan, 1961), 1:273.

21. Frimmel, 'Beethoven', 62.

22. Forbes, *Thayer's Life*, 1:335.

23. Anderson, *Letters*, 1:111.

24. Forbes, *Thayer's Life*, 1:354–55.

25. Anderson, *Letters*, 1:169, 171.

26. Quoted in Frimmel, 'Beethoven', 54.

27. Anderson, *Letters*, 1:242.

28. Ibid., 1:420.

29. Maynard Solomon, *Beethoven* (London: Cassell, 1978), 221.

30. Forbes, *Thayer's Life*, 2:620.

31. Anderson, *Letters*, 2:590.

32. Cooper, *Beethoven*, 146–47.

33. Anderson, *Letters*, 2:766.

34. Ibid., 2:832.

35. Ibid., 2:926.

36. Ibid., 2:967.

37. Cooper, *Beethoven*, 47.

38. Forbes, *Thayer's Life*, 2:807.

39. Ibid., 2:868.

40. Anderson, *Letters*, 3:1080.

41. Ibid., 3:1087.

42. John Warrack, *Carl Maria Von Weber* (Cambridge: Cambridge University Press, 1976), 305.

43. Ibid., 872.

44. Anderson, *Letters*, 3:1135, 1137, 1146.

45. Ibid., 3:1143.

46. Solomon, *Beethoven*, 280.

47. Anderson, *Letters*, 3:1195.

48. Ibid., 3:1197–98.

49. Ibid., 3:1238, 1239.

50. Forbes, *Thayer's Life*, 1:244.

51. See, for example, the analysis in Lewis Lockwood, *Beethoven: The Music and the Life* (New York: W. W. Norton, 2003), 456.

3. *Baden-Baden*

1. I. Burney Yeo, *The Therapeutics of Mineral Springs and Climates* (London: Cassell, 1904), 82.

2. Ibid., 80.

3. Richard Aldous, *The Lion and the Unicorn: Gladstone vs. Disraeli* (London: Pimlico, 2007), 52–55; Philip Montefiore Magnus, *Gladstone*, 4th ed. (London: John Murray, 1963), 74.

4. Hector Berlioz, *The Memoirs of Hector Berlioz*, trans. and ed. David Cairns (London: Gollancz, 1969), 471.

5. C. E. Hallé, ed., *The Life and Letters of Sir Charles Hallé* (London: Smith, Elder, 1896), 258.

6. Ibid., 259.

7. Berlioz, *Memoirs of Berlioz*, 522.

8. J. H. Elliot, *Berlioz* (London: J. M. Dent, 1938), 101.

9. Richard Wagner, *My Life* (London: Constable, 1911), 2:749–50.

10. Ernest Newman, *Life of Richard Wagner* (New York: Knopf, 1946), 4:309.

11. Ivan Turgenev, *Smoke* (London: Heinemann, 1906), 5–6.

12. Ibid., 2.

13. Ibid., 4.

14. Ibid., 175.

15. Ibid., 217.

16. Leonard Schapiro, *Turgenev: His Life and Times* (Oxford: Oxford University Press, 1978), 224.

17. Joan Chissell, *Clara Schumann, a Dedicated Spirit: A Study of Her Life and Work* (London: Hamish Hamilton, 1983), 152.

18. Monica Stegmann, *Clara Schumann* (London: Haus, 2004), 115.

19. Chissell, *Clara Schumann*, 156.

20. Ibid., 158.

21. Ibid., 159.

22. Styra Avins, ed., *Johannes Brahms: Life and Letters*, trans. Josef Eisenger and Avins (Oxford: Oxford University Press, 1997), 301.

23. Jan Swafford, *Johannes Brahms, a Biography* (London: Macmillan, 1998), 309.

24. Ibid., 351.

25. Ada Teetgen, *The Waltz Kings of Old Vienna* (London: Herbert Jenkins, 1939), 165.

26. Hans Fantel, *Johann Strauss: Father and Son, and Their Era* (Newton Abbot: David and Charles, 1971), 196. I owe the *Badeblatt* reference to Peter Kemp.

27. Peter Kemp, *The Strauss Family* (London: Omnibus Press, 1989), 94.

28. Michael Musgrave, *A Brahms Reader* (New Haven: Yale University Press, 1999) 107.

29. F. May, *The Life of Johannes Brahms* (London: Edward Arnold, 1905), 2:37.

30. 'Johannes Brahms in Baden-Baden' in *Johannes Brahms* (Baden-Baden: Brahmsgesellschaft Baden-Baden, 1998), 15.

31. Joseph Wechsberg, *The Lost World of the Great Spas* (New York: Harper and Row, 1979), 63–64.

4. *The Spas of Bohemia*

1. Yeo, *Therapeutics*, 134.

2. Ibid., 133.

3. Ibid., 254–55.

4. Cooper, *Beethoven*, 30.

5. Anderson, *Letters of Beethoven*, 1:385.

6. Ibid., 1:384.

7. Ibid., 1:387.

8. Ibid., 1:389.

9. Forbes, *Thayer's Life*, 2:801–802.

10. Wagner, *My Life*, 127.

11. Ibid., 272.

12. Ibid., 313–14.

13. Ibid., 315.

14. Ibid., 365.

15. Ibid., 366.

16. Ibid., 569–70.

17. Ibid., 570.

18. Ibid., 572–73.

19. Ibid., 574–75.

20. Ibid., 575–622.

21. Ibid., 646.

22. Swafford, *Johannes Brahms*, 614.

23. [John A.] Fisher, *Memories of Admiral of the Fleet, Lord Fisher* (London: Hodder & Stoughton, 1919), 157.

24. Wilson, *CB*, 143.

25. Yeo, *Therapeutics*, 135, 256.

26. Wilson, *CB*, 141.

27. Wechsberg, *The Lost World of the Great Spas*, 165.

28. Jonathan Meades, 'This Year in Marienbad', *The Times*, 2 January 1988, 13.

5. Bad Ischl

1. Kemp, *Strauss Family*, 142.

2. *Johannes Brahms in der Bädern* (Baden-Baden: Stadt Baden-Baden, 1997), 81.

3. Swafford, *Johannes Brahms*, 463.

4. Ibid, 471.

5. Ibid., 484.

6. *Johannes Brahms in der Bädern*, 115.

7. Swafford, *Johannes Brahms*, 496.

8. *Johannes Brahms in der Bädern*, 111.

9. Fantel, *Johann Strauss*, 201.

10. Swafford, *Johannes Brahms*, 613.

11. *Johannes Brahms in der Bädern*, 108.

12. Ibid., 102.

13. The Bad Ischl Museum has a photograph of another house in Kaltenbachstrasse, near Strauss's villa, where it is claimed that Brahms stayed. In fact, Gustav Jenner says that he always stayed in the small apartment in Salzburgerstrasse. Although on one occasion he did find larger lodgings, he never took them up, preferring to stay in his original rooms because of the kindness of his landlords and their children to him.

14. *Johannes Brahms in der Bädern*, 101.

15. I. Keys, *Johannes Brahms* (Portland, Ore.: Amadeus Press, Oregon, 1989), 99.

16. Swafford, *Johannes Brahms*, 580.

17. Letter to Eusebius Mandyczewski, 23 May 1895, *Johannes Brahms in der Bädern*, 99.

18. May, *Life*, 2:262–64.

19. See article on this incident in the *Musical Quarterly* 72, no.1 (1986): 28–50.

20. Grun, *Gold and Silver*, 146.

21. Ibid., 158.

22. This is the date given in Norbert Linke's *Franz Lehár* (Hamburg: Reinbeck, 2001), 60, the most recent and authoritative biography of the composer. Grun's *Gold and Silver* and MacQueen-Pope and Murray's *Fortune's Favourite* both give 1906 as the date for Lehár's first visit to Ischl. Dr Silvia Müller and Dr Michael Lahner ['Von den Operettenwochen zum Lehár Festival', in D. Neumann, ed., *Menschen, Mythen, Monarchen in Bad Ischl* (Bad Ischl: Tourismusverband Bad Ischl, 2008), 66] give it as 1903.

23. Neumann, *Menschen, Mythen*, 66.

24. Grun, *Gold and Silver*, 203.

25. Ibid., 268.

6. Buxton

1. Quoted in Mike Langham and Colin Wells, *The Baths at Buxton Spa* (Leek: Churnet Valley Books, 2005), 21.

2. Ibid., 32–2.

3. William Adam, *Gem of the Peak* (reprint of 1851 edn., Buxton: Moorland, 1973), 284.

4. Granville, *Spas of England*, 2:30.

5. Ibid., 2:35.

6. Langham and Wells, *Baths at Buxton Spa*, 61–62.

7. Granville, *Spas of England*, 2:27–28.

8. Ros McCoola, *Theatre in the Hills: Two Centuries of Theatre in Buxton* (Chapel-en-le-Frith: Caron, 1984), 38.

9. Langham and Wells, *Baths at Buxton Spa*, 92.

10. *Buxton Advertiser*, 8 September 1894.

11. Ibid., 23 October 1897.

12. Horace Fellowes, *Music in My Heart* (Edinburgh: Oliver & Boyd, 1958), 43.

13. Ibid., 44.

14. *Buxton Herald*, 17 August 1898.

15. Ibid., 30 December 1908.

16. Ibid., 27 January 1909.

17. Ibid., 4 August, 11 August, 18 August 1909.

18. Camden, *Blow by Blow*, 35–37.

19. *Buxton Herald*, 22 March 1911.

20. Ibid., 24 May 1913.

21. On the history of the Buxton Festival, see Michael Kennedy, *Buxton: An English Festival* (Buxton: Buxton Festival, 2004).

22. For more on the history and atmosphere of the G & S Festival see the last chapter of my book *Oh Joy! Oh Rapture: The Continuing Phenomenon of Gilbert and Sullivan* (New York: Oxford University Press, 2005).

7. Saratoga Springs

1. Field Horne, ed., *The Saratoga Reader: Writing about an American Village* (Saratoga Springs: Kiskatom Publishing, 2004), 15.

2. Jon Sterngass, *First Resorts: Pursuing Pleasure at Saratoga Springs, Newport, and Coney Island* (Baltimore: John Hopkins University Press, 2001), 11.

3. Horne, *Saratoga Reader*, 37.

4. Ibid., 68.

5. Ibid., 36–37.

6. Ibid., 57.

7. Ibid., 68.

8. Quoted in Evelyn Britten, *The Chronicles of Saratoga*, 26 July 1966, in Archives of City Historian.

9. Horne, *Saratoga Reader*, 115.

10. Publicity material in Archives of City Historian, Saratoga Springs.

11. John G. Saxe, *Poems* (Boston: Houghton, Mifflin, 1882), 49.

12. Sterngass, *First Resorts*, 114.

13. *The Times*, 9 December 1887.

14. Nathan Sheppard, *Saratoga Chips and Carlsbad Wafers* (New York: Funk & Wagnalls, 1887), 227.

15. *Daily Saratogian*, 21 August 1876.

16. In Local History Room, Saratoga Springs Public Library.

17. Britten, *Chronicles of Saratoga*, 17 April 1964.

18. Hugh Bradley, *Such Was Saratoga* (New York: Doubleday, 1960), 246; *A History of Music in Saratoga*, unsigned and undated typescript in Local History Room, Saratoga Springs Public Library, 1942, 3.

19. Edward N. Waters, *Victor Herbert: A Life in Music* (New York: Macmillan, 1955), 294.

20. 'The Musical Convention', *Daily Saratogian*, 9 December 1876.

21. Ms. letter from George Dowing, 16 April 1914, in Archives of City Historian, Saratoga Springs.

22. Ms. Letter from Edmund Tiersel, 20 April 1914 in Archives of City Historian, Saratoga Springs.

23. *Yaddo Newsletter* (Spring 1980), 2.

24. Oscar Levant, *A Smattering of Ignorance* (New York: Doubleday, 1940), 222.

25. Quoted in *A History of Music in Saratoga*, 5.

8. *Coda: Spa Music Today*

1. www.primalwaters.com.

2. www.spa-la-la.com.

3. Kristin Jenkins, 'Deck your Spa with Soothing Music', *Spa Canada*, November 2003, 2–4.

4. Gary Walther, 'Spa Sleuth: The Full Monte', *Luxury Spa Finder* (March 2005), 12, available on line at www.spafinder.com/archive/article.jsp?id=154.

5. See articles on 'The Healing Power of Music' by Annette Foglino in *Spa Finder*, May/June 2002.

Index